CAMBODIA AND LAOS

CAMBODIA AND LAOS

CONTENTS

DISCOVER CAMBODIA AND LAOS 6

EXPERIENCE CAMBODIA 50

EXPERIENCE LAOS 144

NEED TO KNOW 220

Cambodia

Laos

DISCOVER

Man crossing the Nam Song river

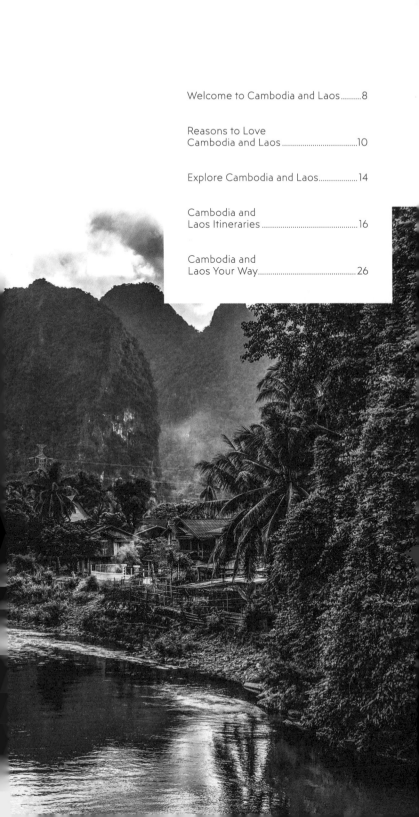

WELCOME TO
CAMBODIA
AND LAOS

Cambodia and Laos have it all: mist-wreathed mountains, white-sand beaches, ancient temples, and lively urban nightspots. Whatever your dream trip to these countries entails, this DK travel guide will prove the perfect companion.

1 French Colonial-era buildings in Kampot.

2 Picturesque white-sand beach in Koh Rong.

3 Rice noodles with herbs and spices in Laos.

4 Boats moored on the river at sunset in Vang Vieng.

Stretching from the rugged borders of China to the scorched shores of the Gulf of Thailand, Cambodia and Laos form the heart of old Indochina. The vibrant capital cities, Phnom Penh and Vientiane, surge with cash and connectivity, but in the smaller towns like Luang Prabang and Kampot an old-world charm endures, with crumbling shophouses, gold-bedecked Buddhist temples, and quiet cafés. The streets abound with rich flavors, from the spicy sizzle of a Khmer barbecue to the steam rising from a hearty bowl of noodle soup.

Out in the countryside, meanwhile, the natural beauty of the region reigns supreme. The roiling Mekong River sweeps past atmospheric settlements and surges through thunderous rapids. Skylines are dominated by fantastical karst outcrops. Deep jungles echo with the calls of birds and gibbons. And towers of weathered stone rise from forest and farmland – the magnificent temple relics that bear testament to ancient civilizations, from little-known Wat Phu Champasak to legendary Angkor Wat.

The sheer diversity of Cambodia and Laos can be overwhelming, but this guidebook breaks the region down into easily navigable chapters, full of expert knowledge and insider tips. We've created detailed itineraries and colorful maps to help you plan the perfect trip. Whether you're here for a flying visit or an extended adventure, this DK travel guide will ensure that you see the very best the country has to offer. Enjoy the book, and enjoy Cambodia and Laos.

REASONS TO LOVE
CAMBODIA
AND LAOS

Lush, intoxicating, and suffused with a certain wild romance – Cambodia and Laos have an irresistible allure for travelers. There are many reasons to love these beautiful countries. Here we pick some of our favorites.

1 THE TEMPLES OF ANGKOR

From the jungle-strangled ruins of Ta Prohm to the majestic towers of Angkor Wat, this vast temple complex in Cambodia ranks high among the must-see wonders of the world *(p86)*.

THE MIGHTY MEKONG 2

The Mekong River is the connecting thread between Cambodia and Laos. Glowing in a Vientiane sunset or traversed on a cruise from Phnom Penh, it is a constant companion to travelers in the area *(p22)*.

3 KAYAKING IN VANG VIENG

Paddling along the Nam Song is the best way to take in the towering karsts, cool limestone caves and ethereal landscapes around Vang Vieng *(p192)*.

CAMBODIA'S COASTAL NATIONAL PARKS 4

Get back to nature in the national parks strung along Cambodia's southern coastline. Explore tangled mangrove forests, snorkel amid teeming coral reefs or stroll along white-sand beaches *(p32)*.

LUANG PRABANG 5

Swamped in greenery, studded with temples, and hemmed by the legendary Mekong, Luang Prabang is straight out of an old traveler's fantasy of Southeast Asia *(p166)*.

CAFÉ SOCIETY, SOUTHEAST ASIAN STYLE 6

Whether it's in a chic Vientiane café *(p165)* or in an earthy barbecue joint in downtown Phnom Penh *(p64)*, watching the world go by from a street-side table is a way of life in Cambodia and Laos.

SI PHAN DON 7

An otherworldly waterscape where the Mekong splits into a maze of channels and islets, Si Phan Don is the place to explore thunderous rapids or stroll along pretty river beaches (p208).

DIVERSE WILDLIFE 8

Cambodia and Laos are home to many tropical species such as gibbons, sun bears, elephants, and tigers. The enigmatic Irrawaddy dolphins can only be sighted in Cambodia.

9 JUNGLE ADVENTURES

Whether it's ziplining through the canopies of Bokeo Nature Reserve (p203), or hiking in the Cardamom Mountains (p134), a jungle journey in the region is an unforgettable experience.

10 PRASAT PREAH VIHEAR

Perched on a dizzying promontory, this stunning 12th-century temple has all of Cambodia at its feet. The intricate carvings are impressive, but the real show-stopper is the view of the plains below *(p114)*.

GASTRONOMIC PHNOM PENH 11

Whether it's a steaming bowl of noodles from a rickety stall in Central Market or a tasting menu in a top restaurant, the Cambodian capital is a haven for foodies *(p64)*.

BEAUTIFUL HANDICRAFTS 12

The mountain villages of northern Laos are known for their highly skilled artisans who create exquisite traditional handicrafts. Phongsali *(p202)* is a good place to pick up jewelry and silverware in particular.

EXPLORE
CAMBODIA
AND LAOS

This guide is divided into two sections covering
Cambodia *(p50)* and Laos *(p144)*. These sections
have been divided into eight color-coded
sightseeing regions, as shown on the map below.

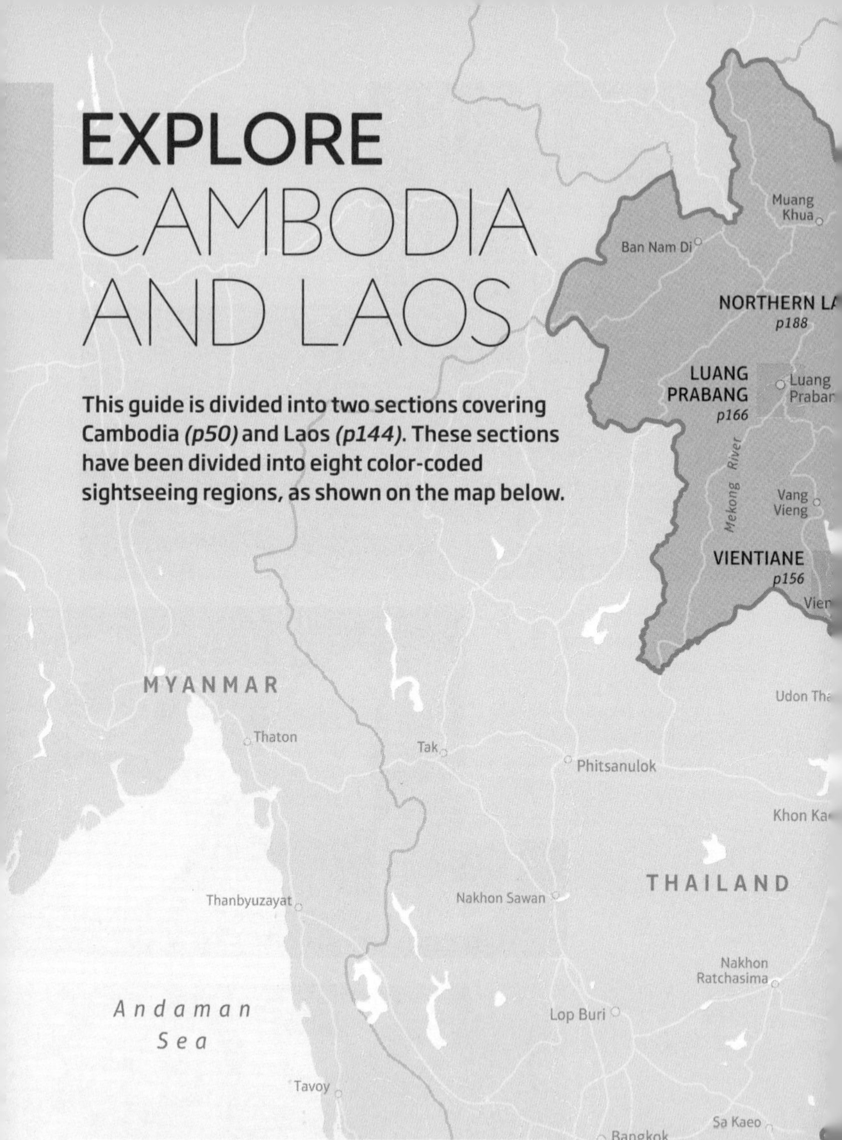

Muang
Khua

Ban Nam Di

NORTHERN LA
p188

**LUANG
PRABANG**
p166

Luang
Prabar

Mekong River

Vang
Vieng

VIENTIANE
p156

Vien

MYANMAR

Thaton

Tak

Phitsanulok

Udon Tha

Khon Ka

THAILAND

Thanbyuzayat

Nakhon Sawan

Nakhon
Ratchasima

*Andaman
Sea*

Lop Buri

Tavoy

Sa Kaeo

Bangkok

Sisc

Chon Buri

SOUTHEAST ASIA

CHINA

BHUTAN

NEPAL

INDIA

MYANMAR

BANGLADESH

LAOS

VIETNAM

THAILAND

PHILIPPINES

*South
China
Sea*

CAMBODIA

BRUNEI

*Bay of
Bengal*

SRI
LANKA

MALAYSIA

SINGAPORE

Indian Ocean

INDONESIA

Chanthaburi

Koh

*Gulf of
Thailand*

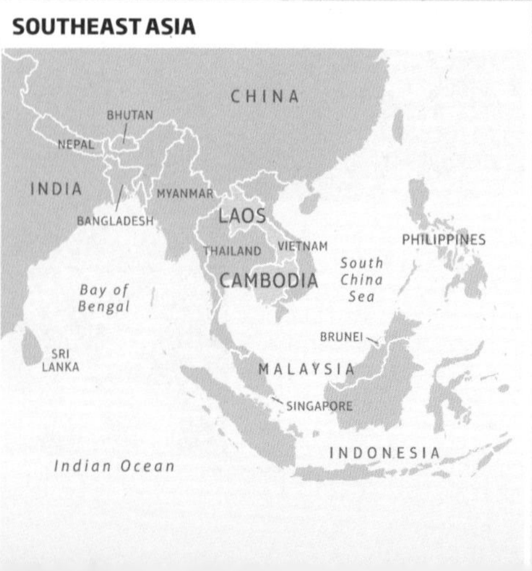

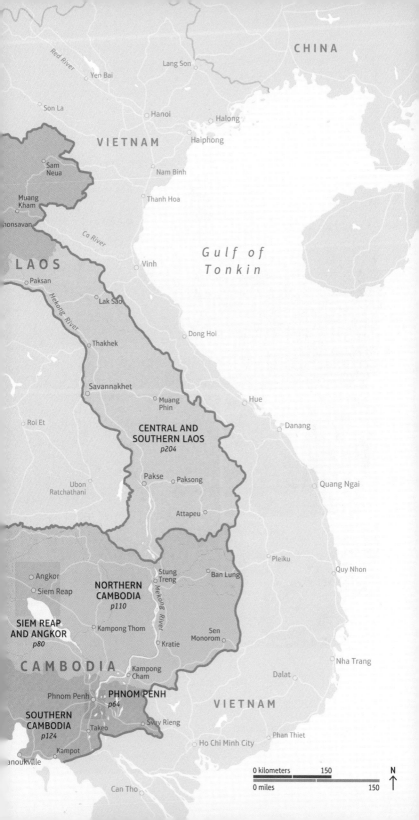

$\longrightarrow$

1 Sunrise over Angkor Wat.

2 Detail of sculpted towers at Bayon.

3 Siem Reap street food.

4 Busy stalls of Angkor Night Market.

Cambodia and Laos brim with travel possibilities, from two-day tours around the big cities to grand odysseys across the entire region. These itineraries will help you to chart your own course through these vibrant and varied countries.

2 DAYS
in Angkor and Siem Reap

Day 1

Morning Get an early start from Siem Reap for a day of temple adventures. Buy your ticket at the main entrance to the Angkor complex, but instead of joining the hordes straining for a snapshot of Angkor Wat, head further north to catch the sunrise at Preah Khan (p106), which is atmospheric and uncrowded at first light. Next, head south to the mighty former city of Angkor Thom (p92). There's hours of exploration to be had here, but focus on the forest of temple towers at Bayon (p96) before the heat rises. To refuel, head to the food court in front of the main entrance to Angkor Wat.

Afternoon Angkor's main attraction is only a short walk away, so after lunch, cross the causeway to enjoy your unforgettable first sight of Angkor Wat (p86). Slow your pace as you explore this magnificent temple, taking your time to admire the lavish carvings along the shaded perimeters. Afterward, continue east to marvel at the jungle-strangled ruins of Ta Prohm (p100). If you still have enough energy, take in the sunset from Phnom Bakheng (p106) – along with hundreds of fellow travelers – before heading back to town.

Evening Reward yourself after a long day of temple-hopping and sample the finest in French-Khmer culinary fusion at the elegant Malis Restaurant (www.malis-restaurant.com/malis-siem-reap), with its lavish set menus.

Day 2

Morning Allow yourself a slower start to the day and, after lingering over breakfast at your hotel, prepare to take the one-hour bus ride to the outlying temple of Banteay Srei (p108). With only one temple to see today, you'll be able to properly appreciate the staggering detail of the carved pink sandstone at this beautiful complex in its isolated rural setting. On the way back to town, stop off at the sobering but informative Cambodian Landmine Museum (p109) for a reminder of Cambodia's troubled recent history. If you're traveling with young children, you might want to skip this and visit the nearby Banteay Srei Butterfly Center (p109) instead.

Afternoon Back in Siem Reap, enjoy a hearty lunch at NGO-run Haven restaurant (Chocolate Rd), then sign up for an afternoon boat trip to Tonlé Sap (p104), the vast lake that lies to the south of Siem Reap. Avoid commercial tours to Chong Kneas and instead head farther out to the Prek Toal Bird Sanctuary or the pretty stilt village of Kampong Phhluk, which is particularly photogenic late in the day.

Evening On your return, hunt out a few souvenirs and sample some tasty street food at the brightly lit Angkor Night Market, before finishing the night with a Tomb Raider cocktail at the bustling Red Piano bar (Bar St).

7 DAYS

A Tour of Cambodia

▌ Day 1

Make Siem Reap your entry point for this week-long odyssey, and fuel up for the journey with a hearty breakfast and tasty coffee from The Little Red Fox Espresso Cafe *(www.thelittlered foxespresso.com)*. Pack a picnic lunch before hitting the road for the four-hour journey north to Prasat Preah Vihear *(p114)*. The views from this dizzyingly located temple make the journey more than worthwhile. Enjoy your lunch from the vantage point on the Pei Ta Da Cliff; you'll feel like Cambodia is at your feet.After you've torn yourself away from the view, head half an hour south to spend the night in the village of Sra Em.

▌ Day 2

Get an early start for the long trip to Battambang. Make a stop at Banteay Srei *(p108)* along the way if you have private transport (the direct journey is six hours); otherwise go straight back to Siem Reap,grab a quick lunch at Il Forno *(www.ilforno.restaurant/siem-reap)*, then hop on a connecting bus for Battambang. Shake out your limbs after the long journey with a stroll through the old heart of Battambang *(p116)*. Walk alongside the Colonial-era shophouses around Pasar Nat and then beside the riverfront. Enjoy a leisurely dinner, then continue south to explore the night market *(St 1)* at dusk.

▌ Day 3

Visit Battambang's Provincial Museum *(p116)* to browse Angkorian statuary before having a light lunch at Lonely Tree Café *(No. 56, St 2.5)*. Flag down a tuk-tuk for a short ride south to Phnom Sampeu *(p117)*, and linger until sundown to see thousands of bats emerging from their hidden roosts. Back in Battambang, tuck into a selection of tapas-style treats at Jaan Bai *(St 2)* before bed.

① Royal Palace, Phnom Penh.
② View from Phnom Sampeau.
③ Boat docking at Kampot Riverside.
④ Colonial-era architecture in Kampot.
⑤ Otres Beach, lined with casuarina trees.

Day 4

Book yourself a seat in an express minibus to Phnom Penh, then sit back and enjoy the six-hour ride along one of Cambodia's better highways. Arrive in the heaving capital in the early afternoon and grab a quick lunch before heading to the ornate Royal Palace and Silver Pagoda complex *(p68)*. Take a sunset cruise on the Mekong from the northern end of Sisowath Quay. Back on dry land, take a tuk-tuk south to the hipster bars along Bassac Lane.

Day 5

Start the day with a Cambodian breakfast of *kuy teav* from one of the stalls in the iconic Art Deco Psar Thmei *(p73)*. Afterward, navigate the busy streets southward to the palatial National Museum *(p72)*. After lunch at Kravanh *(74, St 174)*, take a three-hour bus to the quiet river town of Kampot *(p132)*. On arrival in Kampot, head to Teuk Chhou River. As the sun slips down over the horizon, enjoy a cocktail on the terrace at Rikitikitavi *(www. rikitikitavi-kampot.com)*.

Day 6

Enjoy a lazy morning lounging by the riverside or wandering among Kampot's Colonial-era buildings. Stop off for coffee and cake at the Kampot Pie and Ice Cream Palace *(River Rd)*. In the afternoon, spend a few hours rock climbing at Climbodia *(p132)* and exploring the caves and mountains located just outside Kampot. Take your pick of the bars and restaurants along the riverfront in Kampot.

Day 7

Enjoy the two-hour bus journey to Sihanoukville *(p128)* and while away the final day of your trip lounging on Otres Beach.

7 DAYS
A Tour of Northern Laos

Day 1

Begin your journey with a stroll along the Mekong in Vientiane *(p156)*. Stop for breakfast in one of the riverfront restaurants before heading to the airport to catch a short flight to Phonsavan. After touching down, find your bearings with a walk around the town center. Stop off at the Mines Advisory Group's Visitor Information Center *(p200)* for some sobering insights into the impact of unexploded ordinance on local lives. Stop for dinner at the riverside Kong View restaurant *(183 Souphanouvong Rd)*.

Day 2

Explore Phonsavan's colorful morning market, then take a short bus ride south to the Plain of Jars *(p198)*, beginning your explorations at Site 1. Travel onward to Site 2 and continue to Site 3 on foot, relishing the peaceful countryside along the way. Enjoy delicious steaks

and fried chicken at the popular Cranky-T restaurant *(049 Ban Phonesavanh Xay)*.

Day 3

Fuel up with a hearty early breakfast before embarking on the long six-hour trip through the hills of Hua Phan province to Sam Neua *(p200)*. If you have private transport, detour to the mysterious standing stones at Hintang and look out for the Tat Saloei Waterfall beside the road on the approach to Sam Neua. On arrival in Sam Neua, dine at the basic but friendly Dan Nao Muang Xam restaurant (near the central monument).

Day 4

Start the day with a warming bowl of pho at the riverside market in Sam Neua, then stroll among the stalls, admiring the fabrics and fresh produce. Travel half an hour east of town to tour the astonishing cave complex at Vieng Xai *(p200)*, where

1 The Mekong at Luang Prabang.
2 Pastry market stall in Phonsavan.
3 Sim at Wat Xieng Thong, Luang Prabang.
4 Plain of Jars.
5 Boat trip on the Mekong.

locals and Pathet Lao leaders sheltered to escape US bombing in the 1960s and 70s. Back in Sam Neua, get an early night ahead of a long day on the road.

Day 5

Hit the highway for the long haul west to Nong Khiaw (p201). The stunning mountain scenery more than compensates for the bumpy eight-hour ride. If you have private transport, take a break at the friendly village of Vieng Thong on the edge of the Nam Et National Protected Area, still home to a handful of tigers. Settle in to comfortable riverside lodgings, scrub off the sweat from travel, and enjoy a hearty dinner in one of the village's traveler-friendly restaurants, such as Deen (Ban Sop Houn), with its excellent Indian curries.

Day 6

Spend a lazy morning soaking up the lovely riverside views in Nong Khiaw.

Rent a bike and cycle to the atmospheric Tham Pha Tok caves (p201). Hike up the steep trail to the Sleeping Woman Viewpoint to watch the sun setting over the serried ranks of karst peaks, then stop in for a beer at Q Bar (Route 1c) on the way back to Nong Khiaw.

Day 7

If river boats are running southward, hop aboard for a seriously scenic ride to Luang Prabang (p167); otherwise take the three-hour bus. Luang Prabang will seem like a sophisticated metropolis after your week in the wilds. Take a walk through the old town, ending up at the stupendous Wat Xieng Thong (p170). Buy some souvenirs at the Night Market before making the journey home.

2 WEEKS
Along the Mekong

Day 1

Start your journey in the ultimate Mekong town, former royal capital Luang Prabang *(p167)*. Explore the Royal Palace complex, then stroll along the riverfront to Wat Xieng Thong *(p170)*. Afterward, take a boat tour to Pak Ou Caves, an eerie repository for "retired" Buddha images that can no longer be worshipped on an altar (usually because they are damaged or have been replaced by new images). Circle back and climb to the top of Mount Phou Si *(p176)* in time for sunset. Enjoy live music at Icon Klub *(p178)*, a cozy and atmospheric cocktail bar.

Day 2

Get up in time to watch the solemn Tak Bat ritual *(p177)*, then take the minibus for a four-hour trip south, rolling through stunning scenery to Vang Vieng *(p192)*. On arrival, drift down the Nam Song river – a tributary of the Mekong – in a kayak or tube (oversized rubber ring),

or, if you'd rather stay dry, rent a bike and head out to explore craggy caves. End your day with a stroll along the riverfront before sampling Vang Vieng's impressive array of bars and restaurants.

Day 3

Take a four-hour bus ride to Vientiane *(p156)*, arriving in time for lunch at JoMa Bakery Café *(Setthathirat Rd)*. Explore the lively streets northeast of the river, stopping off at Haw Pha Kaew to admire the bronze Buddha images *(p162)*. If you need refreshment, head a block north to grab a juice at Noy's Fruit Heaven *(Heng Boun Rd)*. Watch the sunset over the Mekong, then browse the handicrafts on offer at the riverfront Night Market *(p163)* and sample some street food.

Day 4

Head to Talat Sao *(p164)*, Vientiane's main market to browse the vast selection of

1 Fisherman casting his net in the early morning light.

2 Hot-air balloons flying over Vang Vieng.

3 Bridge in Luang Prabang.

4 Tak Bat ritual in Laos.

souvenirs. Next, visit the magnificent Wat Si Muang *(p162)*. After lunch in one of the many cafés on Fa Ngum Road, visit the COPE Visitor Center *(p162)* to learn about the impact of 20th-century conflicts on Laos. Grab a table at the lively Chokdee Café *(Fa Ngum Rd)*, for Belgian beer and a bowl of *moules-frites*.

Day 5

Board a bus for the long seven-hour journey southward across the plains of central Laos to Savannakhet. If you can, enjoy a lunch stop at one of the restaurants in Paksan. On arrival in Savannakhet, meet other travelers over a bowl of nachos or a Mexican wrap at Pilgrim's Kitchen *(p213)*, a popular spot overlooking the Mekong.

Day 6

Wander around Savannakhet's center, observing the crumbling Colonial-era

villas. Stop off at Wat Sainyaphum *(p212)*. Charter a tuk-tuk for a foray into the forests of the Dong Natad National Protected Area *(p213)*, northeast of town. Back in Savannakhet, take an evening stroll along the banks of the Mekong, and dine at the waterfront food stalls north of the Chao Mahesak Shrine.

Day 7

Take an early bus to Pakse, then change for a minibus to Champasak. When you arrive, head straight for Wat Phu Champasak *(p210)*. Make your way along the ceremonial causeway to the upper level of this beautifully situated temple, then enjoy the view back east toward the river. Back in Champasak, grab a seat for the show at Cinéma-TukTuk.

$\rightarrow$

Day 8

Continue your southward journey, following the course of the Mekong by bus to the otherworldly islets of Si Phan Don *(p208)*. Having taken your pick of the idyllic accommodations on Don Khon or Don Det, hire a bicycle and set out on a leisurely exploration of these twin islets, linked by a Colonial-era bridge. Nights are dark in Si Phan Don. If you want to join the back packer party, head for the village of Ban Hua Det at the northernmost tip of Don Det.

Day 9

Sign up for either a boat trip or a kayaking tour. Marvel at the thunderous Khon Phapeng Waterfalls *(p209)*, and keep your eyes peeled for Irrawaddy dolphins. After a late lunch, grab a bicycle and ride to the smaller but still thoroughly impressive falls at Li Phi. Choose a prime sunset spot – either isolated Xai Kong Nyai beach on Don Khon, or a laidback guesthouse

restaurant on Don Det's western coastal track, and look out across the water to Cambodia as darkness falls.

Day 10

Say goodbye to island life, then hop on a bus heading for the Cambodian border at Trapaeng Kreil. After crossing the frontier, continue south to Stung Treng *(p122)*. Set at the conflu-ence of the Mekong and the San River, this pleasant town makes a gentle intro-duction to Cambodia. Wander along the riverfront at dusk and get your first taste of Cambodian street food from the nearby stalls.

Day 11

Kit yourself out with a good-quality mountain bike and map from Xplore Asia *(www.cambodiamekongtrail.com)* then chart a course along the network of dirt tracks and backroads that make up the Mekong Discovery Trail. Continue your explorations along the river banks south of town, keeping an eye out for

1 Boat ride from Kratie.
2 Cambodian street food.
3 Cycling the Mekong Discovery Trail.
4 Riverfront lodgings in Don Det.
5 Kayaking in Si Phan Don.
6 Royal Palace in Phnom Penh.

river dolphins. Head back to the food stalls if you fancy more local fare, or relax over a pizza at Ponika's Palace (near the market).

Day 12

Hop on a local minibus for the two-hour ride south to Kratie (p122). Board the local ferry from the Kratie riverfront for the short hop across to Koh Trong – a mid-Mekong islet that offers easy access to rural Cambodia. Rent a bike at the landing stage and make a circuit, taking in the floating village and rustic temples. Enjoy cocktails at Le Tonle Tourism Training Center (724 St 3).

Day 13

Tuck into a breakfast of the local specialty *krolan* (sticky, coconut-flavored rice), then explore the backstreets, looking out for Colonial-era villas. Head north to Kampie, and take a boat trip to view the river dolphins, or sign up for a half-day kayaking tour of the same area with the chance to spot some of the local birdlife.

Enjoy your last slice of provincial Cambodian life, and swap stories with other travelers in one of the cafés between the market and the river in Kratie.

Day 14

The final stage of this Mekong odyssey is the five-hour bus ride south, following the river's course to the Cambodian capital. Experience the culture shock of returning to big city life in Phnom Penh (p64). Wander along the broad riverfront boulevard of Sisowath Quay, then swing inland to the magnificent Royal Palace and Silver Pagoda (p68). Cut back to the waterfront and grab a seat with a sunset view at the lovely Le Moon bar (Sisowath Quay) to give a final toast to the majestic river that has inspired your journey.

Ta Prohm

Locked in the python-like grip of the forest itself, Angkor's Ta Prohm *(p100)* is the ultimate jungle temple. With the mossy masonry and tumbled blocks enmeshed by the roots of huge trees, this one-time monastery conveys a powerful sense of the passage of time.

Trees and moss growing out of the ruins of Ta Prohm in Angkor

CAMBODIA AND LAOS FOR
AWE-INSPIRING TEMPLES

From enigmatic edifices of grey stone, weathered by long centuries and half-hidden by tropical greenery, to living places of worship in the midst of sprawling cities, the magnificent temples of Cambodia and Laos are a testament to the region's rich history and enduring spiritual traditions.

TOP 3 LESSER-KNOWN TEMPLES

Banteay Chhmer
This huge, jungle-swamped complex conveys a real sense of adventure *(p119)*.

That Ing Hang
Buddhist pilgrims flock to this huge temple near Savannakhet *(p213)*.

Koh Ker
With its striking pyramidal centerpiece, Koh Ker *(p120)* is miles from the tourist trail.

Wat Xieng Thong

A city within a city, this monastery is the beating heart of Buddhism in Luang Prabang *(p170)*. The soaring roof finials and vivid mosaics are spectacular, but the real magic lies in its bustling vitality as dozens of saffron-clad monks and novices go about their daily business.

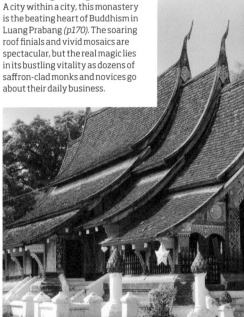

→

The extraordinary gilded exterior of Wat Xieng Thong

Angkor Wat

Probably the most famous temple on the planet and ranking high on many a bucket list, the magnificent Angkor Wat *(p86)* - the world's biggest religious monument - more than matches the hype. With its soaring towers, sublime design, and epic narrative bas-relief panels, this is a true masterpiece carved in stone.

→

Sunrise over Angkor Wat, seen from Phnom Bakheng

Prasat Preah Vihear

Perched atop a prow-like promontory with the lowlands of Cambodia and Thailand stretching far into the hazy distance below, Prasat Preah Vihear *(p114)* is the most spectacularly located temple in the region. The complex, dedicated to the Hindu god Shiva, has been dominating this landscape for a millennium.

←

Young Buddhist monk posing for the camera at Prasat Preah Vihear

Wat Phu Champasak

Set amid the rivers and mountains of southern Laos, this ancient place of worship *(p210)* may not match the scale of Angkor Wat, but its symphony of architecture and landscape reigns supreme. What's more, it gets far fewer visitors than Angkor, and its overgrown terraces offer spectacular views.

→

Wat Phu Champasak surrounded by spectacular scenery

INTRODUCTION TO BUDDHISM

Buddhism sets the tone in Cambodia and Laos. From grand architectural traditions to the columns of alms-seeking monks passing through the streets at dawn, the influence of the faith is everywhere. Buddhism was founded by Siddhartha Gautama, a prince-turned-ascetic in India in the 6th century BCE. It arrived in Southeast Asia, along with Hinduism, around 2,000 years ago, and for centuries the two faiths coexisted as a syncretic mélange. Since the 13th century, however, the Theravada school of Buddhism has been the main religion of Cambodia and Laos, albeit often interwoven with local folk traditions.

DAILY PRACTICE

While Theravada Buddhism teaches that Enlightenment is virtually unattainable, it encourages the acquiring of merit through personal actions and religious practice to ensure higher status in the endless cycle of reincarnation. An obvious formal way to acquire merit is through the offering of alms.

LIVING TEMPLES

Though monks follow organized religious routines, there is no fixed program of service for the general population at wats – which serve as monasteries and temples. Instead the faithful visit when they feel the inclination, bowing or kneeling in respect before images of the Buddha.

↑ Buddhist monks collecting alms during the Tak Bat ceremony in Luang Prabang

THE SANGHA

Becoming a Buddhist monk is not necessarily a lifelong vocation, and many men in Cambodia and Laos join the *Sangha* (monkhood) in their teens for a few months or years – or these days even just a few days – before returning to secular life. There is no ordination for women, though there are orders of lay nuns.

SYMBOLS OF FAITH

Bodhi Tree – The large sacred fig tree under which Buddha meditated for 49 days during his quest to achieve enlightenment. The tree usually symbolizes the path to enlightenment.

Lotus - This aquatic plant represents the progress of the soul toward Enlightenment. Although it is rooted in dirt, the lotus's flowers appear to float above muddy waters, and water easily slides off its petals.

Naga – This serpent-like figure represents wisdom and a protective force.

Wheel of Law – A physical manifestation of the Buddhist doctrine, known as the *Dharmachakra*, which represents the Buddha's path to Nirvana.

1 Image of Buddha underneath a bodhi tree.

2 A lotus-shaped stupa.

3 Seven-headed Naga at Wat Phnom.

4 Wheel of Law behind an image of the Buddha.

↑ Cambodian Buddhist Monks perching on the ruins at Angkor Wat

Mountains

The mountains of Vang Vieng are mightily impressive, while the Annamite Mountains hide shrouded valleys like Vieng Xai (p200). In Cambodia, Kulen Mountain (p108) offers great views near Angkor, while Phnom Santuk (p121) features a temple at its summit. The Cardamom Mountains (p134) represent the largest remaining wilderness in Southeast Asia.

$\longrightarrow$

Dramatic scenery among the mighty Vang Vieng mountains

CAMBODIA AND LAOS FOR
NATURAL
WONDERS

From roiling river rapids and craggy karst mountains to placid lakes and tranquil shores fringed with powdery sand, Cambodia and Laos are home to numerous majestic landscapes. But for all its geographical diversity, the region is bound together as a coherent whole by the Mekong river.

Waterfalls

The rivers of this region are terraced with spectacular waterfalls. Plunging over a cliff in the forested landscapes of Eastern Cambodia, the Bonsraa Waterfall (p123) is a dramatic example, while the spectacular Khon Phapeng (p209) falls in Southern Laos are the widest in the world. There are also gentler cascades perfect for a dip, such as Laos's Tat Sae (p183).

Bonsraa Waterfall, located near Sen Monorom

LEAVE NO TRACE

Cambodia and Laos's popularity with tourists is an economic lifeline, but it also has a significant impact on their fragile ecosystems. This can be mitigated by following some simple precepts. Dispose of your rubbish responsibly or take it away with you; avoid close contact with wild animals and never touch underwater wildlife while diving or snorkeling; and respect local traditions and norms.

Caves

Many caves riddle Laos and Cambodia's karst landscape. A boat journey into Tham Kong Lo cave *(p215)* is surrounded by waterfalls. Many caves are sites of spiritual significance; the temple complex of Phnom Chhnork *(p136)* contains a shrine to the Hindu god Shiva, built in the 7th century.

$\rightarrow$
Boat ride into the mouth of the Tham Kong Lo Lake

Lakes and Rivers

The Mekong river is the lifeblood of Laos and Cambodia. It's also home to the archipelago of Laos's Si Phan Don *(p208)* and Kong Leng Lake *(p215)*. In Cambodia, the wide Teuk Chhou river *(p132)* flows through Kampot, while Tonlé Sap *(p104)* is home to boat villages and mangrove forests.

$\rightarrow$
Khon Phapeng Waterfalls, south of Si Phan Don

Party on the Shores of Koh Rong

Situated a 45-minute boat ride away from the beaches of Sihanoukville, the idyllic island of Koh Rong *(p130)* is Cambodia's seaside set piece. With the ultimate combination of white sands, crystal-clear waters, and a verdant interior, it's little wonder that droves of footloose young travelers flock here to find their own slice of paradise. If music-blasting beach bars aren't your thing, you'll still find a few quiet corners of the island to escape the crowds and take in the scenery.

→

Lively bars lining the beaches of Koh Rong, off the coast at Sihanoukville

CAMBODIA AND LAOS FOR
BREATHTAKING BEACHES

Cambodia's sandy coast gives neighboring Thailand and Vietnam a run for their money with dazzling white sands, coral gardens, and blissfully warm waters. And landlocked Laos isn't left out altogether in the beach stakes: you'll find some unexpectedly lovely coves on the shores of the Mekong.

Bask on the Sands of Otres Beach

Sihanoukville *(p128)* is where tourists first started to descend on Cambodia's beaches in the 1960s. Today, the town draws hordes of holidaymakers from around the world, and it can be hard to find a spot to lay your towel on many of the smaller beaches. But at 2 miles (3 km) long, the seemingly endless expanse of Otres Beach still has plenty of room for all.

←

White sand and turquoise waters on Otres Beach in Sihanoukville

TOP 3 SECLUDED PARADISES

Bokor National Park
This mountaintop escape offers stunning views *(p136)*.

Don Daeng
Quiet beaches pepper this tranquil sliver of land *(p217)*, marooned mid-Mekong.

Koh S'dach
Off the coast of the Botum Sakor National Park *(p137)*, discover peaceful coves that are far removed from the busy resort islands further south.

Watch the River Flow on Don Khon

Laos is full of surprises, not least that a country without a coast has decent beaches. Several river islands along the Mekong have pretty stretches of sand, but the best are undoubtedly those among the many river islets of Si Phan Don *(p208)*.

← View from a beach on Don Khon, the largest of the Si Phan Don islets

Live Like a Castaway on Koh Tonsay, Cambodia

Riding like a ship at anchor in the placid waters south of Kep, pretty little Koh Tonsay *(p142)* - also known as Rabbit Island - has all the palm trees, hammocks, and ramshackle charm you need to create your own desert island paradise.

→ Hammock strung between palm trees on Koh Tonsay

Botum Sakor National Park

Sloping gently down from the foothills of the Cardamom Mountains to the sea, Botum Sakor (p137) is the least visited of Cambodia's coastal national parks. Developers have moved into the western section of the park, but its central forests and eastern mangroves remain untouched. Boat trips here explore the park's creeks and jungle.

$\rightarrow$

Tree-lined beach on the edge of Botum Sakor National Park

CAMBODIA FOR
COASTAL NATIONAL PARKS

Cambodia's southern littoral is still home to swathes of wilderness between the busy beach towns. National parks and nature reserves are strung along the coast, many of them in easy reach of the main accommodation centers. Land and sea lock together here amid some of the best preserved mangrove forests in Asia. The shallow waters and low-lying coastal jungle are home to a vast array of sealife, rare birds, and elusive mammals.

Southern Cardamom National Park

At 1,584 sq miles (4,102 sq km), this huge park sprawls across the four provinces of Pursat, Kampong Speu, Koh Kong, and Sihanoukville, stretching from remote valleys to mangrove shores. It's home to an array of endangered wildlife, including gibbons, bears, and elephants. There is also a plan to reintroduce wild tigers from India, believed to be extinct in Cambodia since 2007.

$\rightarrow$

The Southern Cardamom National Park, the largest in Cambodia

Peam Krasaop Nature Reserve

Just a short ride south of Koh Kong, this is one of the finest places to explore the strange, semiaquatic environment created by mangroves. Walkways thread their way through the thickets here – over either mud or water, depending on the tide. The reserve is also a working community, with a series of traditional fishing hamlets that can be reached by boat via a vast network of narrow channels (p140).

(p140)

← Boat exploring the mangroves of Peak Krasaop Nature Reserve

(p136)

TOP 4 COASTAL WILDLIFE

Hawksbill Turtles
Found in shallow waters, mostly feeding off of sponges.

White-Tip Reef Shark
Growing up to 5 ft (1.5 m) in length, and hunting around shallow reefs, this common shark is not aggressive.

Hermit Crabs
These crabs forage on the muddy foreshores, especially around mangrove forests.

Fishing Cat
Elusive but widespread throughout Cambodia's coastal regions, this small wildcat hunts along the edges of creeks and inlets.

→ Tourists take in the view from the mountains in Bokor National Park

MANGROVES

With elevated roots that provide shelter for a wide array of aquatic and semiaquatic species, mangroves are trees and shrubs that grow in the intertidal zone. Mangrove plants have adapted complex filtration systems to enable them to thrive in salty conditions, and their tangled roots stabilize and protect low-lying coastal regions by preventing the effects of erosion.

Bokor National Park

Though most visitors only see the Colonial-era relics and modern Chinese developments at the old Bokor Hill Station, this large national park (p136) also encompasses mountains, rainforest, and waterfalls. The core of the park is the Elephant Mountains, which angle down toward the sea. Their deep valleys are home to hundreds of bird species, bears, gibbons, and leopards.

Gibbons

The charismatic masters of the forest canopy, seven species of gibbon live in the lush forests of the region. In Laos, see black-crested gibbons in Bokeo *(p203)*. In Cambodia, you can spot rare northern yellow-cheeked gibbons in Veun Sai-Siem Pang Conservation Area, while pileated gibbons are one of eight globally endangered species that can be found in Botum Sakor National Park *(p137)*.

White-handed gibbon swinging from the trees in eastern Cambodia

CAMBODIA AND LAOS FOR
WILDLIFE ENCOUNTERS

Cambodia and Laos are still home to some of Asia's iconic wildlife species. Glimpsing the rarer mammals in the wild requires effort and luck, but you'll spot colorful birdlife on any foray into the countryside. For close encounters, you can visit centers that rescue animals from trafficking and captivity.

An Indochinese tiger at the Phnom Tamao Rescue Center, near Phnom Penh

 INSIDER TIP
Birdwatching

The birds of Cambodia and Laos are much easier to spot than any other species. Hornbills and peafowl inhabit the forests, while the marshy banks of Tonlé Sap are a birdwatcher's paradise. The Prek Toal sanctuary is a major breeding site for wetland birds.

Tigers

The very notion of a tiger is enough to fire the imagination. Although the Indochinese tiger is thought to have vanished from Laos in around 2014, there are plans to reintroduce the big cats in the remote reserves of southern Laos.

Irrawaddy Dolphins

These snub-nosed cetaceans are among the world's most enigmatic animals, revealed in tantalizing glimpses as they break the murky surface of the Mekong River. Irrawaddy dolphins are now deemed functionally extinct in Laos, but there is a good chance of spotting them in parts of Cambodia, with tours departing from Kampie.

$\rightarrow$

Irrawaddy dolphin swimming in the Mekong, spotted from a boat

Sun Bears

With their trademark crescent of yellowish fur on their chest, and their taste for fruit and honey, the sun bear is built for life in the tropical forests. Though elusive, small numbers live in many of the protected areas in Laos, including Phu Khao Khuay, close to Vientiane *(p160)*.

$\leftarrow$

Sun bear perching in a tree in the protected forests of Phu Khao Khuay

TOURISM AND ANIMAL RIGHTS

The political turmoil of the 20th century took its toll on the region's wildlife. Poverty meant poaching, logging, and hunting for cash were common. Today, many animals suffer in captivity, and the tourist industry is often culpable. There are ways to experience wildlife ethically, however. The Phnom Tamao Rescue Center near Phnom Penh does good work, as does the Elephant Conservation Center in Laos.

Elephants

Just a few hundred wild elephants survive today, but they are still the most iconic species in the region. Captive elephants generally don't live happy lives, but ethical encounters are possible around Sen Monorom *(p123)* and Sainyabuli.

$\uparrow$ Elephant enjoying a refreshing dip in protected Elephant Valley, Cambodia

▽ Rock Climbing

The karst landscapes of the countryside offer challenging crags for experienced climbers and also some great, easy-going options for beginners, especially Climbodia *(p132)*, located just outside Kampot. Laos's adventure capital, Vang Vieng *(p192)*, is a top climbing spot, with a number of routes for seasoned climbers and newbies alike.

△ Below the Waves

Cambodia is just as beautiful below the water as above it. Sihanoukville *(p128)* is a good base for diving and snorkeling trips to nearby islands, where turtles, barracudas and nudibranchs can be spotted. Koh Tang is a great spot to swim with larger fish, like leopard sharks and eagle rays.

CAMBODIA AND LAOS FOR
ADVENTURERS

Cambodia and Laos are not all about sedate temple visits or relaxing beach breaks – both countries offer endless possibilities for outdoor adventure, from hikes to kitesurfing too. Local operators are constantly pioneering new activities, so there are always fresh opportunities for thrill-seekers.

△ Mountain Biking

The landscape of Phnom Kulen National Park makes a splendid setting for mountain biking. Check out Tonkin Travel *(tonkin-travel.com)* for options, including a tour to Kbal Spean, a riverbed carved with images of Hindu deities. Mekong also has scenic biking routes connecting the riverside towns via jungle paths and beautiful villages.

▽ Hiking

Through forests echoing with the call of gibbons, or over cloud-bedecked mountains, superb hiking routes lace Laos and Cambodia. The area around Phongsali *(p202)* offers exciting experiences, while the hill town of Muang Sing *(p196)* makes a great base for treks through woods, fields, and villages. In Cambodia, the Mekong Discovery Trail *(p123)* links homestays in the countryside, while offshore islands like Koh Ta Kiev *(p131)* have jungle trails inland.

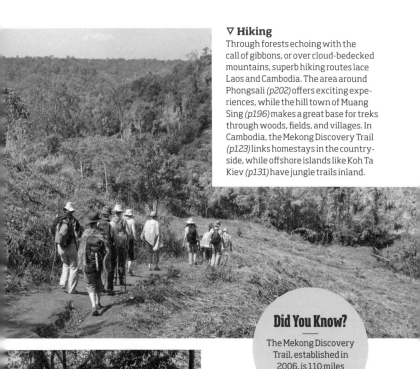

Did You Know?

The Mekong Discovery Trail, established in 2006, is 110 miles (180 km) long.

▽ On the Water

For years, the archetypal aquatic activity in Laos was drifting along the Nam Song river on an inflated inner tube. Nowadays, however, many travelers look for a more active experience, and Vang Vieng has become the kayaking capital of the region. In Cambodia, meanwhile, kitesurfing is a popular activity on the Gulf of Thailand, which provides reliable sea breezes while seldom whipping up dangerously large waves. Kampot's Kep Thmey Beach *(p141)* is an emerging center for kitesurfing, for experts and beginners alike with several operators running courses.

△ Ziplining

Immerse yourself in a forest environment by whizzing through the treetops on a zipline. This activity can be enjoyed by travelers of all fitness levels and at a number of picturesque spots across Cambodia and Laos. Near Luang Prabang, a zipline gives you a bird's-eye view over the terraced waterfalls of Tat Sae *(p183)*, while the Angkor Zipline is a thrilling way to explore the jungles of Siem Reap.

Angkor Sunrise

It's the ultimate Cambodian scene: Angkor Wat reflected in the moat at first light, or bathed in the coppery glow of sunset. The chance to capture this iconic image is irresistible, though you'll find yourself fighting for the perfect shot among hundreds of other snappers. To dodge the crowds, go for a side angle, or head instead to the enchanting Preah Khan (p106).

$\rightarrow$

Iconic image of Angkor Wat reflected in the moat at sunrise

CAMBODIA AND LAOS FOR
PHOTOGRAPHERS

From karst mountains fading into a lavender dusk to the vivid saffron splash of a monk's robes, Cambodia and Laos deliver a welter of striking images. Little wonder, then, that these countries rank high on the wishlists of globetrotting photographers. Whether you're looking to photograph a new angle on a much-snapped temple or to capture the essence of Lao street life, these two countries are paradise for photographers.

Tak Bat Ceremony

Amid the flattened colors before sunrise, the glow of the monks' robes somehow seem all the more intense, so it's no surprise that many travelers are keen to capture Luang Prabang's morning Tak Bat ritual (p177) on camera. However, it's vital to be respectful, unobtrusive, and to avoid using flash – long lenses and fast ISO speeds are the way to go.

The Perfect Waterfall Shot

It's an old favorite when it comes to showing off technical know-how – a waterfall captured at slow shutter speed, with the cascades transformed into a smooth streak of movement. Cambodia and Laos provide plenty of chances to try it out. The Tat Sae falls *(p183)* near Luang Prabang are particularly accessible, and the surrounding trees helpfully reduce light levels.

← see p183

Picturesque Tat Sae cascades, photographed with a slow shutter speed

→

Cycling past crumbling buildings on the streets of Kampot

TOURS AND WORKSHOPS

TOURS AND WORKSHOPS

With endless photo opportunities, Cambodia and Laos are great places for photographers to hone their technical skills and finesse their eye for the perfect image. Several companies run dedicated photography tours in the region, led by experienced professionals. There are also a number of very good one-day workshops that can be joined at short notice, especially around Angkor.

> 💬 **INSIDER TIP**
> **Photo Etiquette**
>
> Many locals are happy to strike a pose for photographers, but asking their permission first is vital – easily done through gesture even when there's no common language. Monks sometimes expect a small cash donation for being photographed, seen as a legitimate form of alms giving.

←

Monks collecting alms during Tak Bat, a popular ritual with photographers

Street Photography

The towns of Cambodia and Laos are full of color, action, and moments of unexpected beauty, and street photography here can reap fantastic results. Colonial-era shophouses in places like Battambang *(p116)* or Savannakhet *(p212)* make brilliant backdrops; food stalls offer striking macro images; and busy markets offer a snapshot of local life.

Luang Prabang's Handicraft Night Market

A gentle introduction to the world of Southeast Asian market commerce, this nightly souvenir bazaar may be thoroughly tourist-oriented, but the vendors avoid the hard sell, making this a fine place to learn the basics of bargaining in a friendly atmosphere *(p180)*.

The handicrafts market outside the Royal Palace Complex in Luang Prabang

CAMBODIA AND LAOS FOR
MESMERIZING MARKETS

Markets are more than just a place of commerce; they're a social institution and an engine house of culinary and craft-based culture. Known as *psar* in Cambodia and *talat* in Laos, they run the gamut from gentle handicraft bazaars to seething produce marts, full of unimaginable foodstuffs.

Angkor Night Market

Lit up like a Christmas tree, Siem Reap's Angkor Night Market is an extravaganza of handicrafts, featuring every imaginable take-home trinket, and a few real treasures for those prepared to hunt. In among the stalls you'll find quirky bars, tasty street food, and unexpected entertainment.

→

Stalls in the Angkor Night Market

 INSIDER TIP
Striking a Bargain

Aim for a small discount when it comes to fresh produce, but remember that opening prices for handicrafts are often way over the odds. Generally, you need to bargain harder in Cambodia than in Laos.

Phnom Penh Central Market

It's the architecture at Phnom Penh's Central Market, known locally as Psar Thmei *(p73)*, that really catches the eye. Set under a striking yellow-and-white Art Deco dome, built in the 1930s and designed by Jean Desbois, it is a maze of stalls selling everything from cheap fashion items to fresh fish. Look out for a wide range of fruits and some fantastic street food in the stalls around the fringes.

→

Phnom Penh's iconic Psar Thmei, also known as Central Market

Talat Dao Heuang, Pakse

Pakse's Dao Heuang is a market experience on a grand scale. With fresh produce delivered from the countryside each morning, dried goods, and every imaginable household item, plus a few handicrafts, there's hours of browsing to be had here *(p216)*.

←

Baguette stall at Talat Dao Heuang in Pakse

Talat Sao in Vientiane

The original shopping center of the Lao capital has undergone a modern makeover in recent years. Most of the cloth merchants, souvenir stalls and shops selling household goods are now found in a modern, air-conditioned building, although there are still some outdoor food stalls *(p164)*.

→

Fresh produce stall at the Talat Sao market in Vientiane

Ban Lung

At the heart of rugged Rattanakiri, Cambodia's farthest-flung province, Ban Lung *(p122)* feels like a true frontier town under a patina of red dust. But its grid of ramshackle streets forms the gateway for treks into the wild spaces of the nearby Virachey National Park, trips to explore thunderous waterfalls and vast crater lakes, and visits to animist cemeteries and friendly local villages.

$\rightarrow$

The suspension bridge at Kachanh Waterfall, near Ban Lung

CAMBODIA AND LAOS
OFF THE BEATEN PATH

The region's must-see attractions draw big crowds, and with good reason, but it only takes a little effort to escape the tourist track. Little-known temples half-hidden in the jungle, village communities making their first forays into ecotourism, and quiet provincial towns forgotten by the tour buses: there are fresh discoveries aplenty to be made in Cambodia and Laos.

Muang Sing

Somehow, travelers to Laos seem to have forgotten about Muang Sing *(p196)* – this is one place that has actually gotten less touristy with the passage of time. But while the former crowds have vanished, the charmingly serene atmosphere, stunning amphitheater of mountains, hiking trails, and diverse communities in the surrounding countryside all still remain.

$\leftarrow$

Looking out across the spectacular landscape surrounding Muang Sing

Koh Kong

This tranquil town offers a true glimpse of provincial Cambodian life, but the real attraction is the chance to trek to the nearby Cardamom Mountains, or take a trip to Koh Kong Island, which has largely escaped development thanks to its location on the frontier with Thailand (p137).

$\rightarrow$

Rowing boat at sunrise on the Piphot river near Koh Kong

Caves of Central Laos

For years, most travelers hurried through the slender midriff of Laos, but there were subterranean marvels here, awaiting discovery. Tham Kong Lo (p215) gets lots of attention these days, but there are other caves that see far fewer visitors, not least the spectacular Tham Lot Se Bang Fai.

$\leftarrow$

Sitting on rocks near the entrance to Tham Lot Se Bang Fai

ESCAPING THE CROWDS

You don't have to travel very far to steer clear of tour groups. The easiest way to get off the beaten track close to places like Siem Reap or Luang Prabang is with your own wheels. A bicycle or motorbike will get you straight onto back-roads with the luxury of stopping whenever you like, or detouring to places that very seldom see an outsider. Southeast Asian roads are not for the faint-hearted, of course, and motorbiking here is not for beginners.

$\uparrow$ Girl wearing traditional Akha Nuqui clothing in Phongsali Province

Phongsali Province

Squeezed in between the borders of Vietnam and China, mountainous Phongsali (p202) is prime hiking territory. The area is a bastion of minority cultures and, with such a vast array of mountain trails to choose from, it's always possible to chart original itineraries that steer clear of tour groups.

Khmer Barbecue

Cambodia may be the true home of barbecue, and a slab of succulent meat or tender squid grilled over charcoal - often accompanied by an ice-cold beer - is the ultimate local comfort food, served in no-frills roadside food stalls in every town.
Where to find it: Sovanna *(2c St 21, Phnom Penh)* and Khmer Grill *(Wat Damnak Rd, Siem Reap)*.

Marinated meat cooked over a Khmer barbecue on roadside food stall

CAMBODIA FOR
FOODIES

Cambodian cookery borrows from the cuisines of neighboring Vietnam and Thailand, stirs in a dash of Chinese influence, sprinkles on a pinch of French heritage, and serves up a spicy fusion that's entirely its own. Rice is the main staple, though noodles run a close second, and both come with a wide range of accompanying soups, curries, and sauces.

TOP 5 FOOD FOR THE FEARLESS

Kan Te (Beetles)
Crispy fried beetles are a Cambodian delicacy.

Jong-Reut (Crickets)
Deep-fried crickets are a popular snack.

Pong Tea Khon (Fertilized Eggs)
Duck and chicken eggs are served complete with an embryo.

Bpoo-Ah (Snakes)
Marinated and grilled snakes are served on bamboo sticks.

A'Ping (Spiders)
Crispy deep-fried tarantula is another local favorite.

Street Food

Cambodia's street food culture is a vibrant circus of flavors, served up with minimal fuss. All the classic Cambodian dishes are designed to be eaten on the go and can be found at street level - including skewered sausages and insects.
Where to find it: Psar Thmei in Phnom Penh *(p73)* and the Battambang Night Market *(St 109)*.

Tables set out at a street food stall in Phnom Penh

Fine Dining

A burgeoning local middle class and a surging tourist economy have provided the impetus for some very sophisticated restaurants popping up in the major cities of Cambodia. Push the boat out with a tasting menu, and choose from classic French dishes or innovative fusions of local flavors and European techniques. **Where to find it:** Topaz *(162 Norodom Blvd, Phnom Penh)*, Malis *(Pokambor Ave, Siem Reap)*, and Jaan Bai *(St 2, Battambang)*.

→

Elegant interior of Malis, featuring Cambodian art and high ceilings

Sweets

Common Cambodian desserts include *borbo skor ta xuan* (a sticky mung bean pudding) and the delicious custard-filled pumpkin slices known as *sankhya lapov*. *Num ansom chek* (banana steamed with rice) is a classic sweet street eat. **Where to find it:** Teuk Skor *(11 St 360, Phnom Penh)* and Khmer Dessert *(51 St 118, Phnom Penh)*.

←

Delectable Khmer shaved ice – made of layers of ice, palm sugar syrup and jelly – served at Teuk Skor

Breakfast

A bowl of streaming hot noodle soup is the standard Cambodian breakfast. Known as *kuy teav*, the dish features flavorsome broth, fresh greens and meat. Another popular breakfast dish is *borbor* (savory rice porridge). **Where to find it:** Street food stalls and Malis *(136 Norodom Blvd, Phnom Penh)*.

→

Breakfast bowl of *kuy teav* (noodle soup)

TOP 4 **TASTY LAO DISHES**

Pho
The Lao version of a hearty noodle soup.

Mok Pa
Pounded white fish is steamed with spices to make this fragrant dish.

Laap
This best-known Lao specialty is a salad made of minced meat.

Or Lam
This noodle broth with smoked meat and greens is a Luang Prabang classic.

Baguettes

Laos has a serious taste for French baguettes. Served filled with pâté, pickles, and salad all over the country, they make for a great lunch or breakfast.
Where to find it: PVO (Fa Ngum St, Vientiane), Annabelle Cafe (Quai Fa Ngum, Vientiane), and baguette stalls on the corner of Th Kitsarat and Th Chao Fa Ngum in Luang Prabang.

→

Delivering freshly baked baguettes to a stall in Luang Prabang

Did You Know?

The key ingredient in any Lao kitchen is *padaek*, a fermented fish sauce with a pungent salty taste.

LAOS FOR
FOODIES

From fried river weed to a reassuringly familiar baguette sandwich, Lao food might not be as well-known as that of its neighbors, but it is delicious and very wide ranging. Spice is key here, and rice and noodles form the basis for most meals, while the influences of Thailand, China, and France produce a fusion that is uniquely Lao.

Noodles

Laos is home to a tangle of different noodle varieties and a wide array of different dishes, but the classic form is *khao poon* (thin, spaghetti-like noodles made from fermented rice), which are used in soups and salads. Thicker Chinese-style wheat noodles are also available.
Where to find it: Khaiphaen (100 Sisavang Vatana Rd, Luang Prabang), Nang Tao (just off Kounxoau Rd, Luang Prabang), and PVO (Kaoyot Village, Vientiane).

←

Boy eating a bowl of *khao poon*, a common type of Lao noodle, cooked in broth

Drinks

The ubiquitous Beerlao is not the only beverage available. Lao lao is a schnapps-like rice liquor found across the country, while those looking for a softer drink will find green tea in vast quantities.
Where to find it: Icon Klub *(Luang Prabang) (p178)*.

Group of tourists enjoying riverside drinks at sunset

Fine Dining

As in neighboring Cambodia, the departing French colonialists left behind a real taste for Gallic cuisine in Laos. These days, old-school French restaurants have been joined by sophisticated new modern joints, forging fusions of local technique and international style.
Where to find it: Dyen Sabai *(Ban Phan Luang, Luang Prabang)* and L'Adresse de Tinay *(Wat Ongteu, Vientiane)*.

Watercress salad with vinaigrette dressing at L'Elephant in Luang Prabang

EXPERIENCE
CAMBODIA

Ta Prohm Temple, Angkor

EXPLORE
CAMBODIA

This section divides Cambodia into four
color-coded sightseeing areas,
as shown on the map below.
Find out more about each area
on the following pages.

THAILAND

Uthumphon
Thisai

Surin

Amphil

An
Ve

SIEM REAP
AND ANGKOR
p80

Sisophon

Angkor

Siem R

Bangkok

THAILAND

Tonlé
Sap

Pattaya

Battambang

Chanthaburi

Pursat

Tumpor

*Gulf of
Thailand*

Koh Kong

SOUTHERN
CAMBODIA
p124

Chrang
Khpos

Khsach
Sor

Kaaong

Kiri Sakor

Kampot

Sihanoukville

CAMBODIA AND LAOS

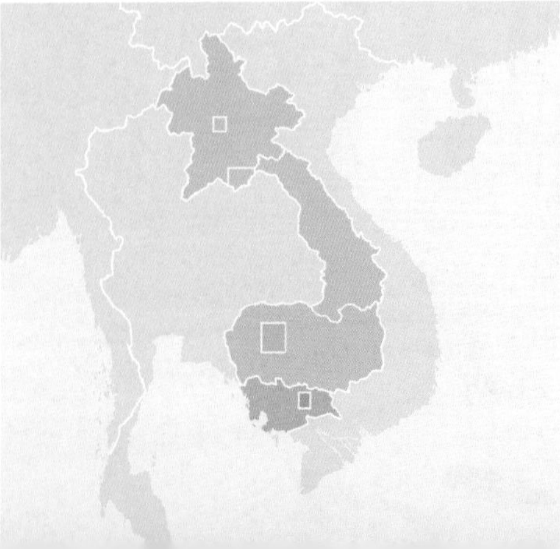

GETTING TO KNOW
CAMBODIA

Beyond the twin poles of the frenetic capital, Phnom Penh, and bustling Siem Reap, gateway to Angkor Wat, Cambodia is still a land of quiet country towns, thickly forested hills, crumbling temples swaddled by the jungle, and arcs of pale sand on the edge of a cobalt-blue sea.

PAGE 64

PHNOM PENH

Set on the sweltering plains of southeastern Cambodia, Phnom Penh is a place of broad boulevards and warren-like markets, combining the endless energy and increasing sophistication of an economically ascendant nation with all the customary color and chaos of Southeast Asia.

Best for
Museums, markets, and sophisticated dining

Home to
The Royal Palace and Silver Pagoda

Experience
Hunting for bargains and sampling food under the Art Deco dome of Psar Thmei (Central Market)

PAGE 80

SIEM REAP
AND ANGKOR

Cambodia's ultimate drawcard is the sprawling temple complex of Angkor, a vast array of centuries-old structures, rising over the forested northern plains. But there's also plenty to do in nearby Siem Reap, a sophisticated town with lively nightlife and great restaurants.

Best for
Exploring the temples of Angkor

Home to
Angkor Wat, Ta Prohm, and Bayon

Experience
A sunset boat ride on Tonlé Sap

NORTHERN CAMBODIA

PAGE 110

Stretching from the Thai border in the west to the Vietnamese frontier in the east, Northern Cambodia is the country's biggest region. This is where old-world traditions survive: in quiet towns packed with Colonial-era shophouses and among little-known temples set in deep countryside. Battambang is the most-visited town in the area, with its photogenic streetscapes and fascinating surrounds, while the easternmost regions, around Sen Monorom and Ban Lung, are perfect for adventures into the wilderness.

Best for
Experiencing rural life in Cambodia

Home to
Battambang and Prasat Preah Vihear

Experience
A ride on the rickety Bamboo train near Wat Banan

SOUTHERN CAMBODIA

PAGE 124

Land gives way uneasily to the sea along Cambodia's southern coast. This is a region of deep inlets and mangroves. It's also home to powdery beaches and paradise islands. Sihanoukville is the original beach destination, complemented by new seashore hideaways among the islands further south. The supremely atmospheric towns of Kep and Kampot also lie on this coast. Inland, meanwhile, an arc of forested hills walls the littoral off from the inland plains, and provides superb opportunities for jungle journeys.

Best for
Beaches and coastal national parks

Home to
Sihanoukville, the southern islands, and Kampot

Experience
Snorkeling in the pristine areas around the southern islands

A YEAR IN
CAMBODIA

JANUARY

△ **Victory Day** *(Jan 7)*. In Phnom Penh, parades and rallies mark the day Khmer Rouge rule ended.
Lunar New Year *(late Jan/early Feb)*. Chinese and Vietnamese communities celebrate the New Year with parades, dragon dances, and fireworks.

FEBRUARY

Meak Bochea *(late Jan/early Feb)*. Almost every temple in the country hosts a candlelit procession in the evening on this major Buddhist festival.

MAY

Victory over Genocide Day *(May 9)*. Somber gatherings commemorate the atrocities carried out by the Khmer Rouge.
△ **King's Birthday** *(May 13)*. Look out for firework displays in most Cambodian towns.
Royal Ploughing Ceremony *(late May)*. Crowds gather at Lean Preah Sre Park in Phnom Penh for this ancient, colorful ritual, marking the start of the rice-planting season.

JUNE

△ **Queen Mother's Birthday** *(Jun 18)*. A low-key public holiday sees kids get a day off school and families gather in parks and public spaces. In Phnom Penh, there is also a fireworks show.

SEPTEMBER

Bon Dak Ben *(mid–late Sep)*. Temples all around the country throng with crowds during this two-week festival dedicated to the spirits of the dead.
△ **Bon Pchum Ben** *(Sep/Oct)*. Keep an eye out for Cambodians making offerings of eggs and money to stave off evil spirits.

OCTOBER

Bon Kathen *(late Sep/Oct)*. A month-long celebration marking the end of the monks' retreat sees offerings made to monks at temples across the country.
△ **Sihanouk's Birthday** *(Oct 31)*. Processions around the Royal Palace in Phnom Penh mark the birthday of Cambodia's late, and much revered, king.

MARCH

△ **Women's Day** (*Mar 8*). Cambodia makes a big thing of International Women's Day, with parades and performances in Phnom Penh.

Mekong River Festival (*mid-Mar*). Held at shifting locations on the Mekong, this three-day festival attracts huge crowds, with boat races and live music.

APRIL

Chaul Chnam Thmey (*Apr 13–16*). The Cambodian New Year is a chance for a nationwide water fight, with much revelry. Wat Phnom in Phnom Penh hosts free festivals.

△ **Visak Bochea** (*late Apr–early Jun*). Head to Angkor Wat for the most impressive candlelit parades, honoring the Buddha's birthday.

JULY

△ **Bon Chol Vassa** (*Jul full moon*). A two-week period of fasting and meditation with young men ordained as monks in temples all over Cambodia.

AUGUST

△ **Khmer Empire Marathon** (*early Aug*). Angkor Wat provides an impressive backdrop for this marathon. There are also half-marathon and fun-run options for less serious runners.

NOVEMBER

Independence Day (*Nov 9*). Commemorating the end of French rule, this national holiday sees a huge ceremony at the independence monument in Phnom Penh, and fireworks over the river.

△ **Bon Om Tuk** (*late Nov*). Head to Tonlé Sap for the biggest boat races and liveliest atmosphere during the nationwide celebration of the end of the monsoon.

DECEMBER

△ **Sea Festival** (*late Dec*). Held in the run-up to New Year in a different coastal town each year, expect live music, boat races, and general revelry.

Angkor Photo Festival (*late Dec/early Jan*). Pop-up exhibitions and installations appear around Siem Reap during this event, one of the biggest photography festivals in Southeast Asia.

1

A BRIEF
HISTORY

From the splendor of Angkor to the unimaginable brutality of the Khmer Rouge, Cambodia has had a tumultuous past. Its strong Khmer identity has endured throughout, seeing it through French colonial rule and into the unprecedented economic developments of the 21st century.

Early Settlers and the Funan Civilization

Almost 9,000 years ago there were already hunter-gatherer communities foraging along the Cambodian coast. Where these earliest inhabitants came from is unclear, but at some point in the subsequent millennia, the Khmer, a group that is thought to have originated in China, moved into the region and migrated along the course of the Mekong. The first urban civilization in Cambodia, known as Funan, sprang up 2,000 years ago, in the southeast delta region. Establishing their capital at Angkor Borei, this state traded far and wide and built extensive canal systems.

1 Print depicting a gateway at Angkor Thom.

2 Canal established by the Funan state.

3 Sanskrit inscription at Lolei Temple, Roluos Group.

4 Angkor Wat.

Timeline of events

6800 BCE
The first settlers begin building shelters along Cambodia's coast.

2000 BCE
Cultivation of rice begins in the region, laying the agricultural foundation for future civilizations.

1st century CE
The Funan state emerges in southern Cambodia.

802
Jayavarman II establishes Angkor and kick-starts the emergence of a Khmer empire.

Indian Influence

During the Funan period, Indian influence seeped into the region through trade, with elements of Indian culture, such as Hinduism, absorbed into Khmer customs and traditions. Between the 5th and 8th centuries CE, small, Indian-influenced city-states, known collectively as Chenla, flourished. Power gradually centralized, culminating in the appearance of the "universal monarch," Jayavarman II, who founded the city of Angkor in 802 CE.

The Angkorian Empire

Angkor was the most important power in Southeast Asia for around six centuries. By the time Angkor Wat was built in the mid-12th century, its territory included what is now northeastern Thailand, southern Laos, and southern Vietnam. By the 14th century, Angkor society had made the shift from Hinduism to Theravada Buddhism. At the same time, outlying territories were beginning to break away and in 1431, Thai armies overran the capital. Over the next five centuries, the vestiges of the Angkorian state declined. By the 19th century, the Khmer homeland was ruled and fought over by its powerful neighbors.

THE HISTORY OF CAMBODIA'S NAME

The Angkorian state was originally known as Kamboja-desa, "Land of the Kambojas," a name of uncertain Indian origin. In colloquial Khmer this became Kampuchea, which the French colonialists turned into Cambodge during the 19th century. This in turn was anglicized as Cambodia, the modern name for the country.

1130–50
Suryavarman II oversees the building of Angkor Wat.

1178–1120
Jayavarman VII builds Bayon and the walled city of Angkor Thom.

1200–50
Conversion of Khmer people to Theravada Buddhism.

1830–49
Thailand and Vietnam tussle for control of Cambodia.

1431
Thai forces attack, and Angkor is partially abandoned.

1

2

The Colonial Era

In the mid-19th century, the French began to seek territorial control of Indochina. The Cambodian royal family decided that a treaty with the French might protect them from the expansionist predations of Thailand. The French Protectorate came into being in 1863 and a second treaty, signed in 1886, gave the French outright administrative control. Anti-French feeling was slow to develop, partly because Cambodian institutions such as the monarchy were left largely untouched.

Independence and Revolt

During World War II, Japanese forces took control of Southeast Asia. In the French territories, the existing administration was left in place. But as defeat became likely, the Japanese encouraged local independence movements. Cambodia was eventually granted independence by the French under its young king, Norodom Sihanouk, in 1953. With the Vietnam War spilling into Cambodia, Sihanouk was deposed in 1970 in a coup led by Lon Nol, the pro-US Cambodian prime minister. Meanwhile, the Communist Party of Kampuchea (Khmer Rouge) was on the rise.

POL POT

Pol Pot (1928–1998), a French-educated former schoolteacher, was originally called Saloth Sar. Later, as leader of the Khmer Rouge, he became "Brother Number One." During his rule, he oversaw the death of millions before the Vietnamese invaded and overthrew him. Never captured, he died in a Khmer Rouge-controlled enclave in western Cambodia.

Timeline of events

1863

King Norodom signs a treaty creating the French Protectorate.

1942

Japanese control of Southeast Asia established, lasting until 1945.

1953

France grants Cambodia independence.

1969

During the Vietnam War, the US bombs Viet Cong bases and supply routes in eastern Cambodia.

Pol Pot's Khmer Rouge

On April 17, 1975, the Khmer Rouge occupied Phnom Penh following a five-year civil war against Lon Nol's forces. Under leader Pol Pot, the group attempted a radical social experiment, abolishing money, education, religion and established economic systems. Huge suffering ensued, compounded by the regime's brutality, with over 20 per cent of Cambodians killed in an appalling genocide. War broke out with Vietnam in the late 1970s, and in 1979 an invading Vietnamese army toppled the Khmer Rouge.

Democratic Cambodia

Vietnamese troops remained in Cambodia until 1989, after which UN forces stepped in to disarm opposing factions and oversee the return of refugees. Elections were held in 1993. The royalist faction won, and Sihanouk was crowned king for the second time, with Hun Sen, leader of the Cambodian People's Party, appointed prime minister. Since 2003, Cambodia has held regular elections. Today, foreign investment, especially from China, pours in, but in some cases – such as the Dara Sakor Project, which sees resorts built in a once-protected national park – it is controversial.

1 King Sihanouk in 1953.

2 Gun piles in Phnom Penh during Khmer Rouge occupation.

3 Tuol Sleng Genocide Museum in Phnom Penh.

4 Hun Sun's son, Prime Minister Hun Manet.

Did You Know?

Sihanoukville is named after King Sihanouk, but the use of the suffix "ville" retains a nod to the French.

1970
A coup replaces Sihanouk with a pro-US regime, led by Lon Nol.

1975
The Khmer Rouge capture Phnom Penh.

1979
Vietnam invades and topples the Khmer Rouge.

2004
Sihanouk abdicates as king and is replaced by his son, Sihamoni.

2023
Hun Manet is sworn in as the new prime minister.

2007
An international tribunal tries surviving Khmer Rouge leaders.

THE FRENCH CONNECTION

Until the mid-19th century, colonial interest in Cambodia and Laos was minimal, mainly consisting of sporadic forays by Catholic missionaries. However, continued aggression by Thailand caused King Norodom to invite the French to make Cambodia a protectorate in 1863; then, in 1886, the French took full administrative control *(p60)*. Laos, too, was steadily absorbed into French Indochina. In both Cambodia and Laos, the French set about reducing the power of each country's monarchy, imposing new taxes, and forcing the local population to speak French. The French withdrew from the region in 1954, but the legacy of French rule is still seen today.

FRENCH ARCHITECTURE

Perhaps the most prominent feature of the French legacy is seen in the Neo-Classical architecture of major towns, where long rows of shophouses, government buildings, and private villas line the streets. In Cambodia, cities such as Phnom Penh, Siem Reap, and Battambang are home to Modernist villas, riverside boulevards, and old French quarters. In Laos, meanwhile, Luang Prabang's National Museum Complex and the Centre Culturel Français represent French-Lao-style architecture. While many Colonial-era buildings have fallen into disrepair over the decades, others have been restored and turned into boutique hotels and restaurants.

> **Perhaps the most prominent feature of the French legacy is seen in the Neo-Classical architecture of major towns.**

↑ Walking past some of the French-era buildings found in Luang Prabang, Laos

TOP 5 FRENCH-ERA CITIES

Phnom Penh
There are many villas and townhouses in the capital, especially along the riverfront (p78).

Battambang
Some of the shophouses and villas here have had a boutique hotel makeover (p116).

Kampot
There's still a strong French influence on the tranquil riverfront in Kampot (p132).

Kep
A former seaside getaway for French officials, Kep still has some villas (p141).

Savannakhet
The buildings in the old quarter are crumbling, although some have been restored (p212).

LANGUAGE AND CULTURE

Though English has taken over as the international language of choice for younger generations, the French linguistic legacy certainly endures. It can be seen in the francophone street signs of Vientiane in Laos, French-language newspapers in both countries, and the lively program of French cultural activities on offer in the major cities. Many Cambodians also continue to play the French game of pétanque, with the country producing world champions in this sport.

↑ A group playing a game of pétanque

THE CULINARY LEGACY

The French culinary influence is most evident in Laos, where croissants and baguettes are popular snacks. Indeed, a baguette – thickly packed with pâté and pickles – is as much a Lao street-food staple as any noodle dish. Many towns still have a bakery producing these quintessentially French bakes. There's also a deep-rooted taste for wine, and you'll find bars in most towns serving French classics that would make the grade in Paris.

↑ Stall selling delicious baguettes in Vientiane, Laos

PHNOM PENH

Phnom Penh, meaning Penh's Hill, derives its name from the legend of Daun Penh, an old lady who discovered four Buddha statues in a hollowed-out tree trunk washed up on the shore of the Mekong. She believed her discovery was a sign that Buddha wanted a new home, so she set the icons on a hill and started to build Wat Phnom, the temple around which the city of Phnom Penh grew.

Due to its strategic position at the confluence of the Tonlé Sap and Mekong rivers, Phnom Penh became the capital of the Khmer Empire in the mid-15th century. The city traded with Laos and China until the 17th century, when it was reduced to a buffer state between the warring Vietnamese and Thais. In 1863, Phnom Penh found itself under French rule, which lasted until 1953, when King Sihanouk finally declared independence.

Phnom Penh fell to Pol Pot's black-clad forces on April 17, 1975; most of the city's population was driven to the infamous Killing Fields of Choeung Ek. Cambodia was liberated by the Vietnamese in 1979 but it was another ten years before Phnom Penh was finally free to manage its own affairs. Having moved past the uncertainties of the 1980s, the city has reinvented itself as a bustling center with world-class boutique hotels and international cuisine.

Around Phnom Penh

- ⓫ Koh Dach
- Phnom Penh International Airport
- *area of main Phnom Penh map*
- Chrey Kaong
- ⓱ Koki Beach ⑨
- ⑧ Killing Fields of Choeung Ek
- Takhmau
- Kampong Tuol
- Tonlé Bati ⑩
- Prek Koy
- Trapeang Khna
- ⓬ Phnom Tamao Wildlife Rescue Center
- Chambak
- ⓭ Phnom Chisor
- Prey Nhoek

0 km 10
0 miles 10

N

PHNOM PENH

Must See

① Royal Palace and Silver Pagoda

Experience More

② National Museum of Cambodia
③ Wat Ounalom
④ Wat Phnom
⑤ Psar Thmei
⑥ Tuol Sleng Genocide Museum
⑦ Psar Tuol Tom Pong (Russian Market)
⑧ Killing Fields of Choeung Ek
⑨ Koki Beach
⑩ Tonlé Bati
⑪ Koh Dach
⑫ Phnom Tamao Wildlife Rescue Center
⑬ Phnom Chisor

Drink

① Le Moon
② Elephant Bar

ROYAL PALACE AND SILVER PAGODA

⊙ E2 ⌂ Samdach Sothearos Blvd ⊙ 8-10:30am & 2-5pm daily

Bearing a striking resemblance to the Grand Palace in Bangkok, Thailand, the Royal Palace, with its gilded, pitched roofs framed by *nagas* (serpents), is one of the most prominent landmarks of Phnom Penh.

Built in the mid-19th century in the classic Khmer style, the Royal Palace is the official residence of Cambodia's reigning monarch, King Sihamoni. The palace was built with French assistance on the site of a former temple on the western bank of the Tonlé Sap River, and is designed to face the rising sun. The Royal Residence is permanently closed to the public, and the Throne Hall is closed during royal receptions.

→

Elaborate exterior of the Royal Palace's Pavilion of Napoleon III

> **The palace was built with French assistance on the site of a former temple on the western bank of the Tonlé Sap River, and is designed to face the rising sun.**

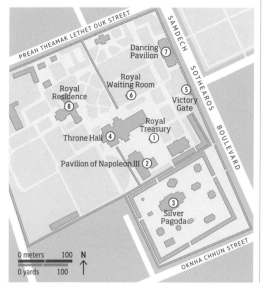

① Royal Treasury

Also called the "bronze palace," this narrow building contains regalia used in royal coronation ceremonies. Highlights include the Great Crown of Victory and the Victory Spear, as well as the Sacred Sword.

② Pavilion of Napoleon III

This pavilion was built for Napoleon III's wife, Empress Eugénie, in Giza. Presented to King Norodom I (r. 1860–1904) in 1876, it was entirely dismantled, shipped to Phnom Penh, and re-erected in the grounds of the Royal Palace.

Today, it is used to display a collection of royal memorabilia, including gifts from visiting dignitaries, paintings, glassware, silverware, and some elaborate silk costumes once worn by royal dancers.

INSIDER TIP
Get a Guide

Visitors can hire English-speaking guides for a fixed price from the ticket counters at the main entrance (situated in the eastern part of the complex). The price is relatively low and it's well worth the money to learn more about the history of the palace.

↑ Cycling past the Throne Hall just outside the Royal Palace walls

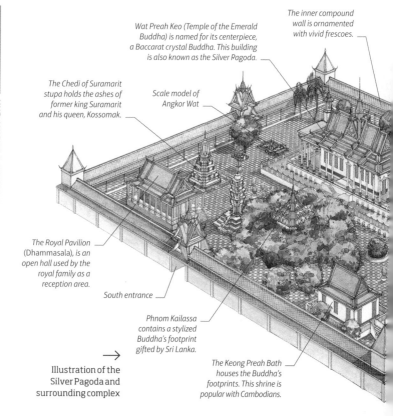

The Chedi of Suramarit stupa holds the ashes of former king Suramarit and his queen, Kossomak.

Wat Preah Keo (Temple of the Emerald Buddha) is named for its centerpiece, a Baccarat crystal Buddha. This building is also known as the Silver Pagoda.

The inner compound wall is ornamented with vivid frescoes.

Scale model of Angkor Wat

The Royal Pavilion (Dhammasala), is an open hall used by the royal family as a reception area.

South entrance

Phnom Kailassa contains a stylized Buddha's footprint gifted by Sri Lanka.

The Keong Preah Bath houses the Buddha's footprints. This shrine is popular with Cambodians.

Illustration of the Silver Pagoda and surrounding complex

③ Silver Pagoda

Also known as Wat Preah Keo, the 19th-century Silver Pagoda, with its intricately curled golden roofs, is a prominent jewel on the city's squat skyline. Surrounded by a courtyard filled with tropical gardens, it is a beautifully calm oasis away from the rush of the city.

④ Throne Hall

Built in 1917 and inaugurated by King Sisowath in 1919, the Throne Hall is known locally as Preah Thineang Dheva Vinnichayyeaah, meaning the Sacred Seat of Judgement. Its design is heavily influenced by Bayon-style architecture (p96), evident from its

cruciform shape and triple spires. The central spire is crowned by an imposing 194-ft- (59-m-) high tower. The roof is adorned with nagas (serpents) and garudas (mythical beasts that are half-man, half-bird). Today, the Throne Hall is used for coronations, and for extending a formal welcome to visiting diplomats.

The Throne Room, accessed from a door to the east, is painted in white and yellow to symbolize Hinduism and Buddhism respectively. It is an excellent example of the harmonious fusion of the two religions, which was encouraged by 12th-century

Interior of the Silver Pagoda, with its stunning Baccarat crystal Buddha

↑ The elegantly lit exterior of the Dancing Pavilion

North entrance

The Mandap is a small library housing sacred texts written on palm-tree fronds. Also of interest is a statue of a bull's head.

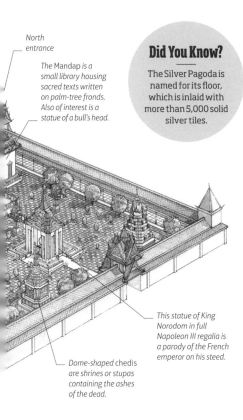

Did You Know?

The Silver Pagoda is named for its floor, which is inlaid with more than 5,000 solid silver tiles.

This statue of King Norodom in full Napoleon III regalia is a parody of the French emperor on his steed.

Dome-shaped chedis are shrines or stupas containing the ashes of the dead.

monarch, King Jayavarman VII. Its ceiling features a beautiful mural depicting the *Reamker*, the Khmer version of the Hindu epic *Ramayana*. A lotus-patterned carpet, donated by China in 1933, perfectly complements the lotus bud floor tiles in the room. The Throne Room also houses the majestic thrones of the king and queen of Cambodia. While the king's throne is small and sits at the front, the queen's is taller and built on a golden stage adorned with *nagas*.

⑤ Victory Gate

Set on the eastern end of the complex, the Victory Gate leads directly to the Throne Hall. Once used only by the king and queen, it is now also used by visiting dignitaries.

⑥ Royal Waiting Room

Situated to the right of the magnificent Throne Hall, Hor Samranphirum, or the Royal Waiting Room, is used by the king and queen while waiting for their ceremonial elephants on Coronation Day. Posts to tether the animals are visible on the east side of the building, as are the platforms used by the king and queen to mount the elephants for the coronation procession.

⑦ Dancing Pavilion

Located near the Victory Gate, the Dancing Pavilion, or Chan Chaya Pavilion, was originally built in 1914 with wood. It was traditionally

used by Cambodian kings to view parades and to enjoy performances of classical Khmer dances. A balcony to the east of the pavilion was used for viewing parades along Sothearos Boulevard, beyond the royal grounds.

Today, the Dancing Pavilion is used for royal celebrations, and royal (as well as state) banquets. The building was memorably used to celebrate the coronation of King Sihamoni in October 2004.

⑧ Royal Residence

Built in the mid-20th century, during the reign of King Sisowath Monivong, by well-known Khmer architect Oknha Tep Nimith Khieu, the Royal Residence is also known as the Khemarin Palace, or the Palace of the Khmer King. Today, it is the home of the present monarch, King Sihamoni, whose presence in the capital is indicated by the blue royal flag, which flies at full mast. The Royal Residence is closed to visitors.

Next to this building stands the royal guesthouse known as Villa Kantha Bopha, which was built in 1956 and named after the late Princess Kantha Bopha, daughter of the former king, Sihanouk. It is used only to house foreign guests.

EXPERIENCE MORE

National Museum of Cambodia

📍D2 🏛Sts 178 and 179 (entrance on corner of Sts 13 & 178) ⏰8am-5pm daily (last entry 4:30pm) 🌐cambodiamuseum.info

Situated in four majestic terracotta pavilions enclosing an enchanting, landscaped courtyard, the National Museum of Cambodia houses the country's greatest display of Khmer statuary. Exhibits range from prehistoric to present-day items, and include Indian sculptures such as a striking eight-armed statue of Vishnu (a Hindu god), and a magnificent cross-legged sandstone statue of the 12th-century king Jayavarman VII. In the courtyard is a stone statue of Yama, the God of Death. The museum also has an excellent collection of local pottery, and bronze statues from the Funan and Chenla periods (p58).

Note that photography is not permitted within the museum. A small shop at the entrance sells books on Cambodian history and archaeology. There's also a pleasant café on the grounds.

→
The richly detailed Great Stupa at Wat Ounalom

Wat Ounalom

📍E2 🏛Samdech Sothearos Blvd ⏰Dawn-dusk daily

Built in 1943, Wat Ounalom is the headquarters and home of the Buddhist *sangha* (order) in Cambodia. In the early 1970s, more than 500 monks lived here. Tragically, the Khmer Rouge murdered the then leader Samdech Huot Tat and threw his statue into the Tonlé Sap River. The statue was recovered after the expulsion of the Khmer Rouge and is now on view on the second floor. The temple's library of over 30,000 precious Buddhist texts, also destroyed by the regime, is slowly being rebuilt. Outside is a beautiful stupa said to contain a hair from the Buddha's eyebrow.

Did You Know?

At 88.5 ft (27 m) high, Wat Phnom is the tallest religious structure in Phnom Penh.

Be wary of self-styled "guides" who insist on showing you around the temple – for a price.

Wat Phnom

📍D1 🏛Norodom Blvd, N of St 102 ⏰Dawn-dusk daily 🎉Cambodian New Year

Built in 1373 to house the Buddha statues found by Daun Penh (p65), who laid the foundations of the shrine on the shores of the Tonlé Sap River, this temple is the highest point in the city. Today, it has something of a carnival atmosphere, with flashing altar lights and kitsch souvenir stalls.

Visitors enter this vibrant house of worship through an easterly *naga* stairway, passing beggars, hawkers, and dogs, cats, and macaque monkeys fed by the monks. The temple's walls are adorned with *Jataka* (stories from the former lives of the Buddha) murals, many blackened by smoke from

→ The immense Art Deco dome of the Psar Thmei covered market

incense offerings. There is a shrine dedicated to Daun Penh behind the *vihara* (temple sanctuary). Nearby, a couple of shrines to Taoist goddesses are popular with the locals, who make offerings of cooked chicken and raw eggs here.

5

Psar Thmei

C2 **E of Monivong Blvd, N of St 63** **Dawn–dusk daily**

Psar Thmei, the city's huge central market, is housed in a fabulous ocher-hued Art Deco building erected by the French in 1937. Its immense central dome is on a scale similar to Hadrian's Pantheon in Rome. Offering an incredible variety of products under one roof, this is a one-stop shop for any visitor. The food section is packed with fresh fruits and vegetables, as well as delicacies such as peeled frogs and fried insects. Four wings radiate from the main building where vendors hawk gold and silver jewelry, watches, electronic goods, Buddha statues, clothes, and fresh flowers. The corridors of merchandise are surprisingly cool, even at midday.

6

Tuol Sleng Genocide Museum

C4 **St 113** **8am–5:30pm daily** **tuolsleng. gov.kh/en**

Hidden down a peaceful side street bordered with bougainvillea, this thought-provoking, and often disturbing, museum was originally a school that was turned into the Khmer Rouge torture headquarters. Tuol Sleng Prison, or S-21, was

the largest detention center in the country. Here, 17,000 men, women, and children were subjected to torture before they were taken to the Killing Fields of Choeung Ek (p76); most did not get that far. When Vietnamese forces liberated Phnom Penh in 1979, they found only seven people still alive at S-21.

The prison has now been converted into a museum; its former cells and gallery are covered with haunting photographs of subjects before and after torture. An exhibition on the second floor of the main building profiles the main instigators of the murderous regime, and displays photos, diaries, and poems written by the victims. The balconies on the upper floors are still enclosed with the wire mesh that prevented prisoners from jumping to an early death. An audio guide helps visitors to understand the brutal history of the Khmer Rouge period.

Visitors need to cover their shoulders and legs while visiting the museum.

7

Psar Tuol Tom Pong (Russian Market)

B5 **S of Mao Tse Toung Blvd** **Dawn–dusk daily**

Also known as the Russian Market because of the many Russians who shopped here during the 1980s, this market is popular with bargain-hunters. A smorgasbord of handicrafts, fake antiques, silk scarves, and musical instruments is available here. Also on sale is a huge selection of fake designer clothing, as well as genuine items made in local factories, all at a fraction of their international prices.

DRINK

Le Moon
This wonderful rooftop bar, at the top of a French Colonial-style hotel, wows visitors with its river views.

E2 **154 Dekcho Damdin St** **le-moon-rooftop.com**

Elephant Bar
Oozing vintage Indochina style, this sophisticated hotel bar serves some of the best cocktails in town.

C1 **Raffles Hotel Le Royal, 92 Rukhak Vithei Daun Penh** **raffles.com**

Colorful rooftops in the east of Phnom Penh

8

Killing Fields of Choeung Ek

🅐D7 🄰5 miles (8 km) S of Phnom Penh 🄾7am–5:30pm daily

Once an orchard of longan trees, this now deceptively peaceful setting was the scene of one of the most disturbing acts of violence in contemporary history. Between 1975 and 1979, in some of the worst excesses of the Khmer Rouge regime, some 17,000 men, women, and children kept as prisoners in the torture chambers of Tuol Sleng Prison, also known as S-21 (p73), were brought here to be killed, often by blunted hoes to save bullets.

Of the 129 communal graves, 49 have been left intact, and it is still possible to chance upon bone fragments and bits of clothing. Signposts close to the graves tell visitors about the number of people buried there; another one marks a macabre tree against which babies were flung by their ankles and killed.

In 1988, a fittingly dignified pavilion was erected within the complex in memory of the 9,000 people found here. Through the glass panels of the pavilion one can see some 8,000 skulls arranged according to age and sex. A museum in the corner of the grounds offers detailed background information, not only on the founders of the Khmer Rouge, but also on its numerous victims, who included doctors, politicians, and actors.

↑ Tonlé Bati lake, a cool and tranquil escape from the city

9

Koki Beach

🅐D7 🄰Off National Hwy 1, 9 miles (14 km) E of Phnom Penh 🚌From Central Market 🚍 🄾Dawn–dusk daily

A romantic picnic spot on a tributary of the Mekong River, Koki Beach is popular with young Khmers, who come here on weekends. The clean sands, stilted huts with thatched roofs, and calm setting make it an ideal place to relax and unwind. Visitors can venture on inexpensive boat trips along the river, or swim close to the sandy beach, where a few people can usually be found braving the waters. There is always plenty of food to be bought from the local vendors who sell a selection of grilled fish, chicken, and fresh coconuts. The beach is also lined with makeshift

restaurants specializing in local food. It is recommended to agree on the price of dishes before settling down to eat.

10

Tonlé Bati

🅐D7 🄰Off National Hwy 2, 19 miles (30 km) S of Phnom Penh 🚍 🄾Dawn–dusk daily

Another popular weekend haunt, Tonlé Bati is a peaceful lake with stilted huts bordering its acacia-shaded shoreline. It is frequented by locals, who find it an ideal spot for a quiet picnic or fishing trip. Adding further appeal are the nearby ruins of Ta Prohm andn Yeay Peau, two beautifully preserved temples built in the late 12th century under King Jayavarman VII.

Ta Prohm's main sanctuary has five chambers, each containing a Shiva *lingam* (phallic monument), as well as basreliefs depicting several *apsaras* (celestial dancing girls). On weekends, the temple grounds play host to musicians and fortune-tellers. Located a short distance from Ta Prohm, Yeay Peau is named after King Ta Prohm's mother. Both sites show signs of damage by the Khmer Rouge.

RIVER CRUISES

The river is Phnom Penh's dominant feature, and a sunset view of the city is a classic experience. A number of companies run evening cruises from the dock on Sisowath Quay. There's a variety to choose from; the standard price is $5 for a one-hour boat ride (including a free drink), departing around 5pm. Smaller boats can also be hired on the spot for private trips, a short way north of the main dock.

→

The crumbling ruins of the ancient temple of Phnom Chisor

11 Koh Dach

⟨D7⟩ ⟨Off National Hwy 6, 4 miles (6 km) N of Phnom Penh⟩ ⟨From Hwy 6⟩

Just a short ride north of the city, this island in the middle of the Mekong is a serene slice of rural Cambodia on weekdays, and a popular getaway for Phnom Penh residents at weekends. The ferry crossing is easily reached by tuk-tuk or bicycle. Once across the water, you'll find a network of quiet lanes through peanut fields and friendly villages. Traditional silk-making thrives here, and there are opportunities to see all stages of the process. The sandy beach has rustic shacks for rent and snack stalls.

12 Phnom Tamao Wildlife Rescue Center

⟨D7⟩ ⟨Off National Hwy 2, 25 miles (40 km) S of Phnom Penh⟩ ⟨From Central Market, then tuk-tuk⟩ ⟨8:30am–5pm daily⟩

Opened in 1995 and set within 10 sq miles (26 sq km) of protected forest, the Phnom Tamao Wildlife Rescue Center is the largest zoo in the country.

Working in collaboration with the Wildlife Alliance's Rapid Rescue team, the zoo is a rehabilitation center for animals (many of them endangered) that have been rescued from illegal wildlife trade. It also cares for, and protects, several rare birds and animals that usually inhabit inhospitable parts of the country, and are therefore difficult to observe in the wild.

These well-nurtured animals are kept in a variety of enclosures. The largest is home to a group of Malayan sun bears. Other species include the world's largest collection of pileated gibbons, a Siamese crocodile, and many fully grown Asiatic tigers. These are best viewed in the afternoon, when they come out from the sheltered areas of their enclosures. You can also book a tour of the center through the Wildlife Alliance (*www.wildlifealliance.org*).

13 Phnom Chisor

⟨D7⟩ ⟨31 miles (50 km) S of Phnom Penh⟩ ⟨From Central Market, then tuk-tuk⟩ ⟨Dawn–dusk daily⟩

An 11th-century sanctuary formerly known as Suryagiri, the temple of Phnom Chisor is

INSIDER TIP
Tuk-tuk for the Day

Rather than paying for single trips, consider renting a tuk-tuk for the day (usually for around $20; negotiate first). The driver will take you everywhere, and wait while you explore different sights or grab a bite to eat. It's far less hassle, and often cheaper.

set upon the eastern side of a solitary hill affording wonderful views of the plains below. Within its crumbling interior stand a few surviving statues of the Buddha, while the carvings on the wooden doors depict figures standing on pigs. Best visited in the early morning or late afternoon, the temple is reached by climbing a flight of almost 400 steps – the path taken by the king of Cambodia 900 years ago. Directly below the summit is the sanctuary of Sen Ravang, the pond of Tonlé Om, and beyond it the Sen Ravang temple, all forming a symbolic straight line to sacred Angkor.

Nearby, beside a pagoda still used for worship, stand two deteriorating brick *prasats* (towers) of the 10th-century temple Prasat Neang Khmau.

A SHORT WALK
RIVERFRONT

Distance 1 mile (1.5 km) **Nearest bus stop** Wat Kos
Time 20 minutes

Phnom Penh's riverfront is distinguished by its Gallic architecture – stucco-fronted, ocher-colored villas, and shuttered townhouses – while the surrounding area is home to many embassies, a number of old municipal buildings built under the French in the 19th and early 20th centuries, and several Chinese-style shophouses. The capital's scenic riverside promenade, Sisowath Quay, is the hub of the city's nightlife, with a variety of restaurants, lively bars, and boutiques. Other interesting places in the area include the Royal Palace and Silver Pagoda, the National Museum, and Psar Kandal – all within walking distance.

Did You Know?

In the dry season, the river flows toward the Mekong, but when it rains it flows toward the Tonlé Sap.

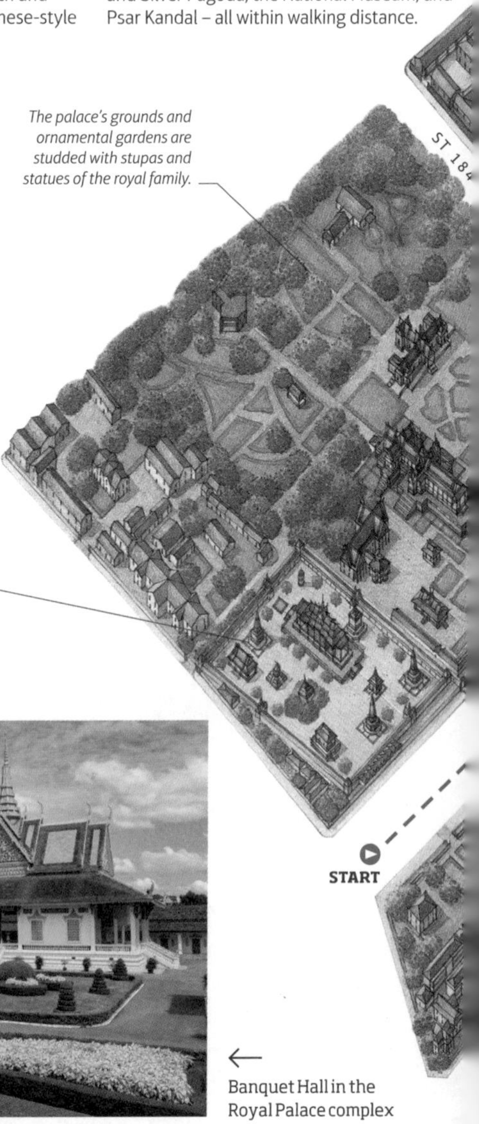

The palace's grounds and ornamental gardens are studded with stupas and statues of the royal family.

ST 184

*Built in the mid-19th century with French assistance, the **Royal Palace** (p68) is home to the current monarch, King Norodom Sihamoni. The adjoining Silver Pagoda houses the highly revered statue of the Emerald Buddha.*

START

← Banquet Hall in the Royal Palace complex

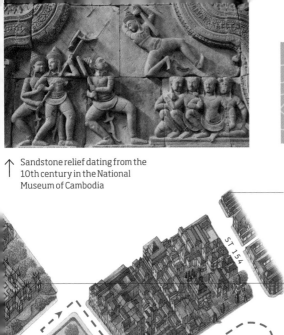

Sandstone relief dating from the 10th century in the National Museum of Cambodia

Locator Map
For more detail see p66

Psar Kandal *is a dry goods market selling everything from electronics to pirated DVDs. Visitors will also find vendors offering fried crickets, a local delicacy.*

ST 154

The four charming terracotta-colored pavilions of the **National Museum of Cambodia** *(p72) house ancient Khmer statuary, ceramics, and bronze statues.*

ST 178

Owned by Cham Muslim silversmiths, who are noted for their fine filigree work, the silver shops on **Samdach Sothearos Boulevard** *sell exquisite belts, jewelry, and other souvenirs.*

SOTHEAROS BLVD

PREAH SISOWATH QUAY

FINISH
ST 184

With no gates or walls, the **Royal Palace Park** *is always available (and free) to visit. This patch of green is a great place to stop for a break or stroll along the dedicated pathways.*

PONHEA YAT

TONLÉ SAP RIVER

The **Preah Ang Dorngkeu Shrine**, *located on the riverfront, is used for a number of ceremonies during festivals.*

PREAH SISOWATH QUAY

Sisowath Quay, *a long, enchanting riverside boulevard, is the perfect place for a stroll. It's also home to lively bars and restaurants offering a wide variety of international cuisine. It serves as a starting point for river festivals and boat cruises down the Tonlé Sap River.*

0 meters   100
0 yards   100

N

SIEM REAP AND ANGKOR

Set on the forested plains of northwest Cambodia, Angkor, the ancient capital of the Khmer Empire, is one of the most magnificent wonders of the world. The mighty Khmer Empire, which extended from the South China Sea almost to Bengal Bay, was founded at the beginning of the 9th century CE by Jayavarman II (r. 802–850). In the following centuries, his successors built magnificent temples such as Phnom Bakheng, Angkor Wat, Banteay Kdei, and Ta Prohm, as well as the bustling city of Angkor Thom. Today, the remains of this metropolis sprawl across 77 sq miles (200 sq km), set between two *barays* (reservoirs).

Four miles (6 km) to the south lies Siem Reap. Once a quiet country town, it has grown into one of Cambodia's most significant tourist centers, is filled with colorful markets, atmospheric bars, some of the finest restaurants in the country, and boutique accommodation fit for a Khmer emperor. Siem Reap is also a base for other excursions in this corner of Cambodia – to lesser-known temples, and to the remarkable floating villages and wildlife reserves of the huge Tonlé Sap lake.

SIEM REAP AND ANGKOR

Must Sees

1 Siem Reap
2 Angkor Wat
3 Angkor Thom
4 Ta Prohm
5 Tonlé Sap

Experience More

6 Phnom Bakheng
7 Preah Khan
8 Preah Neak Pean
9 East Baray
10 Pre Rup
11 Srah Srang
12 Banteay Kdei
13 Prasat Kravan
14 Banteay Srei
15 Cambodian Landmine Museum
16 Banteay Srei Butterfly Center
17 Roluos Group

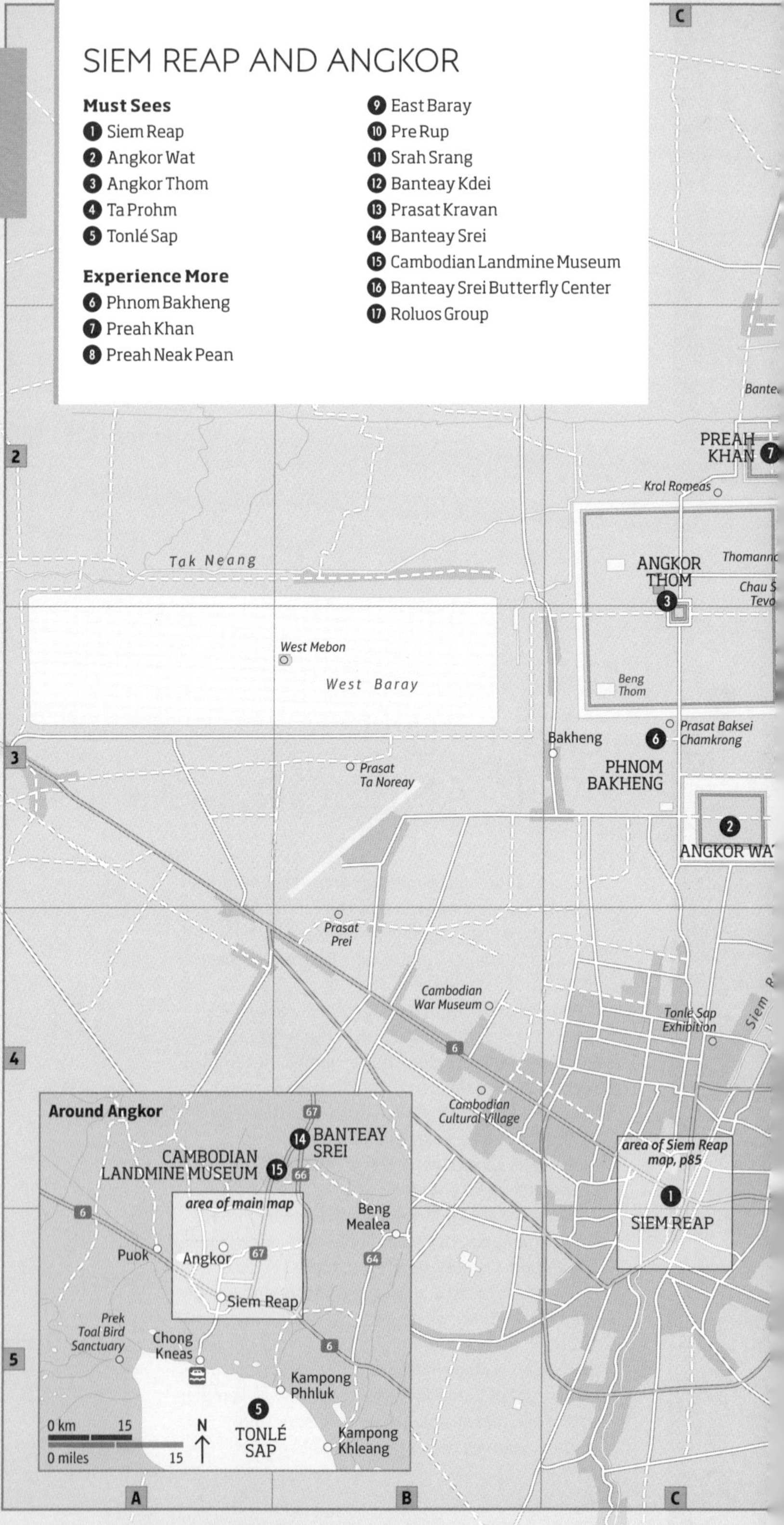

Bante

PREAH KHAN 7

Krol Romeas

Tak Neang

ANGKOR THOM 3

Thomanno

Chau S
Tevo

West Mebon

West Baray

Beng
Thom

Bakheng

Prasat Baksei
Chamkrong

6

PHNOM
BAKHENG

Prasat
Ta Noreay

2

ANGKOR WA

Prasat
Prei

Cambodian
War Museum

Tonle Sap
Exhibition

Siem R

6

Cambodian
Cultural Village

area of Siem Reap
map, p85

Around Angkor

67

14 BANTEAY
SREI

CAMBODIAN
LANDMINE MUSEUM 15

66

area of main map

67

Beng
Mealea

1

SIEM REAP

6

Puok

Angkor

67

64

Siem Reap

Prek
Toal Bird
Sanctuary

Chong
Kneas

6

Kampong
Phhluk

0 km   15

0 miles   15

N

5 TONLÉ
SAP

Kampong
Khleang

↑ Tuk-tuks gathering to transport visitors in Siem Reap's bustling Pub Street

❶

SIEM REAP

 C4 🏠 155 miles (250 km) NW of Phnom Penh ✈🚆 From Phnom Penh & Sihanoukville 🚌 From Phnom Penh or Battambang 🛈 Treang Village, Slorkram Commune; (063)-963-996

Siem Reap literally means Siam Defeated, referring to the Khmer sacking of the great Thai city of Ayutthaya in the 17th century. Once little more than a quiet staging post on the way to Angkor, this bustling city is now a tourist hub in its own right. With lively backpacker bars, bustling markets and sleek hotels, Siem Reap's streets are usually buzzing around the clock.

Cambodia War Museum

🏠 Kaksekam Village, Sra Nge Commune ⏰ 8am-5:30pm daily 🌐 war museumcambodia.com

This museum offers visitors an insightful view of the perils that Cambodia faced during the last three decades of the 20th century. The story of Cambodia's war years is told through a unique collection of war apparatus (including tanks, armored vehicles, and artillery) and rare photographs. Optional tour guides bring the exhibits to life by recounting their personal experiences of the war. The guides don't charge a fee, but tips are always appreciated.

Angkor National Museum

🏠 968 Charles De Gaulle Blvd ⏰ 8:30am-6:30pm daily (Apr-Sep: to 6pm) 🌐 angkornational museum.com

Opened to the public in 2007, the Angkor National Museum is housed in a beautiful sprawling building with well-manicured lawns. The museum comprises eight galleries, each displaying a wealth of ancient Angkorian artifacts. On arrival, visitors first head to the screening of a documentary on the marvels of Angkor entitled *The Story Behind The Legend*.

③
Psar Chaa

🏠 Corner of Pokambor Ave 🕐 Dawn-dusk daily

Once the mainstay of the town's vendors, today Psar Chaa faces competition from shops lining the surrounding streets. Nevertheless, the market continues to be a popular stop for both locals and foreign visitors, who come for its reasonable prices and variety of goods. Popular products include wood carvings, lacquerware, silverware, and groceries.

Artisans Angkor

🏠 Stung Thmey St
🕐 7am-5pm daily
🌐 artisansdangkor.com

A school set up in the early 1990s for under-privileged children, Artisans Angkor teaches children stone carving, lacquer-making, silk painting, and wood sculpting. Visitors can walk through the workshops with a guide who explains the stages of each intricate craft; the tour takes about an hour.

Those keen to see the process of silk farming can head for the school's Silk Farm, 10 miles (16 km) northwest of Siem Reap. The tour takes three hours and buses run from their downtown Craft Centre.

Khmer Ceramics & Fine Arts Centre

🏠 0207 River Road
🕐 8am-6pm daily
🌐 khmerceramics.com

A non-profit, non-government organization, the Khmer Ceramics & Fine Arts Centre was established to reintroduce Khmer's ancient pottery techniques to the country. The center also provides valuable

job opportunities to the people of Siem Reap province. Students are taught for free and are encouraged to set up their own studios. They learn to work with clay, and master the potter's wheel and kilns. Guided tours of the center are given by students, and those interested can also try their hand at the potter's wheel.

Cambodian Cultural Village

🏠 6 Airport Rd, Khum Svay Dang Kum, Krus 🕐 8am-7pm daily 🌐 cambodian culturalvillage.com

The Cambodian Cultural Village is an interesting diversion for visitors who want to learn about Cambodia's demography, religion, and architecture. There are Cham (Muslim), Khmer

(Buddhist), and Phnong and Kroueng (animist) houses, as well as floating villages in the complex. The village also has miniature replicas of famous Cambodian buildings. Occasional shows – such as *apsara* dances and fishing ceremonies – provide an insight into the country's ancient traditions.

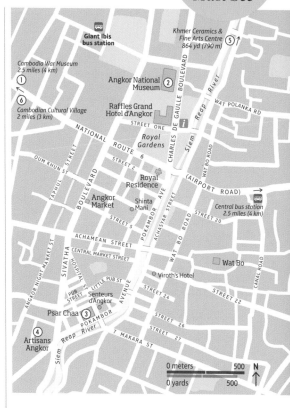

↑ Working with clay at the Khmer Ceramics & Fine Arts Centre

2 ✦

ANGKOR WAT

📍 C3 🚗 4 miles (6 km) N of Siem Reap 🚌 Siem Reap 🕐 5:30am–6pm daily (ticket office from 5am) ℹ️ Khmer Angkor Tour Guide Association, Siem Reap; www.khmerangkortourguideassociation.com

With its tall towers, reflective pools, and epic bas-relief panels, Angkor Wat is one of the most remarkable architectural masterpieces in the world. Set among dense green forests and neat rice paddies, it is the ultimate testament to the sophistication of the ancient Angkorian empire.

The largest religious monument in the world, Angkor Wat literally means the "City which is a Temple". Built during the 12th century by King Suryavarman II, this spectacular complex was originally dedicated to the Hindu god Vishnu. The layout is based on a *mandala* (sacred design of the Hindu cosmos). A five-towered temple shaped like a lotus bud, representing Mount Meru, the mythical abode of the gods and the center of the universe, stands in the middle of the complex. The intricate carvings on the walls marking the temple's perimeter are outstanding and include a 1,970-ft (600-m) long panel of bas-reliefs, and carvings of *apsaras*. The outermost walls and the moat surrounding the entire complex symbolize the edge of the world and the cosmic ocean, respectively. Angkor Wat, unusual among Khmer temples, faces the setting sun in the west, a symbol of death. Some believe this is because Suryavarman II intended the temple as a funerary monument.

↑ Bas-reliefs representing warriors in combat during the Battle of Kurukshetra

→ Monks crossing the causeway toward the main entrance

Timeline

1130–50

△ Suryavarman II presides over the building of Angkor Wat, then probably known as Varah Vishnu-lok, with work coming to an end shortly after his death.

1181–1218

△ After being sacked by the Chams in 1117, the temple is restored and its focus shifts from Hinduism to Buddhism during the reign of Jayavarman VII.

1431

△ The capital shifts to Phnom Penh and most Angkorian temples are abandoned, though a handful of monks keep Angkor Wat itself active until the colonial era.

1860

△ French explorer Henri Mouhot visits Angkor Wat. Though not the first European to see the temple, his account spreads knowledge of the temple worldwide.

PICTURE PERFECT
Angkor Wat

To get a good picture of Angkor Wat reflected in the water, head to the temple shortly before it closes at 6pm, when the five towers are bathed in golden light. Crouch down by the pool to the left of the causeway and start snapping away.

The five towers of Angkor Wat reflected in one of the giant pools in front of the temple ↑

Exploring the Temple

Angkor Wat is a sublime combination of grand impression and minute detail. Although its astonishing overall form is best viewed from afar, particularly from the approaching causeway, up close the staggering complexity and details of the bas-reliefs and statuary becomes apparent. The temple's sacred splendor reveals itself as you pass through each of the concentric enclosing walls.

The third enclosing wall is the place to pause for an anticlockwise circuit of the long, shady galleries lined with intricate bas-relief panels depicting the Hindu epic *Mahabharata*.

Beyond this, visitors pass through a shady, cloister-like section spanning the second enclosure to reach the innermost parts of the temple where the walls are crowded with exquisite *apsara* carvings.

Towering over the complex, the Central Sanctuary is a steep climb, intended to symbolize the difficulty of ascending to the kingdom of the gods. Its four entrances feature images of Buddha, reflecting how Buddhism eventually went on to displace Hinduism at Angkor Wat.

↑ Bas-relief depictions of *apsaras* lining the walls of the second enclosure

Central Sanctuary

The carvings of hundreds of sensual apsaras line the walls of the temple.

The library provides views of the upper levels of Angkor Wat.

→ Illustration of the three central enclosures of Angkor Wat

↑ Visitors making the steep climb to the Central Sanctuary of Angkor Wat

GETTING AROUND THE TEMPLES

There are various ways to get around the temples of Angkor. Though many people visit on organized tours by minibus, traveling independently gives you a lot more freedom. A popular option is to charter a motorbike taxi or tuk-tuk for the day – with many drivers also doubling as informal guides. If you'd prefer to travel under your own steam, it's possible to walk between the major temples, though you'll need to get transport out from Siem Reap at the start. Alternatively, bicycles are available to rent in Siem Reap, and an extensive network of trails winds around the temples.

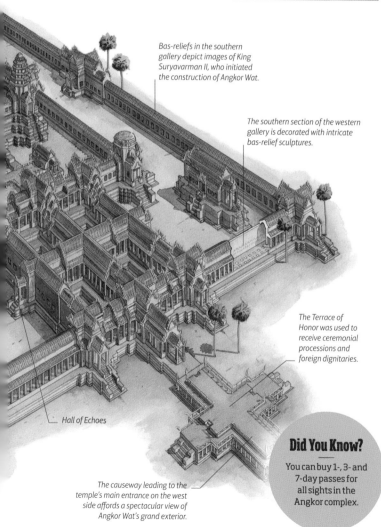

Bas-reliefs in the southern gallery depict images of King Suryavarman II, who initiated the construction of Angkor Wat.

The southern section of the western gallery is decorated with intricate bas-relief sculptures.

The Terrace of Honor was used to receive ceremonial processions and foreign dignitaries.

Hall of Echoes

The causeway leading to the temple's main entrance on the west side affords a spectacular view of Angkor Wat's grand exterior.

Did You Know?

You can buy 1-, 3- and 7-day passes for all sights in the Angkor complex.

ARCHITECTURE OF ANGKOR

Angkor-period architecture generally dates from Jayavarman II's construction of the Khmer capital near Roluos in the early 9th century CE. From then until the 15th century, art historians identify five main architectural styles. The earliest, Preah Ko, is rooted in the pre-Angkorian traditions of Sambor Prei Kuk *(p121)*, to Angkor's east, and the 8th-century temple style of Kampong Preah, relics of which are found at Prasat Ak Yum by the West Baray. Traditional Khmer architecture reached its zenith during the construction of Angkor Wat.

The oldest temple in the Roluos Group, Preah Ko was built in 879. Its distinctive towers and elegant carvings influenced the design of other, later temples in the area.

Unlike the later temples, which were typically built entirely of stone, Preah Ko features a combination of sandstone and brick. The towers were originally covered with plaster, a few traces of which still remain.

Completed in 907, Phnom Bakheng impressively exemplifies the Bakheng style. It was built onto a natural hill, with the terraces and stairways cut into the bedrock. The five towers at the top are arranged in the standard quincunx pattern.

Timeline

Preah Ko (875–90 CE)

▲ The Preah Ko style was characterized by a simple temple layout, with one or more square brick towers rising from a single laterite base. The Roluos Group *(p109)* saw the first use of concentric enclosures entered via the gopura (gateway tower). Another innovation was the introduction of a library annex, possibly used to protect the sacred texts from fire.

Bakheng to Pre Rup (890–965 CE)

▲ The temple-mountain style, based on Mount Meru, evolved during the Bakheng period. Phnom Bakheng *(p106)*, Phnom Krom, and Phnom Bok all feature the classic quincunx layout - a tower on each corner, with a fifth at the center. The Pre Rup style developed during the reign of Rajendravarman II (r. 944-68). It continues the Bakheng style, but the towers are higher and steeper, with more tiers.

↑ An aerial view of Angkor Wat, showing the symbolic layout of the complex

The central tower of Angkor Wat marked the physical and spiritual culmination of the complex – and of the Khmer Empire too.

The towers of Bayon are decorated with faces representing the Bodhisattva Avalokiteśvara, who bears a striking resemblance to Jayavarman VII.

Banteay Srei, built between 967 and 1000 CE, is known for its fine craftsmanship, evident in the detail of the stone lintels.

Banteay Srei to Baphuon (965–1080 CE)

▲ Represented by the delicate and refined Banteay Srei *(p108)*, this eponymous style is characterized by ornate carvings of sensuous *apsaras* and *devadas* (dancers). By the mid-11th century, when Khmer architecture was reaching its majestic apogee, this style had evolved into the Baphuon style, which is distinguished by vast proportions and vaulted galleries.

Angkor Wat (1080–1175 CE)

▲ Art historians generally agree that the style of Angkor Wat *(p86)* represents the apex of Khmer architectural and sculptural genius. The largest and greatest of all temple-mountains, it also houses the finest bas-relief narratives, particularly in the gallery of the third enclosure. The art of lintel carving also reached its zenith during this magnificent period of construction.

Bayon (1175–1240 CE)

▲ Considered a synthesis of previous styles, Bayon - the last great Angkor architectural style - is characterized by a detectable decline in quality. There is more use of laterite and less of sandstone, as well as more Buddhist imagery and fewer Hindu themes. This is the style that was adopted in Angkor Thom, King Jayavarman VII's ambitious capital *(p92)*.

ANGKOR THOM

📍 C2 🏠 1 mile (2 km) N of Angkor Wat; 5 miles (8 km) N of Siem Reap 🕐 5am–6pm daily ℹ️ Khmer Angkor Tour Guide Association; www.khmerangkortourguideassociation.com

Remarkable in scale and architectural ingenuity, the ancient city of Angkor Thom, which means "Great City" in Khmer, was founded by King Jayavarman VII in the late 12th century. The largest city in the Khmer Empire at one time, it is protected by a 26-ft- (8-m-) high wall, and surrounded by a wide moat. Within the city are several ruins, the most famous of which is the atmospheric Bayon temple *(p96)*.

① South Gate

This is the best preserved of the five gateways into Angkor Thom. Its approach is via a causeway flanked by 154 stone statues – gods on the left side, demons on the right – each carrying a giant serpent.

Surrounded by statues of the three-headed elephant Erawan (the fabled mount of the Hindu god Indra), the gate is a massive 75-ft- (23-m-) high structure surmounted by a triple tower with four giant stone faces pointing toward the cardinal directions.

Baphuon

Following over 50 years of restoration, Baphuon opened to the public in 2011. Believed to be one of Angkor's greatest temples, it was built by King Udayadityavarman II in the 11th century. Its striking pyramidal mountain form represents Mount Meru, the mythical abode of the Hindu gods. A central tower with

↑ Exterior of the Baphuon temple, opened to the public in 2011

BAFFLING BAPHUON

French architects began restoring Baphuon in 1959. They dismantled the temple so they could reinforce the structure and put it back together again, a technique called "anastylosis." However, plans identifying the 300,000 pieces were destroyed by the Khmer Rouge in the Civil War. When restoration work began again in 1996, it took over 16 years to complete what architect Pascal Royere called the "largest 3D jigsaw puzzle in the world."

←

Gods lining the causeway leading up to the South Gate

four entrances once stood at its summit, but has long since collapsed.

The temple is approached via a 650-ft- (200-m-) long raised causeway and has four gateways decorated with bas-relief scenes from Hindu epics such as the *Mahabharata* and *Ramayana* (*Reamker* in Khmer). Inside, spanning the western length of Baphuon, is a huge Reclining Buddha. Since the temple was dedicated to Hinduism, this image was probably added later, in the 15th century.

> **The temple is approached via a 650-ft- (200-m-) long raised causeway and has four gateways decorated with bas-relief scenes from Hindu epics.**

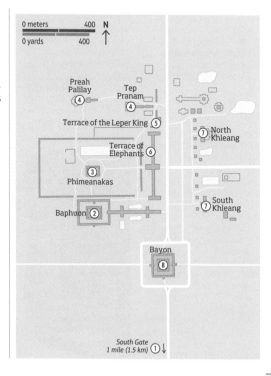

③
Phimeanakas

This royal temple-palace was built during the 10th century by King Rajendravarman II, and added to later by Jayavarman VII. Dedicated to Hinduism, it is also known as the Celestial Palace, and is associated with the legend of a golden tower that once stood here, where a nine-headed serpent resided. This magical creature would appear to the king as a woman, and the king would sleep with her before going to his other wives and concubines. It was believed that if the king failed to sleep with the serpent-woman, he would die, but by sleeping with her, the royal lineage was saved.

The pyramid-shaped palace is rectangular at the base, and surrounded by a 16-ft- (5-m-) high wall of laterite enclosing an area of around 37 acres (15 ha). It has five entrance-ways, and the stairs, which are flanked by guardian lions, rise up on all four sides. There are corresponding elephant figures at each of the four corners of the pyramid. The upper terrace offers great views of the Baphuon to the south.

④
Preah Palilay and Tep Pranam

Two of the lesser, yet still impressive, structures at Angkor Thom, Preah Palilay and Tep Pranam are located a short distance to the northwest of the Terrace of the Leper King.

Preah Palilay dates from the 13th or 14th century and is a small Buddhist sanctuary set within a 160-ft (50-m) square laterite wall. The sanctuary,

which is partially collapsed, is entered via a single gateway, and rises to a tapering stone tower. A 108-ft- (33-m-) long causeway leads to a terrace to the east of the sanctuary, which is distinguished by fine *naga* (serpent) balustrades.

Nearby, to the east, lies Tep Pranam, a Buddhist sanctuary built in the 16th century. This was probably originally dedicated to the Mahayana school. Used as a place of Theravada worship now, it features a big sandstone Buddha image, seated in the "calling the earth to witness" *mudra* (posture).

⑤
Terrace of the Leper King

This small platform dates from the late 12th century. Standing on top of this structure is a headless statue known as the Leper King. Once believed to be an image of King Jayavarman VII, who, according to legend, had leprosy, it is in fact a representation of Yama, the God of Death. This statue is, however, a replica – the original was taken to Phnom Penh's National Museum (*p72*).

The terrace is marked by two walls, both beautifully restored and decorated with exquisite bas-reliefs. Of the two, the inner one is more

remarkable, and is covered with figures of underworld deities, kings, celestial females, *devadas*, *apsaras*, warriors, and strange marine creatures.

The exact function of this terrace, which appears to be

→ Huge sandstone elephants lining the Terrace of Elephants

↑ The remarkable gateway of Preah Palilay

an extension of the Terrace of Elephants, is not clear. It was probably used either for royal receptions or cremations.

 6

Terrace of Elephants

Built by King Jayavarman VII, this structure is more than 950 ft (300 m) long, stretching from the Baphuon to the connecting Terrace of the Leper King. It has three main platforms and two smaller ones. The terrace was primarily used by the king to view military and other parades. It is decorated with almost life-sized images of sandstone elephants in a procession, accompanied by mahouts. There are also images of tigers, serpents, and Garuda – mythical beasts mounted by Vishnu. For a spectacular unobstructed view

of the whole complex, head to the very top of the terrace's middle stairway.

 7

North and South Khleang

These two similar buildings are located to the east of the main road running past the Terrace of Elephants. The North Khleang was constructed by King Jayavarman toward the end of the 10th century, and the South Khleang was built by King Suryavarman I during the early 11th century. The main architectural features of the Khleangs are their stone lintels and elegant balustered windows. Unfortunately, the original function of the buildings is unknown. Khleang, which means storehouse, is a modern designation, and is considered misleading.

APSARA DANCE PERFORMANCES

There is a remarkable continuity between the images of divine *apsara* dancers that decorate many of the temples of Angkor, and contemporary entertainment laid on for travelers. Though the *apsara* tradition declined during the French era, and then suffered Khmer Rouge hostility, it has since been revived. Dancers are trained at the Royal University of Fine Arts in Phnom Penh. The Apsara Theater in Siem Reap *(www. angkorvillageresort. asia/apsara-theatre)* has nightly shows.

Did You Know?

The name Bayon came from local renovators mispronouncing the word "Banyan" (a sacred fig tree).

↑ Buddhist monks and visitors exploring Bayon temple

⑧ 🔄

BAYON

📍C2 🏛Angkor Thom 🕐5am–6pm daily

Located in the heart of Angkor Thom, Bayon is one of the city's most extraordinary structures, epitomizing the "lost civilization" of Angkor. Shaped like a pyramid, this symbolic temple-mountain rises on three levels, and features 54 towers bearing more than 200 huge, yet enigmatic stone faces.

The central sanctuary of Bayon, with its forest of towers, is ringed by an outer enclosing wall, stretching between eight, evenly spaced cruciform bastions. This wall was once a shaded gallery, like that of Angkor Wat. The roof has long since collapsed, but the bas-reliefs remain, and while it is the huge faces on the inner towers that get most of the attention, these carvings are where much of Bayon's unique interest lies. Unlike the reliefs at Angkor Wat, which are dominated by religious narratives, these teem with scenes from Angkorian daily life, as well as tales from local folklore.

Beyond this epic in carved stone, more bas-relief friezes ring the inner enclosing wall before the innermost sanctum with its looming mass of towers. Each tower bears the all-seeing face of Avalokiteśvara. The central structure – a craggy depiction of the mythical Mount Meru – rises from a circular base 140 ft (43 m) above the ground. A large statue of Buddha once occupied the sanctuary but was destroyed when Bayon became a Hindu temple (p92). It has since been restored and is now on display in a small pavilion at Angkor.

> **The central structure - a craggy depiction of the mythical Mount Meru - rises from a circular base.**

↑ Stone faces depicting Avalokiteśvara on the towers of Bayon

THE BODHISATTVA OF COMPASSION

Most archaeologists now believe that the enigmatically smiling faces of Bayon represent Avalokiteśvara, the bodhisattva who embodies compassion and who often appears outside Cambodia as a striking, thousand-armed figure. The fact that they also resemble the king who commissioned the temple, Jayavarman VII (p91), is probably no coincidence, as Southeast Asian concepts of kingship often rested on the identification of a living ruler with a deity.

Timeline

12th century
△ Construction of Bayon begins. It is to be the centerpiece of Angkor Thom, King Jayavarman VII's vast and ambitious new capital city.

13th century
△ Jayavarman VIII, a Hindu king, takes the throne. The temple is altered to reflect the new religion and the Buddha icon in the sanctuary is destroyed.

15th century
△ Angkor Thom is sacked at the hands of the mighty Ayutthaya Kingdom, led by King Borommarachathirat II, and Bayon is abandoned to the jungle.

20th century
△ The École Française d'Extrême Orient starts restoring the temple in the early 20th century. Conservation continues in the 1990s, led by the Japanese government.

History of Bayon

Bayon was the last great state temple built at Angkor, before the empire began its slow, centuries-long decline. It is unique among Angkor's vast array of religious edifices as the only temple originally built to honor Mahayana Buddhism. King Jayavarman VII was one of the most successful of all Angkorian rulers, seeing off regional rivals and consolidating the empire. He also broke with the religious traditions of his Hindu predecessors, and ruled as a Buddhist monarch, dedicated to the Mahayana school. When the time came to command his own mighty contribution to the Angkor cityscape, he ordered the construction of a Mahayana temple, Bayon. After Jayavarman's death, Bayon was retooled for a resurgent Hinduism, with many sculptures adapted. Later, its focus shifted again as Theravada Buddhism came to dominate. But there was no way to erase the vast and essentially Mahayana faces of Avalokiteśvara.

Bas-relief showing a female *devata*, a Hindu deity ↑

> **INSIDER TIP**
> **Visit at Sunrise**
>
> To dodge the crowds, the best time to visit is first thing in the morning, while the rest of the early risers are snapping the sunrise at Angkor Wat, and before the tour buses turn up.

The temple's central towers are decorated with the smiling faces of Bodhisattva Avalokiteśvara gazing out in the cardinal directions.

Outer enclosure

A statue of the Hindu god Vishnu, thought to date from the time of the founding of the temple, is installed in the southern section of the western gallery.

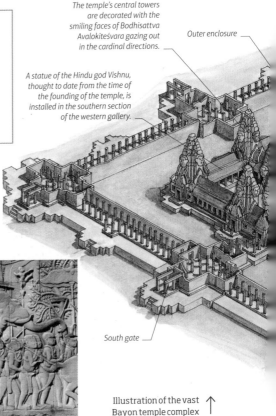

South gate

Illustration of the vast Bayon temple complex ↑

↑ Bas-relief showing a Khmer king on his elephant, marching his soldiers to battle

↑ Inner enclosure of Bayon, seen in early morning light

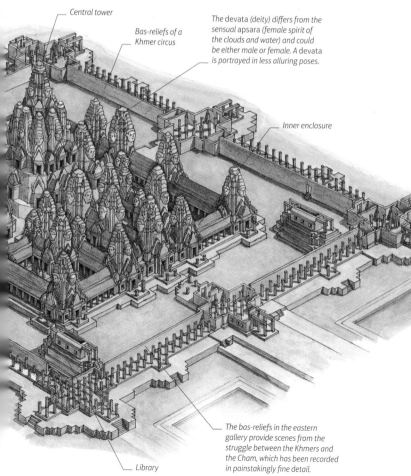

Central tower

Bas-reliefs of a Khmer circus

The devata (deity) differs from the sensual apsara (female spirit of the clouds and water) and could be either male or female. A devata is portrayed in less alluring poses.

Inner enclosure

The bas-reliefs in the eastern gallery provide scenes from the struggle between the Khmers and the Cham, which has been recorded in painstakingly fine detail.

Library

Did You Know?

The monastery once owned an impressive 35 diamonds, 40,620 pearls, and 4,540 precious stones.

④ ⊘

TA PROHM

◍ D3 🏠 1/2 mile (1 km) E of Angkor Thom ⏰ 5am–6pm daily ⓕ Khmer Angkor Tour Guide Association; www.khmerangkortourguideassociation.com

Ta Prohm is what many travelers have in mind when they envisage the temples of Cambodia. With strangler figs sprouting from the crumbling masonry and weathered carvings peering from behind meshed roots, it is one of the most atmospheric ancient monuments on earth.

Originally known as Rajavihara, the "King's Monastery," Ta Prohm was built during the reign of Jayavarman VII (r. 1181–1218). In its day, it was a more like a city than a simple monastic establishment, home to around 12,000 people, including monks, high priests, and 615 temple dancers. Tens of thousands lived in the immediate surrounds to support the monastery's thriving economy. The complex was dedicated to Prajnaparamita, the bodhisattva of wisdom, whose statue was deliberately made to resemble the king's mother.

The current name of the complex, Ta Prohm, means "Ancestor of Brahma," but this has no connection with its original purpose. The monastery was abandoned in the 15th century after the fall of the Khmer Empire, and the jungle began to take over, with the seeds of strangler figs and silk-cotton trees lodging in cracks in the masonry and sending their roots cascading over the crumbling blocks.

↑ Taking a picture of part of the monastery complex at Ta Prohm

The Tomb Raider Tree, so-called for its appearance in *Lara Croft: Tomb Raider*

The monastery was abandoned in the 15th century after the fall of the Khmer Empire, and the jungle began to take over, with the seeds of strangler figs and silk-cotton trees lodging in cracks in the masonry.

Entering the Complex

Most visitors enter the Ta Prohm complex from the west, though the eastern entrance was originally the main point of access. A gopura (tower) rises over the western entrance, with four sculpted faces looking in each cardinal direction, as on the Bayon towers *(p96)*. The faces are thought to represent Jayavarman VII.

The Dinosaur Carving

Just past the entrance to the third enclosure is a small carving that has attracted a lot of heated debate. Set in a small roundel, some claim that it is an accurate depiction of a stegosaurus, suggesting either an inexplicable ancient knowledge of paleontology, or the need for a rethink of evolutionary history. Others say the carving is in fact a rhino with a backdrop of leaves – or even a 20th-century fake.

Iconic Trees

Several specific trees in the complex attract particular attention. The roots of the so-called Waterfall Tree cascade over the galleries of the second enclosure, while the Tomb Raider Tree in the inner enclosure had a cameo in the Hollywood blockbuster of that name. The Crocodile Tree, another much-photographed stranger fig, is on the easternmost gopura.

↑ The dinosaur carving, on a column just past the entrance to the third enclosure

A giant banyan tree engulfs part of Ta Prohm temple

⑤
TONLÉ SAP

 C6-D6

A great blue blot across the map of Cambodia, Tonlé Sap is the watery heart of the nation. This huge lake is a haven for birdlife, a vital source of fish, and the setting for numerous local communities. Short trips from Siem Reap typically only take in the well-touristed floating villages, but those who venture further afield will find mesmerizing scenery where land and water interlock, and vast wetlands teem with waterfowl.

①
Chong Kneas

🏠 9 miles (15 km) S of Siem Reap 🚌 🛈 Gecko Environment Center; www. jinja.apsara.org/gecko

The most accessible floating village from Siem Reap, Chong Kneas can be reached either by road from Siem Reap or by boat. The road trip passes through lush paddy fields and an ancient temple atop Phnom Krom. Chong Kneas has a well-deserved reputation for rampant commercialism and tourist scams, but if you don't have time to explore other, outlying villages, it is still worth a visit for its floating market, catfish farm, and the Gecko Environment Center's informative exhibition on the environmental issues facing the lake ecosystem.

②
Kampong Phhluk

 10 miles (16 km) SE of Siem Reap 🚌 From Chong Kneas

Far less commercial than Chong Kneas – though by no means off the beaten track – Kampong Phhluk is built on stilts amid a half-drowned forest. The boat journey from Chong Kneas through the wetlands of Tonlé Sap is a truly memorable experience. The village offers an insight into life on the great lake. In the dry season, however, the surrounding water usually vanishes, revealing the remarkable supporting stilt structures. A walkway leads through

> ### VISITING THE FLOATING VILLAGES
>
> Most people visit the lake as part of a quick tour from Siem Reap, often stopping off at Chong Kneas. This village, in particular, has a reputation for various tourist scams. Be wary of boat drivers taking you to floating restaurants (even if you're not hungry) and expecting huge tips. Whichever floating village you visit, remember that these are living local communities. It is important to be respectful when exploring the villages and to ask permission before taking photographs of locals.

Stilted houses on Kampong Khleang, the largest settlement on Tonlé Sap

the surrounding trees, and locals offer boat tours of the surrounding area.

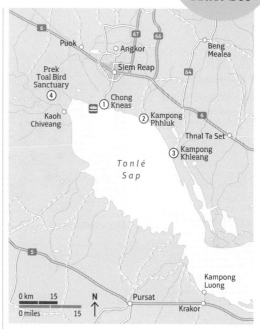

③
Kampong Khleang

⌂ 22 miles (35 km) E of Siem Reap ⛴ From Chong Kneas

Though it is the largest settlement on Tonlé Sap, Kampong Khleang sees fewer tourists than most other lake villages, giving a glimpse of waterside life. The village is built on stilts and pontoons – with most of it floating, including the pharmacy and petrol station. An island situated in the center of the village has a painted pagoda with a macabre depiction of heaven and hell. There is also a flooded forest next to the village.

Did You Know?

You can take a boat from Kampong Chhnag to the little-known floating village of Phoum Kandal.

④ ⊘ ⓜ
Prek Toal Bird Sanctuary

⌂ 19 miles (31 km) S of Siem Reap ⛴ From Chong Kneas

A very important breeding ground for large water birds in Southeast Asia, Prek Toal Bird Sanctuary covers 120 sq miles (310 sq km) on the northwest tip of Tonlé Sap. The seasonally flooded forest abounds with lesser and greater adjutants, milky and painted storks, black-headed ibis, and many other species. The sanctuary is best visited during the dry season (February–April), when migratory birds congregate in large numbers. Most travelers arrange a tour to the sanctuary from Siem Reap.

↓ Storks in a tree in the Prek Toal Bird Sanctuary on Tonlé Sap

EXPERIENCE MORE

6

Phnom Bakheng

📍 C3 🚶 550 yd (500 m)
S of Angkor Thom 🕐 Dawn–
dusk daily

Famous for its sunset views
of Angkor Wat, Tonlé Sap,
and Bayon, the ancient Hindu
temple of Phnom Bakheng
surveys the surrounding plains
from the top of a 220-ft-
(65-m-) high hill. Built by
King Yasovarman I, the
Bakheng complex is one of
the region's first examples
of Mount Meru-style temple
architecture. The complex
was once surrounded by
109 towers spread around
its six tiers; however, most
of them have now collapsed.

STAY

Shinta Mani

Just a stone's throw
from the heart of Siem
Reap, this supremely
stylish hotel also has
excellent responsible
tourism credentials.

📍 C5 🏠 Junction of Oum
Khum and Street 14,
Siem Reap
🌐 shintamani.com

$ $ $

Viroth's Hotel

This greenery-
bedecked boutique
hotel features quality
spa treatments and
cool contemporary
rooms overlooking a
swimming pool.

📍 C5 🏠 Street 23,
Siem Reap
🌐 viroth-hotel.com

$ $ $

↑ Detail of a stone carving
in the atmospheric
ruins of Preah Khan

7

Preah Khan

📍 C2 🚶 Half a mile (1 km)
NE of Angkor Thom
🕐 Dawn-dusk daily

Named for the sacred sword
owned by the 9th-century
King Jayavarman II, the Preah
Khan temple complex was
built by Jayavarman VII
(r. 1181–1218). It is believed
to have been his temporary
capital while Angkor Thom
underwent restoration after
being sacked by the Chams
in 1177. It also served as a
monastery and religious
college with more than 1,000
teachers. Originally dedicated
to the Buddha, this temple
was later vandalized by Hindu
rulers who replaced many
Buddha images on the walls
with carvings of Hindu deities.

Today, the complex extends
over a sprawling 2 sq miles
(5 sq km), and is surrounded
by a 2-mile- (3-km-) long
laterite wall, with four gates
set at the cardinal points. One

→
Sunrise over the
vast ceremonial lake
of Srah Srang

of the main highlights is the
Hall of Dancers, named after
the apsara bas-reliefs that line
the walls. The premises also
have a massive *baray* (reservoir).
The most notable temple in
the complex is the Temple of
the Four Faces. As at Ta Prohm
(p100), Preah Khan is home to
many great trees whose roots
cover and, in places, pierce the
stone structures over which
they grow. Unlike Ta Prohm,
however, the temple has been
extensively restored by the
World Monuments Fund, and
many of the trees have now
been cut down.

8

Preah Neak Pean

📍 D2 🚶 3 miles (5 km) NE
of Angkor Thom 🕐 Dawn-
dusk daily

This monument – a shrine
dedicated to Avalokiteśvara –
is set within the center of a
cruciform arrangement of
sacred ponds. Around the
shrine's base coil a couple of
snakes, giving the temple its

name – Entwined Serpents. Located in North Baray, the temple is built around an artificial square pond, each side measuring 230 ft (70 m), surrounded by four smaller ponds. The central pond represents the mythical Lake Anvatapta, said to be located at the summit of the universe. From it rise the four great curative rivers, each represented here by a different gargoyle at each corner of the pool. The east head is that of a man, the south a lion, the west a horse, and the north an elephant. When the temple was functioning, sacred water would have been diverted through their mouths into the smaller pools and used to heal devotees.

East Baray

◉E2 ◰1 mile (2 km) E of Angkor Thom ◷Dawn-dusk daily

The second-largest of Angkor's *barays*, East Baray measures 4 miles by 1 mile (6 km by 2 km), and was built by King Yasovarman I in the 9th century. Watered by the Stung Treng, it held nearly 13 billion gallons (50 billion liters) of water. While some believe that its purpose was symbolic, representing the sea surrounding Mount Meru, others contend its purpose was for irrigation – it would have been essential to produce three rice harvests a year to feed the population of about one million.

On an island in the middle of the *baray* is the Oriental Mebon temple, built by Rajendravarman II in honor of his parents. Surrounded by three laterite walls, the temple gradually rises to a group of towers dotted with holes that would have supported stucco decorations. At ground level its stairways are flanked by sandstone lions, and at its corners are four sandstone elephants.

Pre Rup

◉E3 ◰3 miles (5 km) E of Angkor Thom ◷Dawn-dusk daily

Dedicated to the Hindu god Shiva, Pre Rup has five lotus-shaped towers. Thought to have been a crematorium, its name means Turning of the Body, which relates to a religious rite of tracing the deceased's outline in his or her ashes.

Srah Srang

◉D3 ◰3 miles (5 km) E of Angkor Thom ◷Dawn-dusk daily

To the west of Pre Rup lies the great reservoir of Srah Srang, or Royal Bath. Built in the 7th century and measuring 1,300 ft by 2,600 ft (400 m by 800 m), it was used exclusively by King Jayavarman V and his wives. On the western side of the lake is a landing platform flanked by two sandstone lions and balustrades bearing a large Garuda on the back of a three-headed serpent. The lake is best visited at sunrise, when water buffalo graze in its shallows, and local children congregate for a swim.

Did You Know?

An 11th-century cemetery with cremated remains in jars was discovered to the northwest of Srah Srang.

↑ Temple buildings on a miniature scale at exquisite Banteay Srei

Banteay Kdei

📍D3 🚗3 miles (5 km) E of Angkor Thom ⏰Dawn-dusk daily

Built in the late 12th century, Banteay Kdei, meaning Citadel of the Cells, lies west of Srah Srang (p107). This Buddhist temple has four entrances, each guarded by Garudas. One of the highlights of this temple is the Hall of Dancers, located in the central corridor.

Prasat Kravan

📍D3 🚗2 miles (3 km) SE of Angkor Thom ⏰Dawn-dusk daily

Dating from the 10th century, this small temple dedicated to Vishnu was built by high-ranking officials during the reign of Harshavarman I. It is located at a slight distance from the capital, Angkor, since only royals could build temples close to the city's center.

The temple, whose name means Cardamom Sanctuary, after a tree that stood here, is particularly remarkable for its brickwork and bas-reliefs, the only such known examples of Khmer art. No mortar was used in its construction, only a type of vegetable compound.

The brick carvings depict Vishnu, his consort Lakshmi, his eagle mount Garuda, a *naga* (serpent), and a number of other divine attendants. The doorways and lintels of all five towers are made up of sandstone. A fine image of Vishnu riding Garuda appears on the southern-most tower, while Lakshmi adorns the northernmost. The central tower has a raised stone that was used to receive water for purification rites.

Banteay Srei

📍C6 🚗20 miles (32 km) N of Siem Reap ⏰Dawn-dusk daily

Located at the foot of the Kulen Mountain, the remote temple complex of Banteay Srei, meaning Citadel of Beauty, is ornamented with exquisitely elaborate carvings executed in pink sandstone. Unlike most other monuments in Angkor, this miniature-scale jewel of Khmer art is not a royal temple. It was built in the 10th century by Yajnavaraha, one of King Rajendravarman's counselors and the future guru of King Jayavarman V.

Rectangular in shape, and enclosed by three walls and the remains of a moat, the central sanctuary contains ornate shrines dedicated to Shiva. The intricately carved lintels reproduce scenes from the Hindu epic *Ramayana*. Representations of Shiva, his consort Parvati, the monkey god Hanuman, the divine cowherd Krishna, and the demon king Ravana are all beautifully etched. Also exceptional are the finely detailed figures of gods and goddesses carved into the niches of the towers. The male divinities carry lances and wear simple loincloths. The goddesses, with their long hair tied in buns or plaits, are dressed in loosely draped traditional skirts, and almost every inch of their bodies is laden with gorgeous jewelry.

Europeans first came across the temple in 1914, and in 1923 four female statues were famously snatched by the future French minister of culture, André Malraux, who

HIDDEN GEM
Phnom Kulen

Around 30 miles (50 km) north of Siem Reap, pilgrims flock to the forest shrines of Phnom Kulen, site of the original Angkor capital, Mahendrapura. There's a beautiful waterfall, a reclining Buddha, and many small temples.

served under President Charles de Gaulle. The statues were recovered and returned soon after.

15

Cambodian Landmine Museum

🅐 C6 🅐 National Hwy 67, 17 miles (28 km) N of Siem Reap 🕒 7:30am–5pm daily 🌐 cambodialandmine museum.org

Founded by former child soldier and self-taught de-miner Aki Ra, this sobering and insightful museum charts the grim history of landmines in Cambodia, and explains their ongoing impact on local lives. The thousands of deactivated mines that Aki Ra and his team have extracted from the countryside along the Cambodian border form part of the display, while a mock minefield gives some sense of the challenges still facing mine clearance workers. The entry fee helps to fund an attached relief center, providing education to children injured by mines.

16

Banteay Srei Butterfly Center

🅔 E1 🅐 National Hwy 67, 16 miles (25 km) N of Siem Reap 🕒 9am–5pm daily 🌐 angkorbutterfly.com

A short way from Banteay Srei, this charming spot is well worth a detour, with hundreds of colorful butterflies drifting through a large netted enclosure. It's a particularly good place to visit with children, who can see the whole butterfly life cycle up close, with caterpillars gorging on foliage and cocoons always ready to hatch. Butterflies are farmed here for export to other centers around the world, providing a sustainable income for local villagers.

17

Roluos Group

🅕 F5 🅐 7 miles (12 km) SE of Siem Reap 🕒 Dawn–dusk daily

This group of temple monuments, the earliest to have been built in the Angkor region, marks the site of Hariharalaya, the first Khmer capital established by Indravarman I (r. 877–89). It takes its name from the small town of Roluos nearby. Three main complexes can be found here. To the north of Highway 6, en route to Phnom Penh from Siem Reap, is Lolei. Founded by Yasovarman I (r. 889–910), this temple stands on an artificial mound in the middle of a small reservoir, and is based on a double platform surrounded by a laterite wall. The four central brick towers have surprisingly well-preserved false doors and inscriptions.

To the south of Lolei, in a serene rural setting, stands Preah Ko, meaning the Sacred Bull. Built by Indravarman I, to honor his parents as well as Jayavarman II (the founder of the Khmer Empire), this temple was dedicated to the worship of Shiva. The main sanctuary consists of six brick towers resting on a raised laterite platform. Close by are

> This group of temple monuments, the earliest to have been built in the Angkor region, mark the site of Hariharalaya, the first Khmer capital.

three statues of the sacred bull Nandi, for whom the temple was named, which are very well preserved, as are the motifs on the lintels, false doors, and columns. They include *kala* (mythical creatures with grinning mouths and large bulging eyes) and *makara* (sea creatures with trunk-like snouts).

Beyond Preah Ko, the huge mass of Bakong, by far the largest of the Roluos Group, is well worth a visit. Originally dedicated to Shiva, it has since become a place of worship for Buddhists. Approached by a pathway that is protected by a seven-headed *naga*, and flanked by guesthouses for pilgrims, the mount rises in four stages. At the summit rests the square central sanctuary, with four levels and a lotus-shaped tower rising from the middle. The mount is surrounded by eight massive brick towers that feature finely carved sandstone decorations.

THE CAMBODIAN CIRCUS

Phare *(https://pharecircus. org)*, Cambodia's homegrown answer to Cirque du Soleil, perform an extravaganza of finely honed acrobatics nightly in Siem Reap. Performers are graduates of a training center near Battambang, created by an inspired NGO to provide opportunities for young Cambodians coming from disadvantaged backgrounds. The troupe now tours internationally, but is still best seen on home ground by Sok San Road.

NORTHERN CAMBODIA

The geographically diverse and remote region of Northern Cambodia shares borders with Thailand to the north and Laos to the northeast. The earliest known evidence of human settlement in the region dates back to 4300 BCE, when hunter-gatherers inhabited caves in the northwest. Between the 6th and 7th centuries, Chenla rulers built several temples in the region. Northern Cambodia was overrun by invading Thai forces on numerous occasions during the 16th and 17th centuries. In the late 18th century, parts of the northwest were annexed by the Thais, and finally returned to Cambodia in 1946. Later in the 20th century, Khmer Rouge forces passed through the region as they retreated north from Phnom Penh, ahead of the Vietnamese Army.

Battambang, the country's second-largest city, is fast emerging as a popular tourist destination. French colonialists arrived in 1907, after the town was returned to Cambodia following a long Thai occupation, and quickly made their mark on the city's streetscape. Battambang still retains many examples of Colonial-era architecture, including the shophouse-lined streets around the Pasar Nat market, the disused railway station, and along the riverfront. The nearby ruins of Wat Banan and Banteay Chhmer make for excellent day trips.

The northeast has a few excellent ecolodges and eco-trekking organizations, while farther south, the town of Kratie is renowned for its sunsets and the Irrawaddy dolphin. The temple ruins of Sambor Prei Kuk and Koh Ker are well worth a visit.

NORTHERN CAMBODIA

Must Sees

1. Prasat Preah Vihear
2. Battambang

Experience More

3. Wat Banan
4. Kamping Poy
5. Choob
6. Ang Trapeng Thmor Reserve
7. Banteay Chhmer
8. Banteay Tuop
9. Koh Ker

10. Kampong Thom
11. Sambor Prei Kuk
12. Phnom Santuk
13. Santuk Silk Farm
14. Kampong Cham
15. Kratie
16. Stung Treng
17. Ban Lung
18. Yaek Lom Lake
19. Sen Monorom
20. Bonsraa Waterfall

① ✎ ⏚ 🖥

PRASAT PREAH VIHEAR

🅐D5 🅰162 miles (260 km) NW of Kampong Thom 🕗8am–4pm daily

Set high on a cliff in the Dangkrek Mountains, close to the Thai border, Prasat Preah Vihear, or Sacred Shrine, enjoys the most spectacular setting of any ancient Khmer temple. Offering some breathtaking views across the lush green plains below, this UNESCO World Heritage Site is believed to have been built on the site of a 9th-century sanctuary dedicated to Shiva, the Hindu God of Destruction.

The greater part of the sprawling complex was constructed during the reigns of King Surayavarman I (r. 1002–50) and Surayavarman II (r. 1113–50), the great builder of Angkor Wat. The earliest surviving parts of the temple, however, date from the 10th century. Following the decline of Hindu worship in the Khmer Empire, the temple was dedicated to Buddhism.

Built in golden sandstone, the temple has an unusual design. The four gopuras (enclosures) are laid out in a row on a north–south axis rather than being structured con-centrically with an eastern orientation (as is usually the case in Khmer temples).

→

Illustration of the third and fourth gopuras of Prasat Preah Vihear

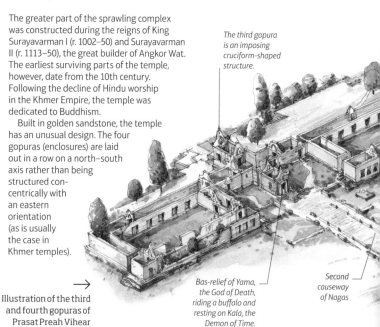

The third gopura is an imposing cruciform-shaped structure.

Bas-relief of Yama, the God of Death, riding a buffalo and resting on Kala, the Demon of Time.

Second causeway of Nagas

↑ View from the fourth gopura over the edge of the Pei Ta Da Cliff

A QUESTION OF OWNERSHIP

Due to its borderland location, Prasat Preah Vihear has long been fought over by Cambodia and Thailand. During Colonial-era border demarcations, the temple was given to Cambodia; however, the Thai authorities seized it in 1954. It was returned after the International Court of Justice confirmed its Cambodian status in 1962, but the dispute flared up again in 2008 and 2013. Since then, tensions have eased, with provisions made for better access to the UNESCO World Heritage Site across the Thai border.

↑ Prasat Preah Vihear
ruins at sunset

→
Bas-relief sculptures in the third
gopura depicting the Hindu
story of creation

Located at the
uppermost level of the
complex are the ruined
Central Shrine and
Prasat (religious hall).

The East Gallery
offers great views
over the Cambodian
countryside.

The West Gallery
is believed to have
functioned as a
scriptural library.

The precipitous Pei Ta Da
Cliff offers spectacular views
of the surrounding plains
1,500 ft (500 m) below.

↑ Apricot-colored Colonial-era buildings on Battambang's Street 1

2

BATTAMBANG

🅰C6 🏠180 miles (290 k) NW of Phnom Penh 🚌NH5, 2 miles (3 km) west of city center 🚉Street 156 ℹStreet 1; www.battambang.com

Battambang is Cambodia's second largest city, but it has the feel of a quiet country town, set along the banks of the Sangker River. The French legacy is plain to see here, with old villas and shophouses hidden down side streets or strung along the riverfront. There are also some impressive art galleries around town. The surrounding countryside is beautiful and verdant, with some fascinating outlying attractions.

1

Battambang Provincial Museum

🏠St 1, Kamkor Village, Svay Por Commune
📞(053)-730-007 🕐8-11am & 2-5pm Mon-Fri

The city's museum is set inside a pretty temple-style building with *so faa* finials on the roof. It houses an eclectic collection of Angkorian and pre-Angkorian statuary, taken from archaeological sites around the region, including some impressive seated Buddhas and many-headed *naga* serpents. There is also a remarkable array of pottery and traditional musical instruments. Information on exhibits is limited, and the displays are not especially well organized, but there are more than enough treasures here to make a visit worthwhile.

2

Psar Nat

🏠St 113

Located right in the center of the city, the striking Art Deco Psar Nat building is filled with a wide variety of stalls, from jewelry specialists to barber shops, and from beauty salons to fruit sellers. With its bold white clock towers (which never seem to be telling the right time), the market building was designed in 1936 by Jean Desbois, the architect behind Phnom Penh's Psar Thmei.

3

Romcheik 5 Artspace

🏠St 201, Romcheik 5
📞(092)-304-210
🕐2-6pm daily

Battambang has a lively gallery scene, with a number of excellent exhibition

↑ Monks on a boat in the Sangker River in Battambang

Wat Ek Phnom

⌂ 5 miles (8 km) N of Battambang ◷ Dawn-dusk daily

Built in the 11th century during the reign of King Suryavarman, this partially collapsed Angkorian temple comprises finely carved *prasats* (towers) mounted on a platform. Much of the statuary has been looted or taken to museums down the centuries, but the root-strangled ruins are atmospheric. Close to the temple is a small, peaceful pond covered with lily pads, a modern pagoda, and a large Buddha statue. The journey from Battambang takes visitors through dense forest, lush rice fields, and bucolic villages dotted with houses where rice paper is made.

EAT

Lonely Tree Café
Excellent pasta dishes are big draws at this stylish restaurant.

⌂ St 121, Battambang
ⓦ thelonely treecafe.com

$$$

Jaan Bai
Come here for tasty tapas-style dishes in support of a good cause.

⌂ St 2, Battambang
☎ (078)-263-144

$$$

Did You Know?

Battambang means "lost stick," after a lost magic stick that was used to usurp a prince.

spaces. One of the best is Romcheik 5 Artspace, set on a quiet street on the east bank of the river. Housed in a stylish modern building with cool, white-walled rooms on two levels, the gallery places emphasis on displaying contemporary art from the local community. There's a permanent exhibition on the upper levels, and regularly changing temporary shows on the ground floor. Expect inventive and arresting paintings, and a few stylish sculptures – all far removed from the classical styles of Cambodia's temples. Works in the temporary exhibition are often for sale, but there is absolutely no pressure to buy.

Phnom Sampeau

⌂ 7 miles (11 km) SW of Battambang ◷ Dawn-dusk daily

Phnom Sampeau, a craggy hill offering superb views over the surrounding countryside, is a beautiful place with a dark history. About halfway up a series of steep steps are the so-called Killing Caves, where shocking atrocities were perpetrated by the Khmer Rouge. In the largest cavern, a glass memorial displays the bones of their victims. Nearby is a statue of a golden Reclining Buddha, and a number of other temples and shrines, tended by a small community of monks, crown the hill. Don't stray from the paths here as there is unexploded ordnance in the area.

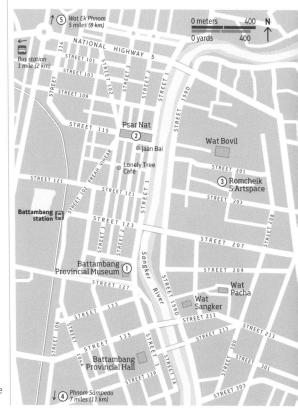

EXPERIENCE MORE

3

Wat Banan

🅰 C6 🚗 17 miles (27 km) S of Battambang 🕒 Dawn–dusk daily

Reminiscent of Angkor Wat in its layout, this mountaintop temple on Phnom Banan is reached by a flight of 358 steps. Flanked by *naga* balustrades, the stone steps lead to five 11th-century *prasats*, which, despite looting in the past, are mostly upright. The views from the top are some of the best in the province, and thirsty visitors can buy drinks from vendors at the summit.

From the temple, visitors can descend a long, narrow staircase to explore a group of three caves with the help of local guides. Flashlights are absolutely essential here as the caves are very dark. Be aware that one of the cave areas is still not fully de-mined and is not safe to enter. The caves can also be quite a tight squeeze, especially if you are visiting with larger tour groups.

4

Kamping Poy

🅰 C6 🚗 17 miles (27 km) W of Battambang 🕒 Dawn–dusk daily

Yet another poignant reminder of the brutal Khmer Rouge, Kamping Poy, also known as Killing Dam, stretches for some 5 miles (8 km) between two hills. More than 10,000 people enslaved under the regime either

Garuda carving flanking the steps to the Wat Banan temple

BAMBOO TRAIN

Battambang's famed bamboo trains were an ingenious local transport solution. Made of bamboo and old motorcycle engines, they ran on abandoned Colonial-era train tracks. The original trains no longer exist, though a short stretch of track has been laid for tourists to ride on near Wat Banan.

---

starved to death or were killed building the now largely worthless dam, which never fulfilled what is believed to have been its aim – to recreate the irrigation system of ancient Angkor. Today, there is nothing left of the site except for the sluice gates and resulting reservoir. The lake is now covered with lotus flowers and used by locals as a picturesque picnic spot. Hawkers on the banks sell lotus seeds, which make a tasty snack. You can also hire a boat, rowed by local boys, to the middle of the lake, but be wary of exorbitant prices.

Boat surrounded by vegetation on the lake below Kamping Poy dam

5 Choob

C6 55 miles (89 km) W of Siem Reap

Located toward the northwestern border with Thailand, the small village of Choob is worth a visit for its renowned sculptors, who sit by the roadside with their wares. Choob's sculptors are celebrated throughout the country for their artistry and are often commissioned by temples to make huge, elaborate sandstone statues that can take months to complete. The village is a great place in which to buy magnificent souvenirs such as miniatures of *apsaras* or statues of the Buddha.

6 Ang Trapeng Thmor Reserve

C5 62 miles (100 km) NW of Siem Reap Dawn-dusk daily

Based around a water storage reservoir – built in 1976 by people enslaved under the control of the Khmer Rouge – this wetland bird sanctuary spans 19 sq miles (49 sq km). A mixture of grassland, forests, and paddy fields, the area was officially declared a Sarus Crane Reserve by royal decree in 2000. The sarus crane is an extremely rare and elegant bird depicted on bas-reliefs at Bayon (p96). Some 300 feed here, along with more than 200 other species of birds, 18 classified as globally threat-ened. Visitors may also chance upon the large fruit bats that inhabit semi-submerged trees on the edge of the reservoir, while those among the very fortunate may see the rare Eld's deer.

It is possible to tour the reserve on a boat if you first register at the Wildlife Conservation Society Office in the adjacent village. While most people visit the reserve on a day trip from Siem Reap, overnight stays can also be organized through the Sam Veasna Center in Siem Reap.

7 Banteay Chhmer

C5 80 miles (130 km) N of Battambang Dawn-dusk daily

Across a causeway, through a tumbledown gate, lies one of the largest and most mysterious temple complexes of the Angkor period. Banteay Chhmer, along with its satellite shrines and vast *baray* (reservoir), was constructed in the late 12th century during the reign of Jayavarman VII. Like the Buddhist-influenced Bayon, it features the enigmatic faces of Avalokiteśvara and is well known for the intricacy of its carvings. However, unlike Bayon, Banteay Chhmer is rarely overrun with visitors, giving those who do come here a very different temple experience. Except for a few families who live and farm around these overgrown ruins, there is often no one else here.

The complex has ceremonial walkways, towers, and courtyards typical of other Angkorian structures, though its two moats have now been made into rice paddies. Vast bas-reliefs on the outer walls depict life 900 years ago – including processions of elephants and scenes of conflict with neighboring Champa. Arrange to stay nearby for a chance to admire the temple at sunrise and sunset.

8 Banteay Tuop

C5 74 miles (121 km) N of Battambang Dawn-dusk daily

Just north of Banteay Chhmer, Banteay Tuop (Army Fortress) is believed to have been built as a tribute to the army of King Jayavarman VII after it defeated the Chams in the 12th century. It originally had five *prasats*; only four towers survive, but they are in good condition, and some still have their original timbers.

There are no buses to Banteay Tuop; from Bantay Chhmer, hire a taxi or ask for a *moto* ride from the market. Visit at dusk if you can: the sunsets here are spectacular.

9

Koh Ker

D5 **81 miles (130 km) NE of Siem Reap** **Dawn–dusk daily**

Hidden in the forests of Preah Vihear province, enigmatic Koh Ker was built during the reign of King Jayavarman IV (r. 928–42), who had moved the capital of Angkor here for a brief period. Not long ago, it was one of the most inaccessible and heavily mined Angkorian temples. Today, however, visitors can safely reach and explore these ruins on a day trip or organized tour from Siem Reap.

The complex has more than 100 temples with 42 significant structures. The most impressive of these is Prasat Thom, a 131-ft- (40-m-) high, 180-ft- (55-m-) wide, seven-tiered sandstone pyramid. Complete with a steep central stairway, it offers dramatic views of the Kulen Mountain and the Dangkrek Mountains to the southwest and northwest, respectively. A giant Garuda (a mythical beast that is half-man, half-bird) statue sits atop the summit. To the southwest of Prasat Thom lies the huge Rahal Baray reservoir, into which the Stung Sen has been diverted to irrigate Koh Ker. Prasat Krahom, the second-largest temple in the complex, is notable for its graceful lintel carvings, and its *naga*-flanked causeway. Also of interest are

the temples Prasat Thneng and Prasat Leung, renowned for the largest Shiva *lingas* (phallic monuments) located in Cambodia.

10

Kampong Thom

D6 **93 miles (150 km) SE of Siem Reap** **Prachea Thepatay St**

Situated at the heart of Cambodia along the banks of the Stung Sen, this busy artery town enjoys trade from the traffic en route to Siem Reap or Phnom Penh. Its original name was Kampong Pos Thom, derived from *posthom*, meaning two snakes.

According to legend, the local population used to make offerings to two large snakes that lived in a cave here. The cave's location has since been forgotten; however, relics of the recent past, namely the pre-Angkorian temple monuments of Sambor Prei Kuk, are increasingly drawing more visitors to this town, as is the quirky mountain temple of Phnom Santuk.

The countryside surrounding Kampong Thom is picturesque, with buffalo lazing in roadside pools, and villagers riding livestock-drawn carts across their farmlands. Look out for homemade effigies outside houses, believed to ward off evil spirits.

THE CHAMS

Villages around Tonlé Sap and in Kampong Cham province are home to Cambodia's largest minority, the Muslim Chams. Numbering around 250,000, the Chams are descended from inhabitants of the former Champa kingdom. Though they suffered appalling persecution under the Khmer Rouge, relations with their Khmer neighbors are generally peaceful. Cham men traditionally wear tartan sarongs and skullcaps.

Koh Ker's Prasat Krahom, with its *(inset)* intricate lintel carvings ↓

Santuk Silk Farm

🅰D6 🚗Hwy 6, 11 miles (18 km) SE of Kampong Thom 📞(012)-906-604 🕐7–11am & 1–5pm Mon–Sat

Just outside the village of Kakaoh, opposite the start of the road to Phnom Santuk, is the Santuk Silk Farm, set up by US Vietnam War veteran Bud Gibbons and now run by his widow, Navin. Visitors can view the various life stages of the silkworm – from egg to caterpillar to cocoon. Cocoons provide the base for the thread, which is spun and woven into attractive *kramas* (scarves) by local girls; the scarves can be bought in the farm shop. Mulberry trees dot the farm, the leaves of which are fed to the silk-worms. An excellent lunch can be arranged if you call ahead.

↑ The temple at the summit of Phnom Santuk mountain

Sambor Prei Kuk

🅰D6 🚗19 miles (31 km) NE of Kampong Thom

Located east of Tonlé Sap Lake in Kampong Thom province, this 7th-century complex of temples was constructed during the reign of King Isanavarman I in the Chenla period *(p59)*. Spread over a large area of semi-cleared jungle, the ruins are all that remain of the ancient capital of Isanapura. There are three main complexes here – Preah Sambor (North Group), Preah Tor (Central Group), and Preah Yeay Poun (South Group). The sun-dappled, rectangular-shaped Lion Temple, guarded by a lion at its entrance, is one of the highlights of these ruins.

Unique to Sambor Prei Kuk are its many octagon-shaped *prasats* (towers). Despite being choked by the roots of strangler fig trees, some of these towers are in excellent condition, with lintels, columns, and pilasters displaying intricate carvings. Large bas-reliefs rendered in brick also represent some of the earliest attempts in this style – amazingly, Sambor Prei Kuk was pioneering new forms of artistry 150 years before the mighty Angkor. Visitors can hire trained guides, who can be found

near the café, to show them around the ruins for a fee. School children often try and tag along to practice their English. A stroll through the ruins will take about an hour. Given the low volume of foot traffic, and the welcome shade provided by the forest, these are rewarding and atmospheric ruins to visit, and can easily be covered in a day trip from Siem Reap.

Phnom Santuk

🅰D6 🚗11 miles (18 km) E of Kampong Thom 🕐Dawn–dusk daily

Rising to a height of 679 ft (207 m) above lush paddy fields, Phnom Santuk is the most sacred mountain in Kampong Thom province. It is approached via a stone pathway of 809 steps, flanked by brightly colored statues. It's quite a taxing climb; you can, alternatively, drive up a steep road that snakes through thick jungle and past a resident colony of macaques. The complex at the summit has a gilded, white-walled central temple. Statues have been carved into the rock face, including Reclining Buddhas measuring up to 33 ft (10 m) in length. Interconnecting bridges between shrines, numerous little caves, statues, and a sculpture workshop add to the appeal. There is also an active monastery here whose friendly monks like to chat with visitors.

STAY

Sambor Village Hotel
With a charming riverside setting and verdant grounds, the airy bungalows here offer a dash of boutique sophistication in Kampong Thom.

🅰D6 🚗Kampong Thom 📞(855)-17-924-612

$⑤$⑤$⑤

Nature Lodge
Rustic cabins, hammocks, and treehouses are just some of the attractions at this fantastic budget resort in peaceful, rural surroundings.

🅰E6 🚗Sen Monorom 🌐naturelodge cambodia.com

$⑤$⑤$⑤

HIDDEN GEM
Preah Rumkel

Close to the Lao border, the serene village of Preah Rumkel hosts an impressive homestay program run by a local NGO (mlup-baitong.org). Guests lodge with local families, and activities include hiking, waterfall swimming, and dolphin-spotting at nearby Anlong Cheuteal.

 14

Kampong Cham

D6 **75 miles (120 km) NE of Phnom Penh** **From Phnom Penh**

Sitting on the west bank of the Mekong River, the city of Kampong Cham takes its name from the exiled Cham people who, pursued by the Vietnamese, settled here in the 17th century. Although it is Cambodia's third-largest city, and the capital of its most populous province, Kampong Cham retains a small-town appeal. The city has a number of run-down French Colonial-era buildings, and the design of the city's grid system has a Gallic feel, with wide boulevards, statue-dotted squares, and a riverside promenade. By night, the city's streets glow with ornate lampposts and illuminated fountains.

 15

Kratie

E6 **43 miles (70 km) NE of Kampong Cham**

Once an isolated backwater and only navigable by boat, this Mekong-bordered town is still a quiet place with a thriving local *psar* (market), dilapidated Indochinese villas, and an easy riverside atmosphere. It's renowned for its beautiful sunsets and sightings of the endangered Irrawaddy dolphin some 9 miles (15 km) north, near the village of Kampie, which can be reached by tuk-tuk or *moto*. The route follows a beautiful riverside stretch, past houses on stilts inhabited by rural families. From Kampie, it is possible to hire a boat or kayak to go out on to the river. Dolphin sightings are more than likely.

Just across the water from Kratie is Koh Trong, a sandbar island in the middle of the Mekong. Here, sights include a floating village, an old stupa, and, perhaps, the rare Mekong mud turtle.

 16

Stung Treng

D6 **87 miles (140 km) N of Kratie**

Originally a Lao-French administered outpost, the town of Stung Treng is now on the tourist map thanks to a new bridge and a cross-country road. Much of Stung Treng province's traffic still moves by water; the province is crisscrossed by several rivers including Tonlé Kong, Tonlé Sepok, Tonlé San, and the mighty Mekong. The town and surrounding countryside have much to offer, with riverine sunset trips operating at inflated prices, and the Chenla period ruins of Prasat Preah Ko a short distance away. Homestay and trekking options are also developing.

 17

Ban Lung

E5 **93 miles (150 km) NE of Stung Treng** **Highland Tour; (088)-988-8098** **tourismcambodia.com**

The country's northernmost region, Ratanakiri province is often referred to as the Wild East, of which Ban Lung is the provincial capital. The town's nickname, *dey krakhorm* – meaning red earth – derives from the red dust here that settles on everything from people's faces to the leaves of trees, giving the place a surreal autumnal feel. Ban Lung is best visited between November and February when the rains have stopped and the dust has not yet become a nuisance. In the wet season, its roads become quite impassable.

Ban Lung is little more than a transportation and accommodations hub for the many riches that lie on its fringes: waterfalls, bottle-green crater lakes, villages, and animist cemeteries. Most guesthouses are willing to organize treks to the waterfalls, of which Ka Tieng

Dolphin-watching boat tour on the Mekong at sunset

is the most impressive. Two-day treks in the Virachey National Park, 30 miles (50 km) to the north of Ban Lung, are also recommended.

18 Yaek Lom Lake

△E5 ◐3 miles (5 km) E of Ban Lung

Believed to have been formed some 700,000 years ago, this volcanic, bottle-green crater lake is the main attraction around Ban Lung. The lake is ringed by thick green jungle and when viewed aerially, it forms a near perfect circle. The area is peaceful and a visit here makes for a memorable day with morning swims and wooden jetties to sunbathe on. Many of the local tribes believe the lake to be an especially sacred place and, according to their legends, monsters inhabit its clear waters. An easily navigable path around the lake can be walked in an hour. Admission to the lake is administered by the local Tompuon tribe, with the money being used toward improving the condition of their villages.

19 Sen Monorom

△E6 ◐230 miles (370 km) NE of Phnom Penh ⊞From Phnom Penh

Capital of Mondulkiri province, Sen Monorom is a picturesque place often referred to as the "

Switzerland of Cambodia" due to its grassy landscape, rolling hills, and two large lakes. The town has a marketplace and a few guesthouses. The area is rich in river valleys, waterfalls, and teal-green deciduous forests, and is also home to tigers, bears, and a number of smaller endangered animals. However, illegal logging and an increase in plantations are driving these animals farther inland, much to the dismay of wildlife conservationists.

Among other attractions around Sen Monorom are one- and two-day treks in and around the Phnong villages, famous for their elephants. Visitors can learn all about these animals in a range of experiences organized by the **Elephant Valley Project,** an excellent ethical sanctuary where former working elephants are free to roam.

↑ Picturesque Bonsraa Waterfall, cascading over basalt lava

Elephant Valley Project
🌐 elephantvalleyproject.org

20 Bonsraa Waterfall

△E6 ◐22 miles (35 km) E of Sen Monorom ◐Dawn–dusk daily

Lying 22 miles (35 km) west of the Vietnamese border and accessed via a toll road from Sen Monorom, Bonsraa Waterfall is now easy to reach. This double-tiered waterfall, plunging some 115 ft (35 m) into dense jungle, is the country's most famous and dramatic cascade. The upper tier is 33 ft (10 m) in width, and although the thundering water is very powerful, the lower, narrower tier, with an 82-ft (25-m) drop, is much more spectacular. To see it from the bottom, cross the river and follow the crooked path weaving down a precipitous stairway. *Motos* can be hired from Sen Monorom to travel to the falls and back.

THE MEKONG DISCOVERY TRAIL

The countryside around the Mekong between Stung Treng and Kratie is crisscrossed by a network of hiking and biking routes known collectively as the Mekong Discovery Trail. Originally a government initiative to introduce the benefits of tourism to rural communities, the trail is now self-sustaining, with homestays in villages, and local operators in Kratie and Stung Treng offering mountain bike hire and organized tours.

SOUTHERN CAMBODIA

The most relaxed, lush part of the country, Southern Cambodia is blessed with dazzling white-sand beaches and richly forested national parks. Stretching from the Thai border in the southwest to Vietnam's Mekong Delta frontier in the southeast, this is a region of myriad attractions. In the north are the relatively inaccessible Cardamom Mountains, a supremely biologically diverse range. Until the late 1980s, these mountains were one of the last strongholds of the Khmer Rouge, whose presence, coupled with the difficult terrain, deterred loggers.

Today, the biggest draws of the area are its pristine beaches and virgin islands. Sihanoukville, with its mix of ramshackle buildings and fancy hotels, continues to draw visitors. The town's fine-sand beaches and turquoise waters are a haven for watersports enthusiasts. Several uninhabited and sparsely populated islands lie just off the coast of Sihanoukville and make for excellent day-trip options.

The region is also home to several wildlife preserves. Peam Krasaop envelops a vast swathe of coastland, with remote waterfalls and mangrove forests, in contrast to the expansive pine forests of Kirirom National Park. The rainforest preserve of Botum Sakor National Park is home to elephants and hornbills, while Bokor National Park's old French hill station has been renovated with a hotel complex. Other attractions include the tiny town of Kep, with its crumbling Modernist buildings, and the captivating temple ruins of Phnom Da in Takeo province.

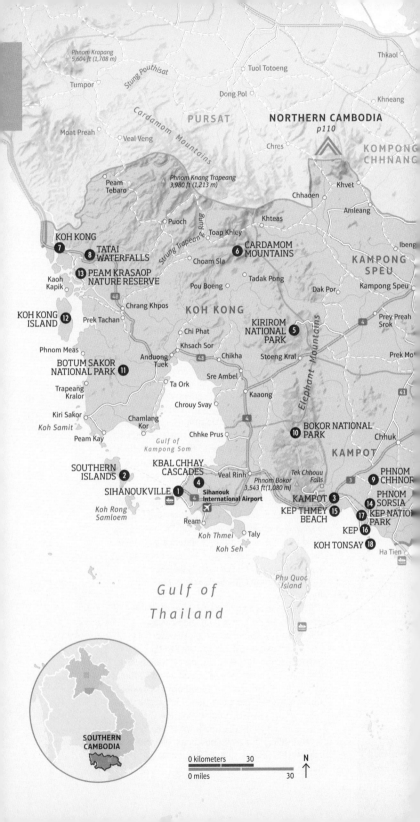

Phnom Krapang
5,604 ft (1,708 m)

Tumpor

Stung Pouthisat

Tuol Totoeng

Thkaol

Dong Pol

Khneang

Moat Preah

Veal Veng

Cardamom Mountains

PURSAT

Chres

NORTHERN CAMBODIA
p110

KOMPONG CHHNANG

Peam Tebaro

Phnom Knang Trapeang
3,980 ft (1,213 m)

Khvet

Chhaoen

Amleang

Puoch

Khteas

Toap Khley

Ibeng

KOH KONG

7

8 **TATAI WATERFALLS**

Choam Sla

6 **CARDAMOM MOUNTAINS**

Tadak Pong

Dak Por

KAMPONG SPEU

Kampong Speu

13 **PEAM KRASAOP NATURE RESERVE**

Kaoh Kapik

Pou Boeng

Prey Preah Srok

Chrang Khpos

KOH KONG

5 **KIRIROM NATIONAL PARK**

Prek Mo

12 **KOH KONG ISLAND**

Prek Tachan

Chi Phat

Khsach Sor

Stoeng Kral

41

Phnom Meas

Anduong Tuek

Chikha

Sre Ambel

Elephant Mountains

BOTUM SAKOR NATIONAL PARK

11

Ta Ork

Kaaong

4

Trapeang Kralor

Chrouy Svay

Kiri Sakor

Koh Samit

Chamlang Kor

Chhke Prus

4

10 **BOKOR NATIONAL PARK**

Chhuk

Peam Kay

Gulf of Kampong Som

KAMPOT

SOUTHERN ISLANDS 2

KBAL CHHAY CASCADES

Veal Rinh

Tek Chhouu Falls

9 **PHNOM CHHNOR**

SIHANOUKVILLE 1

4

Sihanouk International Airport

*Phnom Bokor
3,543 ft (1,080 m)*

3

KAMPOT 3

14 **PHNOM SORSIA**

Koh Rong Samloem

Ream

KEP THMEY BEACH 15

17 **KEP NATIONAL PARK**

Koh Thmei

Taly

KEP 16

Koh Seh

KOH TONSAY 18

Ha Tien

Phu Quoc Island

Gulf of

Thailand

SOUTHERN CAMBODIA

0 kilometers   30

0 miles   30

N

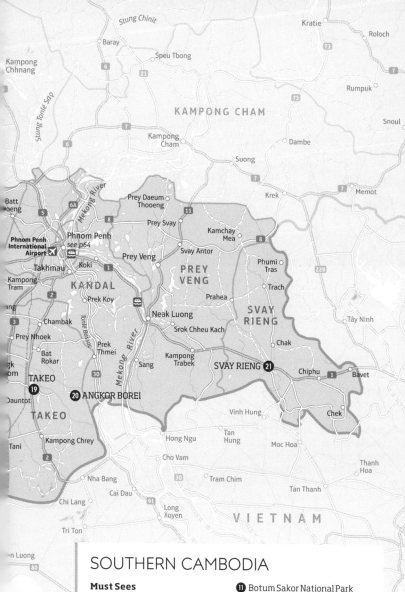

SOUTHERN CAMBODIA

Must Sees

1. Sihanoukville
2. Southern Islands
3. Kampot

Experience More

4. Kbal Chhay Cascades
5. Kirirom National Park
6. Cardamom Mountains
7. Koh Kong
8. Tatai Waterfalls
9. Phnom Chhnork
10. Bokor National Park
11. Botum Sakor National Park
12. Koh Kong Island
13. Peam Krasaop Nature Reserve
14. Phnom Sorsia
15. Kep Thmey Beach
16. Kep
17. Kep National Park
18. Koh Tonsay
19. Takeo
20. Angkor Borei
21. Svay Rieng

↑ Locals paddling in the sea at sunset on Independence Beach

❶

SIHANOUKVILLE

🅰 C7 ✈ 🚌 🏠 112 miles (180 km) SW of Phnom Penh
ℹ Corner of Sopheakmongkol 109 St; (034)-933-894

With its stunning white-sand beaches and azure waters, Sihanoukville is Cambodia's main beach resort. Spread across three districts, the town encompasses a large port and was named after the former king, Sihanouk. Locals, however, refer to it by its old name, Kampong Som. Although the town is of no real architectural interest, it is now the focus of large-scale international investment, and visitors will find excellent facilities including banks, restaurants, bars, and upscale hotels.

①
Victory Beach

🏠 2 miles (3 km) NW of town center

The pretty, white-sand bay of Victory Beach is located directly below Victory Hill. Its southern end is also known as Lamherkay Beach. Victory Beach is about 1000 ft (300 m) long, and its western orientation means that it is perfectly aligned to view sunsets. Late-night venues in the area include a number of casinos, most of which can be found around Victory Hill and the Golden Lion area.

②
Independence Beach

🏠 2 miles (3 km) SW of town center

Another lovely tropical bay, Independence Beach gets its name from the 1960s-era Independence Hotel on the hilltop directly north of this stretch of coastline. It is a mostly privately owned beach, with fine, pale sand and clear water. Visitors can either buy drinks from the hotel's beach café to avoid paying an entrance fee, or head to the small southern section of the bay that is open to all.

###
Sokha Beach

🏠 1 mile (2 km) SW of town center

With its shimmering white sand and the sea a surreal shade of turquoise, Sokha Beach is certainly worth a visit. This crescent-shaped stretch of sand runs for about 1 mile (2 km) between two small wooded bluffs. Directly behind the beach is the sprawling Sokha Beach Resort, which officially owns this stretch of coast. Visitors who want to linger have to pay an entrance fee, which includes use of the resort's pool. The beach has deck chairs and snack stalls operated by the resort.

↑ Water buffalo enjoying the cool sea water on Victory Beach

④
Occheuteal Beach

 1 mile (2 km) S of town center

This beach is the main tourist hot spot in Sihanoukville, and is the closest to the hotel strip. The beach's northern end is heavily built up, with a strip of shack-like bar-restaurants and watersports companies lining the beach. The small rocky cove here, known as Serendipity Beach, is the most pleasant part of Occheuteal Beach, despite there being no sand.

⑤
Prek Treng Beach

 6 miles (9.5 km) NW of town center

Located north of the port, Prek Treng Beach is a fairly deserted, long, thin crescent of sand with shallow blue water. Visitors are advised to bring their own drinks and snacks since there are no facilities available. At high tide, this beach is quite narrow and the shoreline is rocky in places.

⑥
Otres Beach

 3.5 miles (5.5 km) SE of town center

Immediately south of Occheuteal, behind a small headland, Otres Beach is a wonderful golden stretch of sand, lined with graceful casuarina trees. The beach itself is narrow, but it is about 2 miles (3 km) long and dotted with sun loungers, which visitors can use in exchange for a drink or a snack.

Although much of the land here has been bought by developers, for now the place is still pristine. There

STAY

Sahaa Beach Resort
This upscale resort close to the beach has a great restaurant and trendy minimalist bungalows arranged around a handsome outdoor pool.

Otres Beach 1, Sihanoukville
sahaabeach.com

⑤⑤⑤

are a number of small resorts, which offer reasonably priced lodgings close to the beach. The beach is not served by public transport but can be reached by tuk-tuks from the town center, or on foot from Occheuteal Beach.

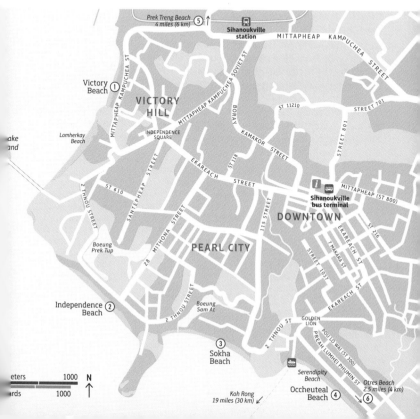

↑ Colorful huts lining a pristine beach on Koh Rong

SOUTHERN ISLANDS

AC7 **⛴**from Serendipity Pier, Sihanoukville; www.speedferrycambodia.com

Fringed with palms and lapped by the warm waters of the Gulf of Thailand, a string of around 20 offshore islands dot the horizon south of Sihanoukville. The larger islands have long attracted paradise-seeking backpackers, and major developers have begun to move in here and there in recent years too. But further afield there are still plenty of pristine pinpricks of land, perfect for living out castaway fantasies.

① Koh Rong

A19 miles (30 km) from Sihanoukville **W**visit kohrong.com

The largest island in the group, Koh Rong has been attracting young backpackers for decades, and the main village, Koh Tuch, has a beach party scene fit to rival those of neighboring Thailand. Nevertheless, there's plenty of space on Koh Rong to escape the crowds, and most of its coast is lined with unspoiled and largely empty beaches. On the western coast, the expansive Long Beach has sugary white sand and great snorkeling just offshore. The forested interior of the island, meanwhile, teems with birdlife.

② Koh Rong Samloem

A15 miles (25 km) from Sihanoukville

With its white-sand beaches, clear turquoise waters, and excellent snorkeling, Koh Rong

Samloem is a vision of tropical paradise. The overall scene is much more sedate than that further north on Koh Rong, making this the perfect destination for those looking to relax, rather than party. The main point of entry – and main accommodation center – is at Saracen Bay on the east coast, a sheltered crescent of sand. Jungle trails crisscross the interior, leading to the pristine Sunset Beach and Lazy Beach on the western coast.

THE KOH S'DACH ARCHIPELAGO

Set in blue seas just off the coast of Botum Sakor National Park, this archipelago draws those looking for a serious island experience. There are 12 islands in total, some little more than a dab of sand and a few palm trees. The main island, Koh S'dach, is home to a fishing community and a small resort. The tiny Koh Totang nearby is popular with those looking to go snorkeling, with day trips on converted fishing boats easily arranged.

③

Koh Russey

 10 miles (16 km) from Sihanoukville

Tiny Koh Russey – also known as Bamboo Island – is just a short speedboat hop from Sihanoukville, and an excellent destination for a day trip, with pristine white beaches and good offshore snorkeling. The island was long occupied by the Cambodian military, before a few low-key guesthouse operators moved in. More recently, it has been handed over to resort developers, but the projects aim to retain the island's paradise atmosphere.

④

Koh Ta Kiev

 12 miles (20 km) from Sihanoukville

Long flying under the radar, Koh Ta Kiev has been attracting far fewer visitors than the bigger islands further from the mainland. Resort development is underway, but for now it's still a fine place to escape the crowds, to lounge on the clean beaches, and to go paddling and kayaking around the rugged coastline. There is also a network of hiking trails through the forest inland.

⑤

Koh Thmei

 19 miles (30 km) from Sihanoukville

Lying within the Ream National Park and separated from the mainland by only a narrow strait, Koh Thmei is a low-lying, thickly forested blot of land. There are no villages, and for many years it was a virtual wilderness, inhabited mainly by birds. Like many other places along the coast here, it is slated for development, but for now it's still an off-the-beaten-track place with some basic accommodations.

Must See

STAY

Song Saa
This superb family-owned resort occupies twin private islands. Its profits are funneled back into the local staff and environment.

Song Saa ⓦsongsaa-private island.com

$$$

Lazy Beach
The bungalows here stand in isolation on one of the prettiest beaches on the island. It's a place designed to fuel castaway fantasies.

Lazy Beach, Koh Rong Samloen ⓦlazybeach cambodia.com

$$$

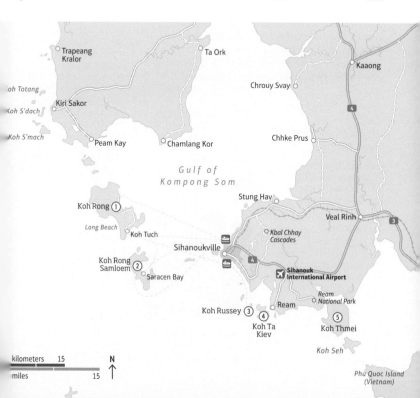

KAMPOT

D7 66 miles (106 km) E of Sihanoukville Off NH33
Off NR3 2 miles (3 km) north of town center; from Phnom
Penh and Sihanoukville River Rd; (033)-6555-541

With a sultry, unhurried air and some fine cafés,
Kampot is one of the most atmospheric towns in
Cambodia. The town's riverside promenade is a
delight at sunset, as fishers cast their lines and
locals enjoy a drink against a backdrop of Bokor
Mountain. Although in a state of decay, the many old
French buildings remain impressive – with louvered
windows, terracotta tiles, and fine balconies.

Kampot Traditional Music School

Plauv Ekareach, 1
Ousaphear Khum 2–5pm
& 5–6:30pm Thu & Fri
kcdi-cambodia.org

South of the town center, this
admirable NGO is dedicated
to caring for disabled and
orphaned children, and pre-
serving traditional Cambodian
arts. Under the Khmer Rouge,
traditional music and art were
nearly annihilated. Many
musicians and artisans were
murdered, while those who
managed to survive fled the
country. Today, however, the
Kampot Traditional Music

School and other NGOs are
using the revival of these forms
of art as a means of rehabilitation for disadvantaged
Cambodians. The school's
opening hours are limited,
and photography is forbidden

↑ Student learning to play
the *roneat ek* at Kampot
Traditional Music School

inside. There is no admission
charge to visit, but donations
are very welcome.

The Riverfront

Kampot is set on the north
bank of the Teuk Chhou River,
and the riverfront promenade
is a great place to stroll and
enjoy some food and drink.
Several large restaurants and
bars line the section just south
of the Old Bridge, while the
stretch farther south provides
ample views of fishers in their
brightly colored boats. Don't
miss the large lotus pond just
behind the museum. There are
several companies offering
sunset boat tours. Set just a
few streets back from the riverfront, Colonial-era shophouses
line the streets just southwest
of the Durian roundabout.

Climbodia

3 miles (5 km) from
Kampot, on the road to
Kep (15 mins by *moto* or
bus from Kampot city
center) 8am–6pm daily
climbodia.com

While climbing isn't the
biggest sport in Cambodia,
there is a small but passionate

Fishing boat on the
Teuk Chhou River
in Kampot

visited after the rainy season,
when the cascades are at
their most impressive. This
is a popular spot for local
picnickers at weekends,
when it can get very crowded.
Families from Kampot come
here to sit on a series of little
bamboo platforms beside
the rapids and take in the
view of the Kampot River.
On weekdays, however, it is
a much more tranquil place.
There are natural pools,
good for swimming in, and
rocky shelves that are ideal
for sunbathing. There are
also plenty of simple open-air
cafés serving tasty local
food. Keen hikers can head
up a steep, rocky path to
Wat Ey Sey, a pretty pagoda
located nearby.

Did You Know?

The Kampot region is
famous for its durian.
A large statue of the
fruit sits on the town's
main roundabout.

group of climbers who have
created their own scene.
However, you don't need to
know the difference between
a bowline knot and zeppelin
bend to get up on the crags of
Cambodia thanks to the folks
at Climbodia. For over a decade,
they've been leading novices
on tours of the caves and
mountains outside Kampot. For
the complete experience, sign
up for the half-day Discovery
Tour ($40), which combines tra-
versing, abseiling, and caving,
finishing off with a series of
rock climbing challenges. All
required gear is provided, and
you will be in the safe hands of
experienced local guides.

④

Tek Chhouu Falls

🏠 5 miles (8 km) NE of Kampot

A popular picnic spot north of
Kampot, the Tek Chhou Falls
are a series of rapids best

EAT

Epic Arts Café
This small café has a
great ethos, with profits
aiding good causes.
It also offers excellent
bagels and meze, plus
moreish cakes.

🏠 Street 730
🌐 epicarts/org.uk

$$$

Twenty Three
Remarkable backstreet
bistro that serves
affordable gourmet
cuisine - great local
craft beer too.

🏠 South of Old Market
📞 (088)-607-9731

$$$

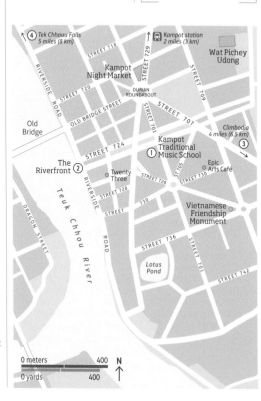

EXPERIENCE MORE

4

Kbal Chhay Cascades

C7 **11 miles (18 km)**
N of Sihanoukville
Sihanoukville; (034)-933-894

The Kbal Chhay Cascades are popular among domestic tourists who come here to see the famous falls; Kbal Chhay featured in the Cambodian movie *Chao Pos Keng Kong* (The Giant Snake).

The falls offer the chance for a refreshing dip – head upstream for rocky ledges and sandy coves perfect for a spot of sunbathing. Note that the water flow reduces toward the end of the rainy season, so there's less chance of a decent swim, and avoid the falls on Sundays, when crowds pick up and litter becomes a problem.

Facilities include snack and souvenir stalls, picnic platforms, and changing booths. Visitors can reach the falls by *motos* and motorcycles.

THE RETURN OF THE TIGER?

The forests of Cambodia were once full of Indochinese tigers, but sadly the 20th century did not treat this iconic species kindly, and decades of war, poaching, and deforestation have taken their toll. The last confirmed sighting of a wild tiger was in Mondulkiri in 2007. Reintroduction efforts are, however, underway, supported by the WWF, and focusing on the extensive wilderness areas in the northeast of the country.

Breathtaking natural scenery at Kiroram National Park ↑

5

Kirirom National Park

C7 **68 miles (110 km)**
NE of Sihanoukville
7am–5pm daily

This intriguing national park occupies a remote plateau about a two-hour drive inland from Sihanoukville. It lies at an elevation of about 2,300 ft (700 m), making the climate here far less oppressive than on the coast, and Kirirom's extensive pine forests reflect this temperate altitude.

Visitors can take advantage of ranger-guided walks to Phnom Dat Chivit, or End of the World Mountain, from which the view of the Elephant and Cardamom mountain ranges to the west is spellbinding. Ox-cart rides and gentle hikes to pretty waterfalls are also popular, and there is a great web of forest trails. Wildlife here includes elephant, tiger, pileated gibbon, banteng, gaur, and sun bear, although sightings are rare.

The park has a basic guesthouse with a restaurant, offering fine views over the forest, particularly at sunset. There is also an upscale resort with manicured lawns that is popular with weekenders from Phnom Penh.

6

Cardamom Mountains

C7 **73 miles (119 km)**
SE of Koh Kong **From Koh Kong** **Wildlife Alliance, Chi Pat; www.chi-phat.org**

The largest wilderness in mainland Southeast Asia, the Cardamom Mountains cover an area of 3,900 sq miles (10,100 sq km). Two regions in these mountains have been officially protected: the Central Cardamom Reserve, which extends across an area of 1,549 sq miles (4,013 sq km), up to Pursat province; and the Southern Cardamom Reserve, covering 557 sq miles (1,443 sq km) east of Koh Kong.

These mountains sustain several distinct forest environments and a wide variety of wildlife. Lower elevations, which are dominated by dry forests and deciduous trees, support large numbers of mammals, including the elephant, tiger, and sambhar deer. This region is also one of the last remaining homes of the Siamese crocodile.

Rainforests at higher altitudes are prime territory for endemic species such as the Cardamom banded gecko. Around 1,400 bird species have also been recorded here. However, the rise of activities such as hunting, illegal logging, and land clearance are putting tremendous pressure on these habitats. Renowned environmental activist Chut Wutty was shot and killed in 2012 while guiding journalists reporting on deforestation here.

Koh Kong tour operators can help visitors to plan trips to the foothills of the Southern Cardamoms. An ecotourism program has been established at Chi Phat village, 13 miles (21 km) upriver from the riverside port of Anduong Tuek and 61 miles (98 km) south of Koh Kong. It offers mountain biking, hiking, and birdwatching. Wildlife Alliance, an NGO working for environmental conservation, organizes boat trips to the Chhay Tameas rapids, 4 miles (6 km) from Chi Phat. The remote park station at Thma Bang, a two-hour drive west of the Tatai River, offers basic accommodations.

7
Koh Kong

🅐C7 🅐137 miles (220 km) NW of Sihanoukville 🚌🚤

The dangers posed by the Khmer Rouge, coupled with the difficult journey through the Cardamom Mountains, led to Koh Kong being neglected for years. Its fortunes are now changing thanks to a road that links the town to the NH4 and to the rest of the country. The town has grown to cater for the increased influx of tourists crossing from Thailand – the border is just 6 miles (10 km) away. Koh Kong is a good base for ecotourism – trips up jungle-fringed rivers and through mangrove forests can be organized from here.

About an hour upriver from Koh Kong, Koh Por Waterfall has a gorgeous rainforest setting. There is safe swimming below the falls, but care should be taken above the main drop because currents can be strong after heavy rain.

Between December and June, hiking is possible on trails along the riverbank.

8
Tatai Waterfalls

🅐C7 🅐12 miles (19 km) E of Koh Kong 🚤From Koh Kong

Set amid lush green jungle, the Tatai Waterfalls lie upstream from the bridge spanning the Tatai River. During the rainy season, the falls have powerful rapids, while the dry season presents opportunities for dips in rocky pools. Visitors can reach the falls by kayak, hiking trails, or boat, as well as by *motos* hired in Koh Kong. Nearby, along the Tatai River, are two excellent ecolodges.

↑ Serene river views in the foothills of the Cardamom Mountains

9

Phnom Chhnork

📍D7 🚗5 miles (8 km) NE of Kampot 🕐8am–5pm daily

Situated on a small hill that rises from the pancake-flat plain east of Kampot, Phnom Chhnork is a renowned Hindu cave-temple. It is approached by a walk through muddy rice paddies and the temple is reached by a flight of stone steps. The atmospheric cave contains a 7th-century Funan brick temple dedi cated to Shiva, the God of Destruction. The temple was built as a sanctuary amid the stalagmites and stalactites that are formed within the cave. This temple is accessible by a hired *moto* or tuk-tuk from Kampot.

10

Bokor National Park

📍C7 🚗26 miles (42 km) N of Kampot

One of Kampot province's main tourist attractions, Bokor National Park covers 610 sq miles (1,581 sq km) of rainforest, grasslands, and deciduous forest. Although illegal logging has decimated large tracts of the park's southern section, Bokor remains home to the Indian elephant, tiger, leopard, pangolin, Asiatic black bear, Malayan sun bear, pileated gibbon, slow loris, and pig-tailed macaque. Some 300 bird species also inhabit the park, including the gray-headed fish eagle and the spot-bellied eagle owl.

Bokor's attractions also include the atmospheric Bokor Hill Station, which featured in the 2002 Matt Dillon movie *City of Ghosts*. Set atop the 3,543-ft- (1,080-m-) high Phnom Bokor, the station was for many years an abandoned Colonial-era resort, and included the remains of a once-magnificent 1920s four-story hotel and casino. Renovated and reopened in 2018, it makes a welcome stop for lunch or coffee after a long drive around the often foggy mountain On clear days, there are stunning views

↑ Ruins of a church in the middle of Bokor National Park

over Kampot to the Gulf of Thailand, although this is a rarity as the summit is usually blanketed in mist. Close by lie the ruins of an old Catholic church, which has withstood years of warfare and occupation by the Khmer Rouge. Although the church's interior is now gutted and the stonework is encrusted with orange lichen, the altar is still intact.

Bokor Palace, also known as the Black Palace, lies 6 miles (10 km) east of the Bokor Hill Station. Once the residence of King Sihanouk, it's now a ruin, though the marble floors, tiled bathrooms, and fireplaces are still intact.

Most organized tours to the park include a visit to the pretty Popokvil Waterfall,

---

💬 **INSIDER TIP**
Rent a Scooter

Various companies offer guided tours to the Bokor National Park, but the best way to see the park is to rent a scooter in Kampot and go it alone. Take care on the windy roads, and pack a sweater as it can be cold on the mountain.

STAY

Asian Hotel

A long-running Koh Kong favorite, the best rooms at this simple, well-maintained budget hotel have views across the river.

📍C7 🏠Street 1, Koh Kong 🌐asian kohkong.com

⑤⑤⑤

Cardamom Tented Camp

This glamping resort combines wilderness experiences, such as kayaking and trekking, with comfortable surroundings. Multi-night packages only.

📍C7 🏠Trapeang Rung 🌐cardamomtented camp.com

⑤⑤⑤

> **Beach Three is a blissful and idyllic virgin beach where only the wind, the waves, and birdsong interrupt the silence.**

3 miles (5 km) northeast of the hill station. Its two tiers are separated by a shallow pool that can be paddled through. It's usually not deep enough to swim in; however, the swirling mist and cool air make this a pleasant spot.

---

 ⑪

Botum Sakor National Park

🅰C7 🏠63 miles (102 km) S of Koh Kong 🚊🚻 ℹ(034)-933-894

Occupying the bulbous peninsula between Koh Kong and Sihanoukville, the Botum Sakor National Park encompasses a large area of coastal land and low-lying rainforests, grasslands, and mangroves.

There is a park is home to a huge range of wildlife, including elephants, fishing cats, sun bears, leopards, and pileated gibbons. Although leopards and elephants are rarely spotted, you are almost guaranteed a sighting of amphibians such as tree frogs, and birds like the white-bellied sea eagle. The park has been a bone of contention between developers and environmentalists. The latter argue that development plans are contrary to Botum's status as a national park, and hence disastrous for its wildlife.

Despite this, large areas of mangroves have been logged and the park has been reduced in size by 139 sq miles (360 sq km), around half of its original area.

There is limited road access to the park, but hikes and boat trips can be organized from the park headquarters, located 2 miles (3 km) west of Anduong Tuek. These boat trips pass through mangrove forests teeming with mud crabs and kingfishers.

---

⑫

Koh Kong Island

🅰C7 🏠16 miles (26 km) S of Koh Kong 🚌From Koh Kong

A tropical paradise being eyed for development, Koh Kong Island features beaches lined with coconut palms and other vegetation. Its transparent waters and pale,

powdery sands form seven perfect beaches, although Beach Three, backed by a lovely lagoon, is the one to head for. This is a blissful and idyllic virgin beach where only the wind, the waves, and bird-song interrupt the silence. Several species of sea turtle nest here, but visitors are unlikely to encounter them as they usually arrive at night. Snorkeling is good, with excellent visibility and clear views of schools of mirror fish.

There is no regular transport to Koh Kong Island. Visitors will need to organize a boat trip from Koh Kong, and register at the island's police checkpoint before heading to the beaches. The traveling time to Beach Three by speed-boat is 75 minutes. Long-tail boats, on the other hand, take around 2 hours and 45 minutes. It's advisable to carry insect repellant because sandflies can be a nuisance here.

↑ Clear waters and white sand at a pristine beach on Koh Kong Island

Aerial view of one of Koh Kong Island's beaches

13

Peam Krasaop Nature Reserve

🅰C7 🚗4 miles (6 km) S of Koh Kong

Covering an area of over 93 sq miles (240 sq km), Peam Krasaop Nature Reserve is one of the most important and internationally recognized mangrove environments in Southeast Asia. The mangroves not only protect the coastline from erosion but also support a wealth of flora and fauna. The extensive mud flats here provide a crucial habitat for invertebrates, and a rich feeding ground for waders such as the spotted greenshank and Asian dowitcher.

Concrete walkways have been constructed through

↑ Exploring the mangrove forests in Peam Krasaop Nature Reserve

the forest, allowing visitors a closer look at the wildlife, which includes mud crabs, storks, and cranes. The preserve is also home to pangolins, monkeys, bats, and deer. Fishers have also reported occasional sightings of saltwater crocodiles.

The main walkway leads to a 49-ft- (15-m-) high lookout tower in the settlement of Boeng Kayak, at the main gateway to the preserve, offering excellent views of the estuary and mud flats. Boats can be hired for trips into Koh Kong Bay at the entrance gate, and early-morning trips might

provide the best chance to spot the endangered Irrawaddy dolphin.

14

Phnom Sorsia

🅰D7 🚗11 miles (18 km) E of Kampot ⏰7:30am–5pm daily

A religious hill complex, Phnom Sorsia consists of a vividly painted Buddhist temple, and a karst outcrop riddled with caves. A staircase leads up to the temple, to the left of which is the first cave, with a stalagmite resembling an elephant's head, giving the cave its name – Rung Damrey Sor, or White Elephant Cave. To the east lies Bat Cave, filled with thousands of bats. The walk up to the summit leads to a stupa and scenic views.

15

Kep Thmey Beach

🅐D7 🅰Near the tip of the Kep Peninsula 🚌

Located about a 20-minute drive southwest of the quiet town of Kampot is the center of Cambodia's kiteboarding scene and a hot spot for thrill-seekers. Kep Thmey beach's shallow waters and strong wind provide the perfect conditions for kiteboarding, and visitors from all around Southeast Asia and beyond flock to these shores to enjoy this sport. **Cambodia Kiteboarding** is the only local operator run by an expat Dutchman who grew up in the Kingdom. It offers gear for hire and lessons by certified instructors as well. The best time to take to the water is from December to February, which is the dry season. Or, if you don't mind the rain the wind, June to September are also favorable months. The lessons are best suited for ages 9 to 65, and all skill levels – from beginners to experts – are welcome.

Cambodia Kiteboarding
🔗cambodiakiteboarding.com

 16

Kep

🅐D7 🚆109 miles (175 km) S of Phnom Penh 🚌

Once known as Kep-sur-Mer, the town of Kep was an upscale resort for the rich and influential of French Indochina in the 1930s. The town was overrun by the Khmer Rouge in 1975, who torched most symbols of colonial prosperity.

Today, the area is little more than an overgrown village in a scenic location, set on a lofty forested headland with the sea on three sides. In the last ten years, however, it has become Cambodia's most successful micro-resort, with ecolodges and guesthouses mushrooming across town.

Despite the damage done by the Khmer Rouge, the town's Modernist concrete villas remain Kep's best-known attraction. Although charred and ruined, these structures are fascinating reminders of a more prosperous time.

Kep Beach is about 1 mile (2 km) long and made up of imported yellow sand, which needs to be regularly topped up due to erosion. The bay's waters are extremely shallow and quite safe for children, although adults may have to wade a long way out for a decent swim. Coconut Beach, a short distance east of Kep Beach, is popular with both locals and visitors.

The region's most renowned dish, the delicious and spicy Kep pepper crab, is served in every restaurant on the strip known as Crab Market, north of town. There are several pepper farms nearby where visitors can see the vine-like plant, and also buy the famous and pungent Kep peppercorn.

Did You Know?

Peppercorns picked green turn black when they dry out. Red peppercorns are left on the vine for longer.

↓ Snorkeling in the shallow waters off Kep Beach

Kep National Park

 D7 1 mile (2 km) NW of Kep From Kep

One of the smallest protected preserves in Cambodia, Kep National Park occupies the hilltop directly behind Kep town *(p141)*. A 5-mile- (8-km-) long concrete trail loops around the hillside, passing through an evergreen forest, and takes about three hours to walk. On the way, you will pass views of Kampot and Angkoul Beach, a picturesque pagoda, and finally Sunset Rock, which offers fine vistas over the sea to Koh Tonsay. The park can be reached by motorbike from the bottom of the hill.

Koh Tonsay

D7 4 miles (6 km) S of Kep From Kep

Located just off Kep, Koh Tonsay, or Rabbit Island, is so called because its profile is said to resemble that of a rabbit. Although now undergoing development, the quiet island is inhabited by around 200 people, who make a living by fishing and harvesting coconuts and seaweed.

It is possible to walk around the entire island in just a couple of hours. The main attraction is a lovely sheltered beach with a narrow strip of golden sand – great for swimmers. There are about half a dozen bungalow operations, all offering simple accommodation in wood-and-thatch huts, most without private bathrooms. Several have restaurants with well-stocked bars. Visitors can also make trips to the nearby islands of Koh Pos and Koh Svai.

Takeo

D7 48 miles (77 km) S of Phnom Penh Street 4; (032)-931-323

A provincial capital, Takeo is located on the fringe of a vast flood plain that forms a vital wetland area. Although not on the tourist map, Takeo's broad streets are visited by those en route to the impressive early Khmer temple of Phnom Da, not far from town. As a result, the town has several facilities, including modest hotels and a couple

↓ Panoramic view of the gorgeous golden beach on Koh Tonsay island

> It's well worth trying Takeo's culinary specialty, *bong khorng* – giant prawns fried with garlic and lemon juice

of banks with ATMs. There are not many impressive sights here, although the lakeside promenade has a certain charm, including a dilapidated pier. The Provincial Museum, a short distance from the lakefront promenade, also deserves a visit for its local archaeological exhibits. It's well worth trying Takeo's culinary specialty, *bong khorng* – giant prawns fried with garlic and lemon juice – which is served at many restaurants and street stalls.

Angkor Borei

D7 13 miles (21 km) E of Takeo From Takeo

A highly enjoyable boat ride from Takeo takes visitors to the small riverside settlement

of Angkor Borei, one of the oldest pre-Angkorian sites in Cambodia. This scruffy, isolated town was earlier known as Vyadapura, capital city of the ancient Hindu kingdom of Funan, but the town's unpaved streets and general air of poverty provide little evidence of its illustrious past. Many of the residents are Vietnamese – the border is just a few miles to the east.

The **Angkor Borei Museum**, located on the canal bank, is a reminder of the area's former glory. This interesting museum has a small, eclectic collection of artifacts from the region, including Funan-style ceramics that date back 2,000 years; *lingas* (phallus-shaped Hindu statues); a 6th-century Standing Buddha; a 12th-century sandstone statue of Lakshmi; and ancient images of the gods Shiva and Vishnu.

A 2-mile (3-km) boat ride south from Angkor Borei, Phnom Da is an exquisite, partially ruined temple. Standing on the summit of an isolated hill, it has exceptional views over lush, green paddy fields across to Vietnam, 5 miles (8 km) away, and over the wetlands to Takeo.

Phnom Da's ruins, rising to a height of 59 ft (18 m), are approached by 142 steps. The temple's red-brick foundation dates from 514 CE, and its intricate carvings have been weathered by centuries of rainfall, while the walls are cracked and penetrated by plants. Despite its dilapidated condition, there still remains much to admire – carved pillars, bas-reliefs of *nagas*, and an imposing stone doorway. However, most of the carvings have been taken away to museums in Phnom Penh and Angkor Borei. Below the temple are several caves. These are said to have been used as cremation sites by the Khmer Rouge, but today they are used as religious shines.

Angkor Borei Museum

 Riverbank, Angkor Borei ☎ (012)-201-638
🕐 8am–4:30pm daily

㉑
Svay Rieng

🅐 E7 📍 70 miles (113 km) SE of Phnom Penh 🚌 From Phnom Penh

A provincial capital roughly half way between Phnom Penh and Ho Chi Minh City in Vietnam, the town of Svay Rieng is bypassed by most travelers, except those desperately in need of a meal or a drink. The Vietnamese border at Bavet is a short journey from here.

THE BOMBING OF NEAK LUONG

On August 6, 1973, American bombers destroyed the town of Neak Luong, north of Angkor Borei on the Mekong, in an attempt to stop the Khmer Rouge advancing on Phnom Penh. The bombing – later portrayed in the iconic 1984 movie, *The Killing Fields* – killed almost 150 Cambodian civilians. Some commentators argue that the attack on Neak Luong provided a powerful propaganda coup for the Khmer Rouge, ultimately fueling their successful takeover of Cambodia.

EXPERIENCE
LAOS

Fisher and his raft on the Mekong River

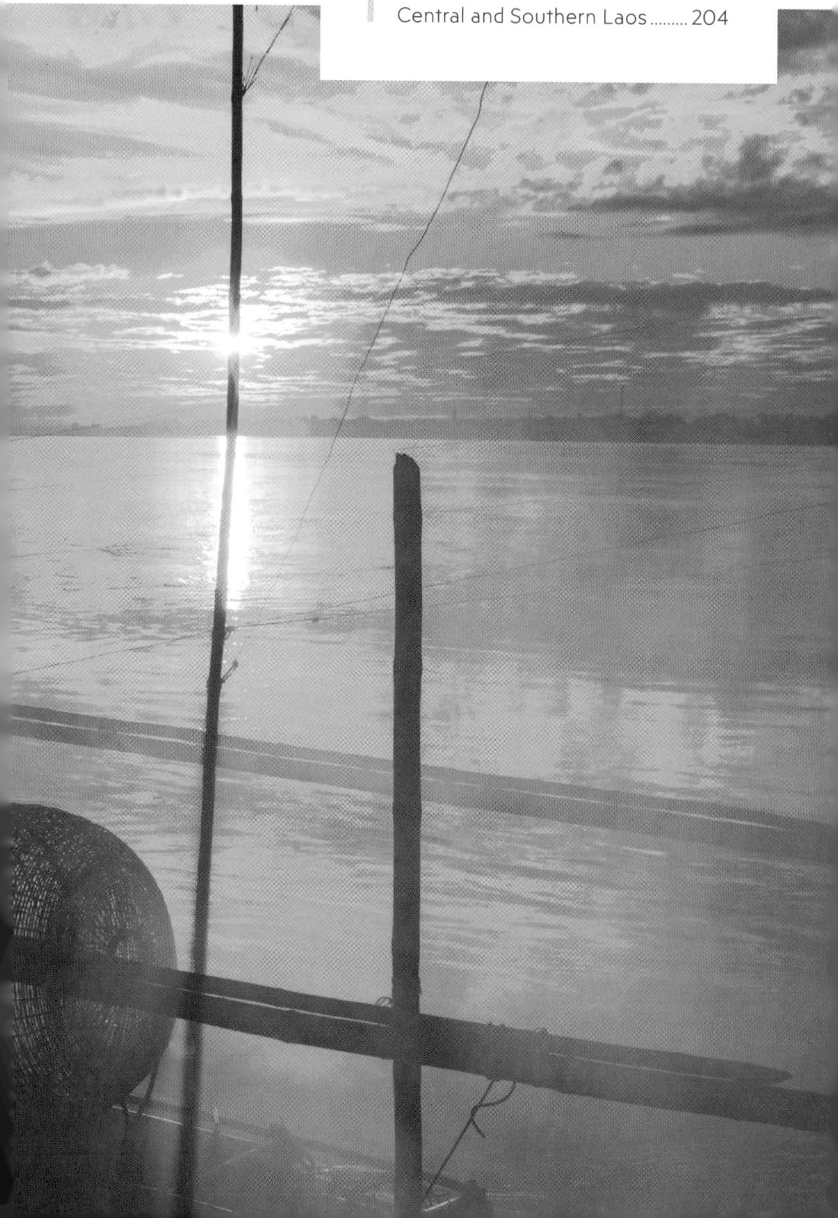

EXPLORE
LAOS

This section divides Laos into four
color-coded sightseeing areas,
as shown on the map above.
Find out more about each area
on the following pages.

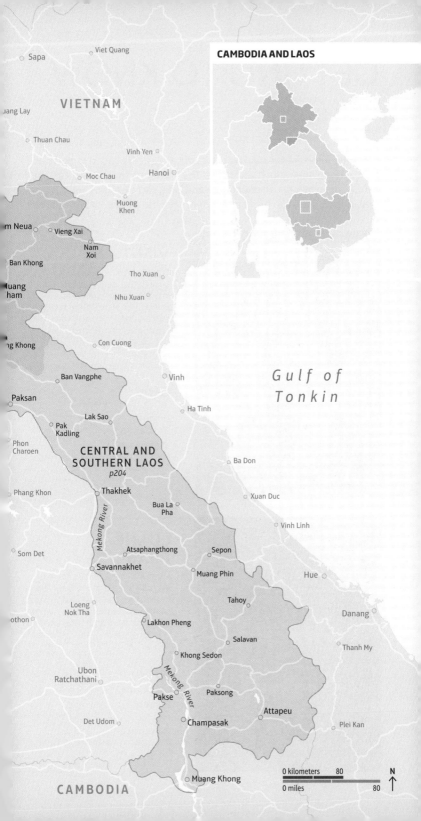

GETTING TO KNOW
LAOS

Gold and green are the abiding colors of Laos – in the gilded temples and the overwhelmingly lush landscape. The Mekong is the country's main artery, defining its north-south orientation and long, narrow form. Laos is supremely slow-paced, and even the capital, Vientiane, has a quiet, provincial feel.

PAGE 156

VIENTIANE

Languid, low-rise Vientiane trails far behind other Southeast Asian capitals in the urban mayhem stakes, which makes it one of the most relaxing of the region's cities for visitors. With lingering French accents in its street signs and café culture, and a fine array of gold-clad temples, it often keeps travelers hanging around far longer than they planned.

Best for
Temples, museums, and street food

Home to
Phu Khao Khuay National Protected Area

Experience
Making Lao dishes on a local cookery course

PAGE 166

LUANG PRABANG

Luang Prabang is perhaps the most atmospheric town in Southeast Asia, set on the banks of the fast-flowing Mekong and crowded with temples. The morning Tak Bat ritual highlights the importance of religion here, as do the rhythms of daily worship at Wat Xieng Thong.

Best for
Buddhist culture

Home to
Wat Xieng Thong and the Royal Palace Complex

Experience
Browsing for treasures at the Night Market

NORTHERN LAOS

In Northern Laos narrow roads wind between surreal karst outcrops, and a network of interlocking ridges provide the backdrop for dizzying cultural diversity. In the hills around Phongsali a web of hiking routes gives access to welcoming rural villages and communities, while the forests of Bokeo resound with the calls of wild gibbons. Tangible history here comes in the form of the mysterious Plain of Jars, but the whole region often feels like it belongs to a softer, slower-paced Southeast Asian past.

Best for
Hiking amid dramatic karst landscapes

Home to
Vang Vieng, Muang Sing, and the Plain of Jars

Experience
Kayaking along the Nam Song in Vang Vieng

CENTRAL AND SOUTHERN LAOS

Central and Southern Laos is essentially the eastern half of the Mekong catchment – a narrow strip of territory with low-lying plains that rise eastward into serried ranks of hills. Riverside towns here are full of decaying Colonial-era shophouses, the rugged landscape is riddled with vast limestone caverns, and in the far south the Mekong fragments into a riverine archipelago of other-worldly islands. There are also vast expanses of protected forest here, still stalked by a handful of wild tigers.

Best for
Exploring caves and national parks

Home to
Si Phan Don, Wat Phu Champasak, and Savannakhet

Experience
Gazing up at bizarre stalactites during a boat trip into the Tham Kong Lo caves

A YEAR IN
LAOS

JANUARY

Boun Khun Khao *(late Jan/early Feb)*. A true festival of the countryside – look out for feasting and music at rural temples as farmers give thanks for the rice harvest.

△ **Lunar New Year** *(late Jan/early Feb)*. In Vientiane and Savannakhet, the Chinese community marks the New Year with colorful street parties and fireworks.

FEBRUARY

Boun Wat Phu Champasak *(Feb full moon)*. Head to Wat Phu Champasak for three days of performances and entertainment.

△ **Boun Makha Busaa** *(Feb full moon)*. Candle-carrying cavalcades of worshipers descend on Buddhist temples in Vientiane and other large towns.

Boun That Sikhot *(Feb full moon)*. A revered temple south of Takhek is the focus of a huge fair.

MAY

Labor Day *(May 1)*. Commemorations for victims of World War II are held throughout the country.

△ **Boun Visakha Busaa** *(May full moon)*. Marking the Buddha's enlightenment, candlelit processions move through the streets at night.

JUNE

△ **Children's Day** *(Jun 1)*. With the monsoon gearing up, this day marks the beginning of the long school holidays, with children's parades and parties.

OCTOBER

Boun Ok Pansa *(mid-Oct)*. The rains end, monks come out of retreat and receive new robes and alms bowls, and processions emerge from every temple.

△ **Boun Souang Heua** *(mid-Oct)*. Head for the Mekong in Vientiane or Luang Prabang the day after Ok Pansa to see the most extravagant of all the autumn dragon boat races.

SEPTEMBER

△ **Boun Khao Salak** *(Sep full moon)*. Lavish offerings of food are presented at Buddhist temples, especially in Luang Prabang, during this ceremony to honor the deceased.

MARCH

Women's Day (Mar 8). International women's day is a public holiday in Laos, with events to draw attention to women's issues in Vientiane and Luang Prabang.

△ **Boun Pha Vet** (late Mar/early Apr). Temples all over Laos are particularly vibrant, as the Buddhist Jataka tale is recited and monks are ordained.

APRIL

△ **Boun Pi Mai** (Apr 14–16). In the heat of spring, Laos celebrates its New Year, with good-natured water fights on the streets.

JULY

△ **Boun Khao Pansa** (early Jul). As the monsoons properly begins, monks go into retreat in their monasteries, and there's a general uptick in religious observance across Laos.

AUGUST

△ **Boun Haw Khao Padap Din** (Aug full moon). A somber and serious religious festival, with offerings and prayers for the deceased. In Luang Prabang, the dragon boat racing season begins.

NOVEMBER

△ **Boun That Luang** (Nov full moon). Huge crowds descend on the Pha That Luang temple in Vientiane for a week-long festival and street fair.

DECEMBER

National Day (Dec 2). Flag-waving, parades, and speeches in Vientiane commemorate the founding of the LPDR in 1975.

Boun That Ing Hang (early Dec). The inner sanctum of the revered That Ing Hang temple near Savannakhet is opened to worshipers and a huge fair takes over the precincts.

△ **Luang Prabang Film Festival** (early Dec). With free screenings, talks, and workshops, the arthouse cinema scene of Southeast Asia gets a five-day showcase in Luang Prabang.

A BRIEF
HISTORY

Though it has often been at the mercy of its powerful neighbors, and though its borders were only drawn by outsiders during the political upheavals of the 20th century, Laos has a royal history stretching back hundreds of years. This dynastic past still underpins national identity in the republican present.

Prehistory

Around 4,000 years ago, knowledge of rice cultivation made its way along the Mekong from China, and settled civilizations developed in Laos, including the mysterious megalithic culture that established the Plain of Jars in around 500 BCE.

The Arrival of the Tai and Angkorian Control

From the 8th century, various Tai peoples (ancestors of modern Thais and Lao) followed a similar route from southern China, partly displacing the earlier Mon-Khmer-speaking inhabitants. In the 13th century, most of Laos fell under the control of the

1 Engraving of early settlers cultivating rice.

2 Plain of Jars.

3 Buddha icons at Wat Si Saket in Vientiane.

4 Depiction of a temple in Vientiane after the city was torched by the Siamese.

Timeline of events

500 BCE

A Mon-Khmer kingdom emerges near Champasak in the south; a megalithic culture flourishes around the Plain of Jars in the north.

900–1300 CE

Most of Laos is controlled by Angkor.

1353

Fa Ngum founds the Lao kingdom of Lan Xang and introduces Theravada Buddhism.

1563

Lan Xang capital shifts to Vientiane to escape Burmese threats of attack.

1637–49

Laos enjoys a period of prosperity during the reign of King Suriya Vongsa.

Cambodian kingdom of Angkor. When Angkor went into decline in the following century, a major new regional power began to emerge in the form of the Sukhothai kingdom of Thailand.

The Rise of Lan Xang

In the 1340s, the Angkor rulers sent a young Lao prince named Fa Ngum, who had grown up in exile in Cambodia, north to reassert their influence in Laos. But instead of becoming a Angkorian vassal, Fa Ngum created his own independent Lao state known as Lan Xang, "Land of a Million Elephants," with a capital at Xiang Dong Xiang Thong (modern-day Luang Prabang). He also introduced Theravada Buddhism to the region.

Fragmentation and Foreign Incursions

Though Lan Xang endured for several centuries, the threat from neighboring states was ever present. In 1560, the capital moved to Vientiane and prosperity followed, but succession disputes in subsequent centuries saw the country divided into four feuding principalities. By the 19th century, Thailand dominated central and southern regions, and Vietnam controlled the north.

WHAT'S IN A NAME?

Outsiders often get in a muddle over how to pronounce Laos's name. "Lao" is an adjective, used to describe things from Laos, including the language and the people. In English, the name of the country itself is correctly pronounced to rhyme with "mouse." The full official name is the Lao People's Democratic Republic – though locals refer to the country as Muang Lao, "Land of the Lao."

1641
Dutch merchant Gerritt van Wuysthoff produces the earliest first-hand European account of Laos.

1700
Lan Xang divides into four semi-independent principalities, heavily influenced by Thailand.

1771
Burmese armies sack Luang Prabang.

1782
Siam (modern Thailand) seizes power in Vientiane.

1828
The Siamese army burns down Vientiane.

1

2

French Rule

From the mid-19th century, the French began to annex parts of
Southeast Asia. In 1893, they used threats of violence to force
Thailand to abandon its claims to all territory east of the Mekong.
Luang Prabang – a surviving fragment of Lan Xang – became a
French protectorate with its king left in place. The rest of the
country was under direct colonial administration. The French
put little effort into developing Laos, though they introduced
forced labor and heavy taxes; while Laotians did revolt against
the French, these protests were usually small and localized.

World War II

During the Japanese occupation of Southeast Asia in World
War II, the colonial administration of Laos – now allied to Japan
via the Vichy France regime – remained in place. However, in
1945, as an Allied victory became inevitable, the Japanese
rounded up French officials and pushed King Sisavang Vong,
a lifelong supporter of French rule, to declare independence.
As soon as the French returned in 1946, he reneged on this
declaration, but Laos was nonetheless granted partial independence in 1949, and then full independence four years later.

KAYSONE PHOMVIHANE

Born into a
Vietnamese family
near Savannakhet,
Kaysone Phomvihane
(1920–92) gave up his
law degree studies to
join the anti-colonial
struggle in Vietnam,
and was then a key
figure in the develop-
ment of the Pathet Lao.
He became the first
prime minister of the
Lao People's Democratic
Republic in 1975,
serving until 1991.

Timeline of events

1907
A treaty
establishes
current borders
of Laos with
Thailand.

1893
French seize Lao territories
east of the Mekong.

1954
Laos gains full independence;
a conference in Geneva makes
provisions for national unity.

1945
Encouraged by the
Japanese, the Lao king
reluctantly declares
independence.

1964
US begins
bombing
Communist
targets in Laos.

The Shadow of the Vietnam War

Post-World War II Lao politics was dominated by royals. Princely wrangling led to a split in the original resistance movement, Lao Issara ("Free Lao"), with the Communist Pathet Lao ("Land of Lao") coming to prominence. Throughout the 1950s, the Royal Lao Government (RLG) and a Pathet Lao-led opposition tussled for power, with sporadic violence. From 1964 to 1973, the US dropped more than 2 million tons of bombs on eastern Laos in an unsuccessful attempt to cut North Vietnamese supply lines. The US also sponsored a proxy war against the Pathet Lao. In 1975, however, the Communists forcibly took control of the country and created the Lao People's Democratic Republic (LPDR).

Modern Laos

Since 1975, the government has remained in the control of the Pathet Lao-founded Lao People's Revolutionary Party. However, since the early 1990s there have been many changes. A long Vietnamese military presence has come to an end; the historically fraught relationship with Thailand has improved; Buddhism has resurged; and tourist numbers have soared.

1 King Sisavang Vong in 1949. ↑

2 Communist troops in Laos in 1959.

3 Communist statue in Vieng Xai.

4 Laborers building a new road in 2011.

Did You Know?

Laos is the only landlocked country in Southeast Asia.

1975
Communists seize power; King Sisavang Vatthana abdicates, and the Lao People's Democratic Republic comes into being.

1994
As relations with Thailand improve, the first bridge spanning the Mekong is opened.

1988
Vietnamese troops officially withdraw from Laos as the Cold War draws to a close.

2023
Laos suffers an economic crisis largely caused by over-borrowing from China.

2021
Laos celebrates the opening of the Boten-Vientiane railway, connecting the country with China.

VIENTIANE

The capital of Laos, Vientiane is also Asia's smallest capital. Located on a bend in the wide Mekong River, the city has survived numerous changes over the centuries. More than 1,000 years ago it was a Khmer trading post. In the 16th century it became the capital of the Lao kingdom, but was ultimately destroyed by the Siamese in 1828. French colonialists appropriated the country as part of their Indochinese empire in the late 19th century, and Vientiane was chosen to be their administrative capital. During the Cold War (1945–91), the city was flooded with refugees while the rest of the country witnessed intense bombing, and it suffered during its time under the Soviets.

Vientiane has undergone rapid changes during the last couple of decades. The strict Communist stance of the country was relaxed after the collapse of the Soviet Union in 1991, and new business ventures sprung up around the city. Many Lao exiles also returned to reclaim properties they had abandoned as they fled the Communist regime, and they are now re-establishing homes and businesses here.

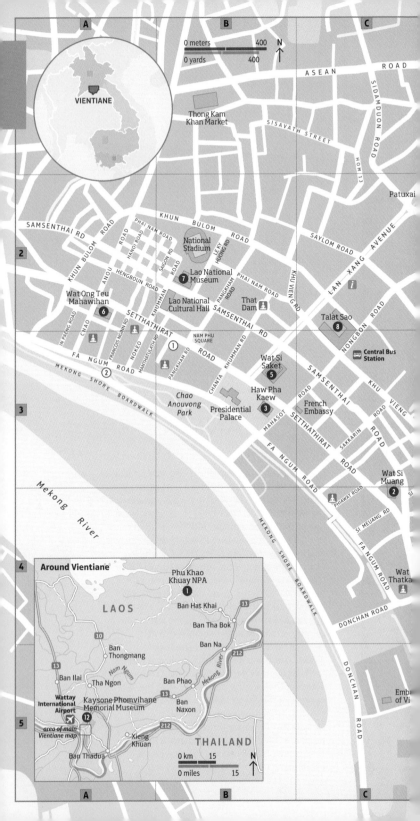

VIENTIANE

Must See

1 Phu Khao Khuay National Protected Area

Experience More

2 Wat Si Muang
3 Haw Pha Kaew
4 COPE Visitor Center
5 Wat Si Saket
6 Wat Ong Teu Mahawihan
7 Lao National Museum
8 Talat Sao
9 Patuxai
10 Wat Sok Pa Luang
11 Pha That Luang
12 Kaysone Phomvihane Memorial Museum

Eat

① JoMa Bakery Café

Shop

② Night Market

PHU KHAO KHUAY NATIONAL PROTECTED AREA

⚑C3 **⌂30 miles (48 km) NE of Vientiane** **🚌From southern bus terminal to Ban Tha Bok** **ℹ️Information National Tourism Administration; (021)-212-251**

Though it's within easy striking distance of Vientiane, this large and beautiful wilderness area sees surprisingly few visitors. Thickly forested, traversed by meandering rivers, and home to a few friendly villages, this is one of the most accessible protected areas in Laos, with an impressive array of wildlife.

Covering an area of more than 770 sq miles (2,000 sq km), Phu Khao Khuay begins a short way northwest of Vientiane. The main entrance is off Route 13, just before the village of Ban Tha Bok. With a rented vehicle, it is possible to explore independently, and guides are available at local villages, though most people visit on an organized tour.

The village of Ban Hat Khai is the main settlement within the protected area. There is homestay accommodation here, and it is an ideal place to arrange boat tours and jungle hikes. Some 3 miles (5 km) north of Ban Hat Khai lies the beautiful Tat Xai waterfall, which is a popular picnic spot at weekends. Another waterfall can be found at Tat Leuk, further west. Ban Na, 4 miles (6 km) southwest of Ban Tha Bok, is a village with lush paddy fields and an elephant observation tower. Elephants are seldom spotted these days, but other wildlife is frequently glimpsed at the nearby salt lick.

↑ Kayaking with a bamboo canoe at Tat Leuk

←

Wildflowers in the tropical rainforest at Phu Khao Khuay

WILDLIFE IN THE PARK

Phu Khao Khuay is home to a wide range of forest animal species, including sun bears, clouded leopards (left), white-cheeked gibbons, macaques, wild dogs, and several species of deer. There are two small herds of wild elephants (one living near Ban Na, the other near Nam Mang), and occasional rumors of tigers. There is also a wealth of birdlife, including the endangered green peafowl.

Did You Know?

Phu Khao Khuay means "buffalo horn mountain," and is named after one of the park's mountain peaks.

Waterfall in Tat Leuk, to the west of Phu Khao Khuay National Protected Area ↑

EXPERIENCE MORE

The beautifully landscaped gardens of the museum offer a verdant respite from the heat of central Vientiane.

2

Wat Si Muang

📍C4 🏛Convergence of Setthathirat & Samsenthai rds ⏰8am–5pm daily

One of the best-known temples in Vientiane, Wat Si Muang houses the *lak muang*, or city pillar, installed here by King Setthathirat in 1563 after he moved the Lao capital from Luang Prabang to Vientiane. Razed by the Siamese when they sacked the city in 1828, the temple was later rebuilt.

Today, the temple is a vibrant place of worship and considered particularly auspicious by devotees who come here to perform a variety of rituals. The current sim (ordination hall) dates from 1915 and is divided into two chambers. Inside the front chamber, devotees are blessed by a monk with holy water and a *baci* string (a string tied to the wrist to channel good luck). After this, worshipers with a particular wish prostrate themselves before what was once a Buddha image, but is now only a melted lump, having been damaged when the Siamese set the temple on fire. The inner sanctum houses the city pillar, now gilded and wrapped with a sacred cloth. Incense is burned here and candles are lit as offerings to the city spirit.

Behind the temple are the laterite remains of an ancient Khmer religious site, next to which a statue of Vientiane's guardian goddess, Sao Si, is located. Legend has it that when the city pillar was installed, Sao Si jumped beneath it to appease malevolent spirits and to bring good fortune to the city. Today, worshipers make fervent offerings to commemorate her sacrifice.

3

Haw Pha Kaew

📍B3 🏛Setthathirat Rd ⏰8am–noon & 1–4pm daily

Once the exclusive temple of Lao kings, Haw Pha Kaew is no longer a functioning Buddhist temple, but a national museum of splendid Buddhist art.

Ironically, it is named after a precious piece of religious art, the Pha Kaew (Emerald Buddha), which is no longer here. Made of jade, it is as important an icon as the Phabang (*p167*) in Luang Prabang. However, it was seized by the Siamese in 1779, and has remained in Wat Phra Kaew in Bangkok ever since. A signboard expresses, in Lao and English, the Lao peoples' indignation at this act.

The main attraction of this impressive museum is the magnificent collection of bronze Buddhas on a terrace surrounding the building. These have been collected from various temples in the country. Artifacts inside the building include smaller Buddha images, Khmer stelae, bronze frog drums, and a large Seated Buddha image.

← Buddha statue decorated with gold leaf at Haw Pha Kaew

4

COPE Visitor Center

📍D4 🏛Khu Vieng Rd ⏰9am–6pm daily 🌐copelaos.org

The vast tonnage of explosives dropped on Laos by the US military between 1964 and 1973 continues to have a devastating impact. Unexploded ordnance (UXO) still lies in fields and forests, leading to numerous deaths and injuries each year. The Cooperative Orthotic & Prosthetic Enterprise (COPE) NGO works to support the injured, and this insightful, understated exhibition – in its own building on the grounds of the Centre for Medical Rehabilitation hospital – puts their efforts in context. Documentaries are screened in a cinema built to resemble a wartime bunker, and well-structured displays guide visitors through the country's grim history. The exhibit featuring dozens of suspended cluster bombs – the main type of ordnance dropped on Laos – is particularly sobering.

Tiny Buddhas in niches and larger statues lining the cloister at Wat Si Saket

7

Lao National Museum

📍B2 🏠Samsenthai Rd
🕐8am–noon & 1–4pm daily

Once known as the Lao Revolutionary Museum, and derided by foreigners for its overt propaganda, the Lao National Museum now offers fascinating exhibits (all well displayed and illuminated, with captions in English). The museum traces the history of the country from prehistoric times to the present.

The displays, showcasing artifacts from both the Lao Pako archaeological site and the Plain of Jars *(p198)*, and the Khmer- and Buddhist-era exhibits, are excellent. The Buddhist-era room features a rare Thai Lue Buddha image, which resembles an animist icon. Life-sized re-creations of the Khmer lintels of Wat Phu Champasak *(p210)* are impressive, as are the original Hindu artifacts from the temple, including Shiva and Ganesha statues. The modern-era exhibits mainly comprise photographs of key figures of the revolution. The second floor has a display on minority cultures.

5

Wat Si Saket

📍B3 🏠Setthathirat Rd
🕐8am–5pm daily

The oldest wat in Vientiane, built in 1818, Wat Si Saket was spared the destruction wrought by the Siamese when they burned the rest of the temples in the city. The architectural feature that makes this temple unique is the cloister, or covered gallery, surrounding the central sim. The inner walls of the cloister are filled with more than 2,000 Buddha images arranged in symmetrical niches facing the sim. The sim itself has an exquisite five-tiered roof; restored by the French twice, it has a distinctly European finish. One of the highlights of this enchanting ancient collection of Buddhist art is a *háang song nam pha*, a *naga*-headed trough. It is kept in the covered gallery and used for pouring holy water over the Buddha images during Lao New Year.

6

Wat Ong Teu Mahawihan

📍A2 🏠Setthathirat Rd
🕐8am–5pm daily

This wat's name, meaning Temple of the Heavy Buddha, derives from the 19-ft- (6-m-) tall bronze Buddha statue, dating from the 16th century, within the sim. The site is believed to have been used for religious purposes since the 3rd century. Khmer stelae are housed in a *sala* (open-sided hall) within the complex. Monks from all over Laos come to study in the school housed in the wat, and visitors can strike up an enlightening conversation with these erudite young men.

↑ Monks taking a break from their studies at Wat Ong Teu Mahawihan

Talat Sao

C2 **Corner of Lan Xang Ave & Khu Vieng Rd** **8am–6pm daily**

No longer a traditional produce market, Talat Sao, known as the Morning Market, comprises a large, partly 1960s-built mall with a warren of stalls attached. It is a popular shopping destination for locals and visitors, not least because the mall has air-conditioning. Among outlets for electronic goods and homewares are shops selling a range of handicrafts, antiques, jewelry, 24-karat gold ornaments, and traditional textiles; the beautiful handwoven silk and cotton *pha sins* (wraparounds) worn by Lao women make attractive souvenirs. Look out for magnificent hand-worked silver belts and silver ornaments such as bracelets and earrings. Bargaining is *de rigueur*, but beware overpricing: antiques and gemstones are best left to those with sound knowledge of such items, since fakes abound. However, some of the reproduction antiques, generally from Vietnam, are quite attractive, and usually priced and sold as repro.

The food court on the third floor of the mall is an ideal stop for weary shoppers.

Visitors eager to experience a bustling Lao market selling fresh local produce should head for Khua Din, to the east of Talat Sao just past the bus station.

Patuxai

C2 **Lan Xang Ave** **8am–5pm daily (for tower only)**

At first sight, the Patuxai, meaning Victory Gate, brings to mind the Arc de Triomphe in Paris. The monument was constructed in 1964 to commemorate the lives lost during the course of the Lao Civil War, fought between 1953 and 1975. It is made out of concrete rumored to have been donated by the Americans, who intended it to be used in the construction of a new airport, earning the arch the nickname of the "vertical runway."

The arch is adorned with the typically Lao mixture of Buddhist and Hindu iconography, along with bas-reliefs of *apsaras* facing fierce demons from the Hindu epic, *Ramayana*. A spiral staircase leads to the top of the monument. En route visitors will pass dozens of souvenir shops that specialize in T-shirts. Once at the top, visitors are rewarded with excellent views across Lan

Xang Avenue toward the Mekong River. The Patuxai is best visited early in the morning in order to avoid the heat and the tour bus crowds.

 10

Wat Sok Pa Luang

E5 **Off Khu Vieng Rd** **8am–3pm daily**

A visit to this simple wat, in a quiet outer suburb, presents an interesting alternative to visiting the grand temples that line the streets of Vientiane. The compound of the wat, whose name means Forest Temple, is filled with shady trees. Just outside the entrance to the wat is a house offering traditional massages as well as herbal saunas (available in the afternoons, every day of the week). The temple also offers courses in Vipassana, which is a type of Buddhist meditation.

 11

Pha That Luang

F1 **That Luang Rd** **8am–5pm daily**

This important religious monument, whose name means the Great Stupa, is also the symbol of Lao nationhood. Its image appears on the currency as well as the national seal. Some date the site to the 3rd century, when a shrine was built here to

← The Patuxai, a memorial to those who lost their lives in the Lao Civil War

↑ Festival dancers at Pha That Luang, the Great Stupa

house a relic of the Buddha. Excavations have indicated the existence of a Khmer site here from around the 12th century, built long before Pha That Luang was erected in its present form. King Setthathirat ordered its construction when he moved the Lao capital from Luang Prabang to Vientiane in the mid-16th century. After the Siamese razed the city in 1828, the site was abandoned, and bandits seeking gold and jewels later destroyed the edifice. The French rebuilt it in the 1930s with the aid of drawings made by French explorers who had visited the abandoned site in 1867.

Today, Pha That Luang lies within a large compound behind a statue of King Setthathirat, and is flanked by two Buddhist temples. The gloriously gilded main stupa reaches 148 ft (45 m) above ground level, and is surrounded by three platforms of decreasing size, each of which is surrounded by rows of smaller stupas and lotus petal-shaped crenellations. A cloister on the outermost wall contains both Lao and Khmer Buddha images. Boun That Luang (p151), held here in November, is among the most important festivals in Vientiane, and lasts for several days.

  12

Kaysone Phomvihane Memorial Museum

B3 **NH13, Ban Sivilay, Muang Saythani** **8am–noon & 1–4pm daily**

Located on the main road south of Vientiane, this museum is divided into two parts. The first is a grandiose memorial to the late president and founding father of Communist Laos, Kaysone Phomvihane (p154), and the second is the actual house in which he lived after the Communists seized power in 1975. The memorial is a huge, well-kept hall that includes a scale model of the late president's childhood home in Savannakhet (p212), and various items of revolutionary memorabilia. More interesting, however, is his home, which is located on what was once a US military and CIA base, which the Pathet Lao occupied after its former occupants were ousted. It is a modest, single-story bungalow and has been kept exactly as it was when Kaysone Phomvihane resided here, with his library, work table, and other personal items on display. The house is a short distance from the memorial hall, but staff are happy to guide visitors there.

EAT

JoMa Bakery Café
This stylish café does excellent breakfasts; it's also a perfect spot to while away a lazy afternoon over coffee and tasty pastries.

B3 **Setthathirat Rd** **joma.biz**

$$$

LUANG PRABANG

Nestled amid verdant mountains on the banks of the Mekong, Luang Prabang is as enticing for its natural beauty as for the resplendent golden facades of its many wats. Located on a compact peninsula formed by the confluence of the Mekong and its tributary, the Nam Khan, Luang Prabang is the former royal capital of Laos. In 1353, Fa Ngum, a Lao prince who had been exiled to the Khmer capital of Angkor, returned and established the first Lao kingdom here. He named it Lan Xang Hom Khao, meaning "Kingdom of a Million Elephants and the White Parasol," aptly reflecting the kingdom's military power and royal status. Shortly thereafter, Fa Ngum's Khmer benefactors sent the sacred Phabang, a golden Buddha image, from Sri Lanka. It is from the Phabang that the city has taken its current name. Although the country's administrative capital was moved to Vientiane in 1545, Lao royalty continued to reside here until the Communist takeover in 1975. Over the next decade and more, the city plunged into desolation as thousands of people left it to escape the Communist regime. Luang Prabang finally reopened to the world after the fall of the Soviet Bloc in the 1990s. In 1995, the city was designated a UNESCO World Heritage Site, and today it remains the uncontested cultural capital of Laos.

LUANG PRABANG

Must Sees

1. Wat Xieng Thong
2. Royal Palace Complex

Experience More

3. Mount Phou Si and That Chomsi
4. Wat Siphoutabath
5. Traditional Arts and Ethnology Center
6. Wat Mai Suwannaphumaham
7. Wat Xieng Mouan
8. Wat Choum Khong
9. Wat Pa Phai
10. School of Fine Arts
11. Wat Nong Sikhunmuang
12. Wat Sene
13. Wat Si Boun Huang
14. Wat Khili
15. UNESCO Maison du Patrimoine
16. Wat Aham
17. Wat Visounarat
18. Wat Manolom
19. Wat That Luang
20. Wats on the West Bank
21. Santi Chedi
22. Ban Phanom
23. Ban Xang Khong
24. Tat Sae Waterfalls
25. Tat Kuang Si Waterfalls

Eat

1. Tamarind
2. Dyen Sabai
3. Tangor

Drink

4. Icon Klub
5. Maolin Tavern

Shop

6. Handicraft Night Market

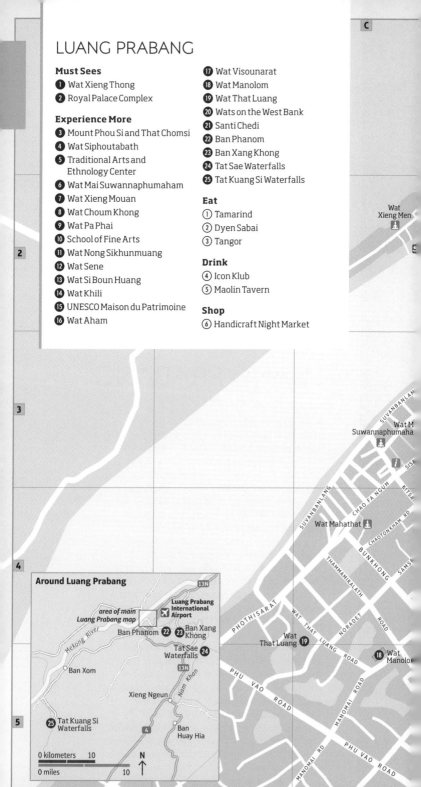

Around Luang Prabang

area of main Luang Prabang map

Luang Prabang International Airport

13N

Mekong River

Ban Phanom — 22 23 — Ban Xang Khong

Tat Sae Waterfalls — 24

Ban Xom

13N

Xieng Ngeun

Nam Khan

4

Ban Huay Hia

Tat Kuang Si Waterfalls — 25

0 kilometers   10
0 miles   10

N

Wat Xieng Men

Wat M Suwannaphumaha

Wat Mahathat

Wat That Luang — 19

Wat Manolom — 18

SUVANBANLAN

SISV

CHAO FA NGUM

KITSA

SUVANBANLANG

CHAOTONKHAM RD

BUNKHONG

THAMMAMIKALATH

SAMSE

PHOTHISARAT

WAT THAT LUANG ROAD

NORADET ROAD

MANOMAI ROAD

MANOMAI RD

PHU VAO ROAD

PHU VAO ROAD

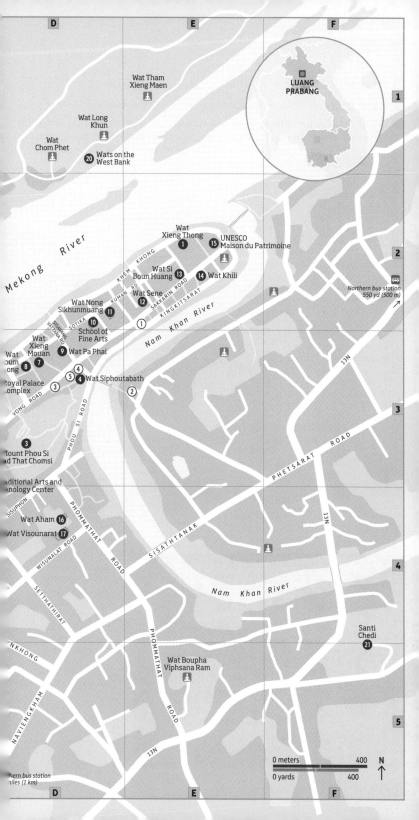

D | E | F

LUANG PRABANG

Wat Tham Xieng Maen

Wat Long Khun

Wat Chom Phet

20 Wats on the West Bank

Mekong River

Wat Xieng Thong **1**
15 UNESCO Maison du Patrimoine

KHEM KHONG

Wat Si Boun Huang **13**
14 Wat Khili

XUMAN RD

Wat Sene **12**

SAKKARIN ROAD

Wat Nong Sikhunmuang **11**

SOTIKA VATTANA RD

KINGKITSARAT

10 School of Fine Arts

①

Northern bus station 550 yd (500 m)

Wat Xieng Mouan **7**
9 Wat Pa Phai

Wat oum ong **8**

5 **4**
4 Wat Siphoutabath

3 Royal Palace Complex

②

VONG ROAD

PHOU SI ROAD

Nam Khan River

13N

3 Mount Phou Si and That Chomsi

SISUPHON

Traditional Arts and Ethnology Center

Wat Aham **16**
Wat Visounarat **17**

WISUNALAT ROAD

PHOMMATHAT ROAD

SETTHATHIRAT

SISATHANAK ROAD

PHETSARAT ROAD

13N

ANKHONG

Santi Chedi **21**

Wat Boupha Viphsana Ram

PHOMMATHAT ROAD

NAVIENGKHAM

13N

0 meters 400
0 yards 400

N

Southern bus station
miles (1 km)

D | E | F

1

WAT XIENG THONG

⊙ E2 **🏠 Between Sakkarin Rd and the Mekong River** **🕐 6am–6pm daily**

With its soaring roof finials, glittering mosaics, and bone-white *chedis*, Wat Xieng Thong is one of the most impressive religious complexes in Laos. But what makes the place so atmospheric is its dynamic sense of religious life, with monks and worshipers energetically going about their daily business.

Considered by the locals to be the most important symbol of their country's religious heritage, Wat Xieng Thong, meaning Gold City Monastery, is notable for the brilliant colored-glass mosaics that adorn the exterior of several of the main buildings within the temple complex. These mosaics depict standard Buddhist iconography, such as lotus blossoms, as well as scenes from Buddhist scriptures and the daily lives of the Lao people. Look out for graphic depictions of the punishments received in the various levels of Buddhist hell, including liars being strung up with hooks through their tongues, and murderers being boiled alive. The sim (ordination hall) was built in 1560 by King Setthathirat, and the temple enjoyed royal patronage until 1975. It has served as a coronation venue for several Lao kings.

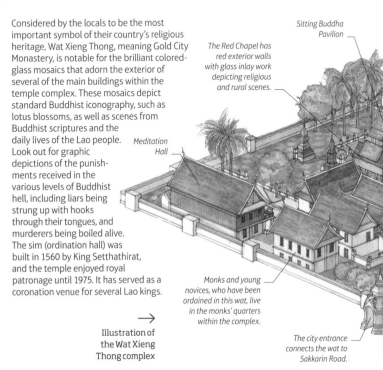

Sitting Buddha Pavilion

The Red Chapel has red exterior walls with glass inlay work depicting religious and rural scenes.

Meditation Hall

Monks and young novices, who have been ordained in this wat, live in the monks' quarters within the complex.

The city entrance connects the wat to Sakkarin Road.

→
Illustration of the Wat Xieng Thong complex

💬 **INSIDER TIP**
Visit Early

The temple gets very busy from around 10am onward. To see it at its best, with just monks and private worshipers for company, arrive promptly at dawn before most of the tourist crowds descend.

←
The sweeping roof lines of the gilded sim at Wat Xieng Thong

→ Interior of the Red Chapel, with its bronze Reclining Buddha

Holy texts and the Phaman (a Buddha image believed to have the power of invoking floods) are housed in the Tripitaka Library.

Boat shelter

Apart from its sweeping roof lines, the sim has a stunning Tree of Life mosaic.

The Elephant Head Fountain spouts lustral water that is collected by devotees to wash Buddha images in their homes.

The massive drum inside this pavilion is sounded on special prayer days.

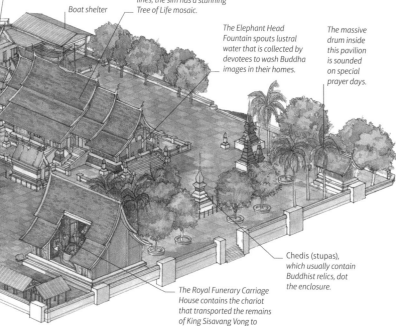

Chedis (stupas), which usually contain Buddhist relics, dot the enclosure.

The Royal Funerary Carriage House contains the chariot that transported the remains of King Sisavang Vong to his cremation.

Timeline

1828

▽ The Tripitaka Library is added to a complex that has gradually grown around the original sim over the course of three centuries.

1961

▽ The last major bout of construction gets underway, with the drum tower and carriage house added, and renovations to the older buildings.

1559–60

▵ Just three years before the royal capital shifts to Vientiane, King Setthathirat orders the construction of a wat to honor 8th-century King Chanthaphanith.

1887

The Chinese bandit group, the Black Flag Army, invades, but Wat Xieng Thong is saved from harm by the bandit leader, a former monk.

LAO TEMPLE ARCHITECTURE

A wat complex usually consists of several buildings in addition to the main ordination hall or sim. The sims in Lao wats differ from place to place and are constructed with variations in the style and design of the roof. While the sims of Luang Prabang-style wats are noted for their multi-tiered roofs, which almost reach the ground, the Vientiane style features tall and narrow roofs. The Xieng Khuan style, on the other hand, is known for low, single-tiered roofs. The primary decorative color of Lao wats is gold, symbolizing the light of the sun. Stencils, bas-reliefs, mosaics of colored glass or tiles, and painted murals are all used, both to create geometric patterns and to depict religious teachings. Syncretism, or the mixing of various faiths and cultural beliefs, abounds in these places, and elements of both Hinduism and animism are easy to find.

WAT COMPLEX

The layout of a wat reflects its diverse functions, which are not limited to worship. The word wat derives from the Sanskrit word for enclosure, and these sometimes vast complexes can include schools, community centers, and even health clinics. All wats are surrounded by an exterior wall, and all buildings, except libraries, are built on the ground, not on stilts. Most wats include monks' quarters, a temple, a sanctuary housing a large image of Buddha, and a place of learning.

→

A *hor kang*, a structure housing the wat's ceremonial drums, used to call monks to prayer

Monks' quarters

Small chapels often contain images of the Buddha.

The hor tai *is a temple library housing sacred scriptures.*

DECORATIVE ELEMENTS

A variety of murals, carved wooden panels, stencils, gilded statuary, and glass mosaic tiles are used to adorn wats.

Murals
Wall paintings in wats are usually hand-painted or stenciled. They depict tales from the *Jataka* and the *Phra Lak Phra Lam*, the Lao version of the Ramayana.

Dok Heuang Pheung
This is the name for the triangular gable area above the front door of a sim.

Dok So Faa
Metallic roof decorations, often depicting parasols or pagodas.

So Faa
These are roof finials that point upward, often in the shape of a *naga* (serpent).

① Gold-stenciled murals at Wat Xieng Thong.

② *Dok heuang pheung.*

③ *Dok so faa* on the sim at Wat Xieng Thong.

④ *So faa* on the top of the sim at Wat Xieng Thong.

The sim is the ordination hall, where devout worship takes place and monks are ordained.

As the main focus of worship, the sim is often elaborately decorated.

← The layout of Wat Xieng Thong in Luang Prabang

Did You Know?

The Phra Bang Buddha, seen as a symbol of the right to rule Laos, is said to bring bad luck to unworthy rulers.

ROYAL PALACE COMPLEX

D3 **Sisavang Vong Rd** **8:30am-11:30am & 1:30pm-3:30pm Wed-Mon**

Once the center of the royal city, this riverside palace sits in the shadow of Mount Phou Si. Designed by French architects and built in 1904, the main buildings blend the Beaux Arts style with traditional Lao elements. When the monarchy was overthrown in 1975, the country's Communist rulers converted the palace into the National Museum.

National Museum

The center of the complex is the palace itself, an elegant single-story building built in a double cruciform layout. The palm-lined ceremonial approach leads to a gable above the main entrance decorated with a gilded relief of a three-headed elephant protected by a parasol and surrounded by intertwined *nagas* – the symbol of the Lan Xang Hom Khao Kingdom.

Visitors pass through the royal reception room, home to murals painted by French artist Alex De Fautereau in the 1930s. These are idyllic representations of life in old Luang

↑ Ceremonial driveway leading to the main entrance of the National Museum

EAT

Tangor
Just around the corner from the Royal Palace, this stylish lunch spot uses local, seasonal produce to create a tasty fusion of French and Asian cuisine.

🏠 63 Sisavang Vong Rd
Ⓦ thetangor.com

Ⓢ Ⓢ Ⓢ

↑ Wat Ho Phra Bang at sunset, with the Luang Prabang Night Market in the foreground

Prabang. Behind the throne room, which is decorated with mosaics, lie the former private quarters of the royal family. The furniture in both the king's and queen's bedchambers remains and is surprisingly spartan. The final stop is a hall reserved for diplomatic gifts, notably some moon rocks and a plaque from US President Richard Nixon. This hall also has two large portraits of King Sisavang Vatthana and Queen Kampoui, painted by a Soviet artist.

Royal Palace Car Collection

An open-fronted pavilion houses the private fleet of Sisavang Vong and Sisavang Vatthana. The collection includes a pair of cream-colored Lincoln Continentals, shipped in from the USA in the 1960s, and a 1958 Edsel Citation.

Wat Ho Phra Bang

To the left of palace's main entrance lies Wat Ho Phra Bang. This gilded temple is akin to the older sacred architecture of Luang Prabang, but it is a modern structure, only completed in 2011 to house the Phra Bang Buddha. This 33-inch (83-cm) statue is made of an alloy of gold, bronze, and silver. Legend has it that it was brought to Southeast Asia from Sri Lanka

↑ Novice monks admiring a statue of King Sisavang Vong in the grounds of the Royal Palace

sometime in the 1st millennium CE to aid the spread of Theravada Buddhism.

Royal Ballet Theatre

The modest white building to the left of the main gate is home to the Royal Ballet Theater. Before the abolition of the monarchy, the palace housed a royal dance troupe, which appeared during court rituals and entertained the king. In 1999 a troupe was reformed by the provincial government, and dancers now lay on two-hour performances four nights a week.

> A gable above the main entrance is decorated with a gilded relief of a three-headed elephant.

EXPERIENCE MORE

Mount Phou Si and That Chomsi

📍 D3 🏛 Sisavang Vong Rd
🕒 8am–6pm daily

Meaning Sacred Mountain in Lao, Mount Phou Si is perhaps the best-known landmark in Luang Prabang. The hill, and the 79-ft- (24-m-) high That Chomsi (a four-sided stupa), on its summit, are visited by locals on the first day of the Lao New Year.

There are three sets of stairs leading to the summit – one from the Royal Palace Complex (p174), where the entry fee is collected, another from the Nam Khan's side, and a third that winds up from behind Wat Siphoutabath. Visitors will find a couple of old temples on the lower slopes of the hill as they make their way up the 328 steps leading to That Chomsi.

The stupa, dating from 1804, is more impressive when seen from afar; the adjacent sim is rather basic. There are resting places en route but the stunning views of the city from the top make the climb worthwhile.

Wat Siphoutabath

📍 D3 🏛 Phou Si Rd
🕒 8am–5pm daily

This Thai-style temple, constructed in 1851, takes its name from the stylized Buddha footprint located above the temple on the path to Mount Phou Si. In the same compound as Wat Siphoutabath is another temple, Wat Pa Khe, whose name is sometimes used to refer to the whole complex. Of particular interest are the bas-relief carvings of Dutch merchants on the doors and

Monks descending the steps from the stupa atop Mount Phou Si

window shutters of the two temples. Well executed and in typical Lao style, they are depicted wearing tricorn hats with feathers, tall boots, and with a parrot on each shoulder. The window shutters show a long-haired Westerner with a dog at his feet.

Traditional Arts and Ethnology Center

📍 D3 🏛 Between Dara Market and Mt Phou Si
🕒 9am–6pm Tue–Sun
🌐 taeclaos.org

This museum, housed in the restored home of a French judge at the base of Mount Phou Si, offers an excellent insight into the cultures of Laos. Guided tours are offered by prior arrangement. The museum focuses on the preservation and interpretation of traditional arts, crafts, lifestyles, and culture. Its permanent collection displays more than 200 objects from 17 minority groups. These include clothing, religious artifacts, and household objects, as well as jewelry. The museum's fair-trade shop sells handicrafts made by local artisans at competitive prices. There is also an excellent café serving food and drinks, with great views of the distant mountains.

> ### HANDICRAFTS
>
> Luang Prabang is a great place to hunt out handicrafts, with both high-end treasures and inexpensive souvenirs readily available in the shops. Fabrics to look out for include Hmong cotton throws and runners with intricate designs and geometric patterns. More quirky items include jewelry and cutlery made from recycled bomb casings, and sa paper, made from the bark of mulberry trees.

Luang Prabang's daily Tak Bat ritual is an impressive spectacle, but it's important not to treat it as a mere photo opportunity. Behave as you would at any religious ceremony: dress modestly, stay quiet, and keep a respectful distance from participants. If you insist on taking photos do so unobtrusively and without using a flash.

Wat Mai Suwannaphumaham

Q C3 **A** Sisavang Vong Rd
C 8am–5pm daily

Among the most important wats in Luang Prabang, the Wat Mai Suwannaphumaham temple has an opulent exterior covered in red, black, and gold stencil. Inaugurated in 1788, its construction took almost 70 years. While restorations have taken place several times, it is one of the few temples in Luang Prabang to have survived in its original form. The wat is revered because it was, for decades, the home of the Pha Sangkharat, the most senior monk in Laos. It is also important because the sacred Phabang statue (p167), the guardian talisman of Luang Prabang, was kept here between 1894 and 1947.

The structure of the wat is influenced by both the Luang Prabang style and vernacular architecture. Its sim has an impressive five-tiered roof with gilded bas-reliefs on the front veranda. Vivid scenes from the national epic of the Lao people, *Phra Lak Phra Lam* – a deity-filled tale from one of Buddha's former existences – cover some panels, along with scenes of Lao village life.

Wat Xieng Mouan

Q D3 **A** Sotika Kuman Rd
C 8am–3pm daily

The construction of this temple was ordered by King Chantarath (r. 1851–72) in 1853 to house some particularly melodious temple drums that he had acquired. Consequently, the original name of the temple meant Monastery of the Melodious Sounds. For reasons lost in time, the name has changed to mean Monastery of the Amusing City. A school on the premises of the temple, inaugurated by UNESCO with a grant from the Norwegian government, aims to preserve traditional art forms in Laos.

Novice monks produce various forms of traditional arts and crafts, such as stenciling, wood carving, lacquerwork, and cement sculpture. These products are on display in a small exhibition hall. The sim of the temple features a veranda encircling the entire building, with impressive columns in the front.

Did You Know?

Legend has it that Buddha visited Luang Prabang, and prophesied that it would one day become a wealthy capital.

Fabulously ornate doorway at Wat Xieng Mouan ↑

Wat Choum Khong

D3 **Sotika Kuman Rd**
8am–5pm daily

Located next to Wat Xieng Mouan, Wat Choum Khong is accessible via a passage that connects the two compounds. It was originally constructed in 1843, though the temple has been restored several times since, most recently with the help of students from the school in Wat Xieng Mouan. According to legend, the wat takes its name from an image of the Buddha, which was cast here from a bronze *khong* (gong). A variety of modern but attractively styled Buddha images depicting the various *mudras* (hand positions) used in classical Buddhist statuary have been placed among the rows of shrubs and trees within the garden of this temple, which is particularly verdant and well kept. The ordination hall of the wat is in classic Luang Prabang style, with a heavily gilded lintel above the center of three elaborate front doors, eaves with curved brackets, and recessed windows.

→ Seated Buddha at Wat Choum Khong

Wat Pa Phai

D3 **Off Sisavang Vattana Rd** **8am–5pm daily**

The name of this wat means Bamboo Forest Monastery, but the origin of this appellation is unclear. The original date of its construction is also debatable, placed either at 1645 or 1815. There is a Siamese influence on the architectural style of the wat, apparent from the narrow base and high, steep roof lines. The main feature is the ornate pediment surrounding the doorway to the sim, decorated with a protruding peacock motif festooned with colored glass mosaic tiles. This archway rises in three successive levels, and *nagas* mingle with birds in flight. The door panels depict a leaping figure of Rama holding a staff, trouncing the head of a lion.

🔟 School of Fine Arts

D2 **Sotika Kuman Rd** **(071)-212-047** **8am–4pm daily**

Signposted in French as the École des Beaux Arts, this single-story building in a tree-filled compound dates from the 1920s, and is an excellent example of the Colonial-era architecture of the period. With an aim to promote traditional Lao art, the School of Fine Arts offers a four-year certificate program for students who have completed their secondary education. Specialized courses include painting, sculpture, graphic art, ceramics, metalwork, traditional drawing, and lacquerwork. There is also provision for an 18-month internship (post-graduation) in a student's hometown. The school plays a major role in ensuring the continuation of traditional art and craft in Laos. There is also an exhibition center in the complex that displays and sells beautiful paintings, carvings, and sculptures made by the students.

⓫ Wat Nong Sikhunmuang

D2 **Sotika Kuman Rd** **8am–3pm daily**

Originally constructed with wood in 1729, during the reign of King Inta Som, Wat

DRINK

Icon Klub

Less a club and more a cozy bar, this popular spot is located behind wooden shutters in an elegant old house. The cocktails are excellent, as is the live guitar music.

D3 **Sakkarin Rd** **iconklub.com**

$$$

Maolin Tavern

This brick-walled bar has an unpretentious atmosphere with a pool table. There's also a great range of local and imported beers.

D3 **Sisavangvong Rd** **(856)-2059-485-241**

$$$

↑ Vividly painted red and gold exterior of Wat Sene

Nong Sikhunmuang was completely destroyed by a fire in 1774. The only surviving artifact from the original temple is a bronze statue of the Buddha known as Pha Sao Ong Sanesakid. The statue was originally brought here by a local merchant whose raft grounded mysteriously near the temple after a harrowing journey downriver from Thailand.

The current structure, restored by Thai artisans in the 19th century, is rather contemporary, and painted in bright colors. Of architectural interest is the elaborate roof referred to as *dok so faa (p173)*; its 15 parasols suggest a royal connection since parasols are symbolic of royalty in Laos. Staircases on either side of the temple are adorned with *naga* balustrades.

This temple attracts many Buddhist visitors, particularly during festivals, because of the Pha Sao Ong Sanesakid. Now housed in the wat's sim, the sacred statue is said to be endowed with special powers to grant the wishes of supplicants.

Wat Sene

Q E2 **⌂ Sakkarin Rd**
⊙ 8am–5pm daily

This Thai-style temple was built in 1714, and restored in 1957 to commemorate the 2,500th year of the Buddhist era. Located prominently on Sakkarin Road, the central road of Luang Prabang, this is the first in a series of temples that line the street for about 650 ft (200 m). With a stunningly beautiful exterior of bright red and gold, the wat is well-known as the storage space for two of the largest and most attractive boats used in the annual Souang Heua boat racing festival *(p150)*. The sim is similarly painted a brilliant red, and covered with stencils depicting a menagerie of mythical animals. The interior

> ## Did You Know?
>
> Wat Sene - Temple of 100,000 Treasures - is said to have been built with 100,000 stones from the Mekong.

of the wat is also intricately decorated. A smaller chapel at the front of the wat houses a Standing Buddha image and an immense drum and gong. These are used to signal the *wan sin* (holy days) of Buddhism. An adjacent upright carved stone tablet portrays a stylized footprint of the Buddha.

Wat Si Boun Huang

Q E2 **⌂ Sakkarin Rd**
⊙ 8am–5pm daily

Located just up the street from Wat Sene, past Wat Sop, this temple is said to have been constructed during the reign of King Sotika Kuman (r. 1749–68). The four columns in front of the veranda of the relatively small sim carry lotus petal capitals. Notable here is the gable above the superbly decorated doors depicting a Buddhist symbol known as the *Dharmachakra*, or the Wheel of Law *(p29)*, which symbolizes rebirth. The roof of the wat, typical of the Luang Prabang style, has only two tiers, but its edge is lined with elegant and understated replicas of classical temple roof finials, known as *so faa*.

Wat Khili

E2 **Sakkarin Rd**
8am–5pm daily

This wat is a rare example of the ornate style of temples built in the mountainous Xieng Khuang province. Its full name, Wat Souvanna Khili, can be translated to mean Monastery of the Golden Mountain. It was built in 1779 by Prince Chao Kham Sattha, who came from that region, and its construction is said to have established a good relationship between the two rival principalities of Xieng Khuang and Luang Prabang.

The Xieng Khuang style of sim is characterized by a wide and low profile. The front wall of Wat Khili's sim is decorated with six beautiful Tree of Life mosaics – smaller versions of the now famous mosaic on the back of Wat Xieng Thong's sim (p170). The wat's window shutters are ornately carved with various depictions of Prince Siddhartha, later known as the Buddha, while the gables above are alive with bas-reliefs of zoomorphic phantasmagoria. Near the front of the wat stands an incongruous two-story building blending Colonial-era and traditional Buddhist styles of architecture.

Wat Aham

D4 **Phommathat Rd**
8am–5pm daily

This wat is situated outside the main peninsular grid of the Old Town, across the street from a charming residential neighborhood of winding lanes. There are two huge banyan trees in the temple grounds, said to house the spirits of the guardian deities of the city, Phu Noe and Na Noe. The

---

UNESCO Maison du Patrimoine

E2 **Sakkarin Rd**

Located at the far northern end of the Luang Prabang peninsula, the UNESCO Maison du Patrimoine is an imposing but graceful structure that provides a contrast to the Buddhist temples and simple residences that characterize the neighborhood. This two-story building, dating from 1932, was once the Customs House of the ruling French colonial government. From here, duties were levied on all Lao exports, the most lucrative of which was opium.

This attractive building now belongs to the Lao government, and is the headquarters of UNESCO consultants who advise local authorities on urban conservation, and on the administration of the World Heritage Site status that was bestowed on Luang Prabang in 1995. Now referred to as La Maison du Patrimoine, or Heritage House, the large windows and high ceilings of the building present an excellent example of Colonial-era architecture.

Although the interior is not open to the public, visitors are welcome to take a leisurely stroll through the large and well-kept garden surrounding the building.

---

shaggy-haired and red-faced effigies representing these spirits are kept in the grounds of the temple, and are carried at the head of a procession during Lao New Year. The green compound also houses an attractive sim with statues from the *Phra Lak Phra Lam* epic guarding its front doors. The Corinthian-style columns of the sim are artistically decorated with lotus buds, while the gable on the back of the sim is decorated with murals depicting the Buddha addressing his followers.

Wat Visounarat

D4 **Phommathat Rd**
8am–5pm daily

Named after King Visounarat (the king who was then on the throne), this temple was originally constructed in 1512, making it the oldest surviving Buddhist place of worship in the city. Located adjacent to Wat Aham, and connected to it by an arched passageway, the temple is also known as Wat Visoun. The door panels on the sim depict Hindu deities, and a gilded screen inside portrays a battle from the Hindu epic *Ramayana*.

In front of the temple's sim lies one of Luang Prabang's most famous landmarks, *that makmo*, meaning watermelon stupa. Officially, however, it is

---

SHOP

Handicraft Night Market

There are some real treasures to be found among the souvenirs on offer in the open-air market that sets up at 5:30pm each evening in the heart of town.

D3 **Sisavang Vong Rd**

→

Scenes from the life of Buddha and his first disciples at Wat Manolom

referred to as *that phatum*, meaning lotus stupa, named for its bulbous, hemispherical shape. The original stupa was razed by Chinese Black Flag Haw marauders in 1887 and was rebuilt in 1898 under the patronage of King Sakkarin Kamuk. In 1914, it was struck by lightning, revealing a cache of gold, bronze, and crystal Buddha images that the marauders had missed. These treasures are now on display at the Royal Palace Complex (*p174*).

Wat Manolom

⬛ C5 ⬛ Manomai Rd ⬛ 8am-5pm daily

Located on the site of an earlier temple raised by King Fa Ngum, the founder of the Lan Xang Dynasty, Wat Manolom is situated in a quiet residential area 1 mile (2 km) west of the center of the Old Town area of Luang Prabang. For almost 11 years it served as the first home of the sacred Phabang statue (*p167*). The current sim was built in 1972 and has an intricately engraved door at the northern entrance, flanked by a pair of lions. A revered statue of the Buddha –

made of bronze, 20 ft (6 m) high, weighing 2 tons (2,000 kg), and badly damaged by Chinese Black Flag Haw marauders in 1887 – is now housed inside the sim. This long-eared statue is Thai-Sukhothai in style. Inside the wat compound is a group of gold stupas resembling the famous Pha That Luang (*p165*) in Vientiane.

Wat That Luang

⬛ C4 ⬛ Wat That Luang Rd, near Phu Vao Rd ⬛ 8am-5pm daily

Built in 1818, this temple located fairly close to Wat Manolom is one of the most important in Luang Prabang. The wat houses the ashes of King Sisavang Vong (r. 1904–59), whose funeral chariot is kept in Wat Xieng Thong (*p170*). That Luang means Royal Stupa, and the *dok so faa* ornamentation with the 15 parasols on the roof of the sim denotes the temple's royal status. The sim is noteworthy for its gold and silver-lacquered door panels depicting various divinities. Next to it is an elegant stupa, now weathered black.

EAT

Tamarind

This is one of the best places in town to try traditional Lao dishes. The tasting platters are a specialty, and the service is excellent. The restaurant has a cookery school offering day and evening classes, the former including a shopping trip to the market.

⬛ E2 ⬛ Kingkitsarat Rd ⬛ tamarindlaos.com

Dyen Sabai

Tables are set in individual bamboo pavilions at this secluded restaurant across the Nam Khan river. It specializes in innovative modern Lao cuisine.

⬛ E3 ⬛ Ban Aphai ⬛ dyensabairestaurant. wordpress.com

20

Wats on the West Bank

D1 **West Bank of the Mekong River** **From Wat Xieng Thong or behind the National Museum Complex** **8am–5pm daily**

Boatmen on the river steps of Wat Xieng Thong (p170) can be hired to take you across to the west bank of the Mekong, where there are several rural wats. The first is Wat Long Khun, the Monastery of the Happy or Blessed Song, where prospective kings of Laos would meditate before their coronation. Interesting but faded murals depict Chinese gentlemen in elaborate costumes. A short distance upstream lies the small, abandoned cave-shrine of Wat Tham Xieng Maen.

A path downstream along the river from Wat Long Khun leads to the bottom of a hill. From here a steep flight of steps ascends to Wat Chom Phet, which is more renowned for its spectacular views than its architectural or cultural interest. The last stop, Wat Xieng Men, is about 2 miles (3 km) downstream. Although it can be reached on foot, it is much easier to go by boat. Built in the second half of the 16th century, the wat's small but well-proportioned

sim has an elaborate three-tiered roof, with separate eaves covering the front veranda. The portico above the front door is intricately decorated, as are both the exterior and interior columns.

21

Santi Chedi

F5 **3 miles (5 km) E of Luang Prabang** **8am–5pm daily**

Built in 1988 with donations from an affluent Lao living abroad, Wat Phra Pone Phao, popularly known as Santi Chedi (Peace Pagoda), is a forest meditation retreat. A particular favorite with most visitors to Luang Prabang, this golden, bell-shaped stupa is visible from various spots in the city. Located on a hilltop along the banks of the Nam Khan, it offers excellent views of the city, particularly from the upper story of the outer terrace, which make it worth the climb. En route to the terrace are walls decorated with brightly colored murals. As well as the standard *Jataka* tales that recount the lives and deeds of Buddha, these murals portray, in detail, the gruesome punishments awaiting sinners in hell.

Making decorative *sa* paper in Ban Xang Khong ↑

22

Ban Phanom and Mouhot's Tomb

B2 **4 miles (6 km) E of Luang Prabang Tomb** **9am–5pm daily**

Ban Phanom is populated by people of the Thai Lue community, who traditionally inhabit the areas around Luang Nam Tha and Muang Sing. The Thai Lue were required to serve the palace as weavers and dancers, since their women were famous for both these skills. Although their dance traditions eventually disappeared,

Golden stupa of Santi Chedi, overlooking the Nam Khan ↑

the weaving of both cotton and silk continues today. The locals sell their goods from their homes or at the village craft center.

About 3 miles (5 km) beyond Ban Phanom, approached by an unpaved but well-marked road, lies the tomb of the French explorer Alexandre-Henri Mouhot. The first Westerner to visit Luang Prabang, Mouhot contracted malaria and died there in

ALEXANDRE-HENRI MOUHOT (1826-61)

The French explorer Mouhot was the first to bring Angkor Wat to international attention. It was his vivid description (published in English after the French showed little interest in his journals) that spread the word about the glories of Angkor in Europe. Mouhot later continued his travels in Luang Prabang, which he described as "a little paradise."

1861, aged 35. His tomb was discovered in 1990 and restored by representatives from his hometown in France. The simple, whitewashed tomb, surrounded by trees, has a small statue of the explorer standing nearby.

23

Ban Xang Khong

🅰B2 ⏰3 miles (5 km) E of Luang Prabang 🕒9am–5pm daily

A picturesque village nestled on the banks of the Mekong River, Ban Xang Khong is a haven for traditional Lao art and craft. The village was originally known for its intricate weaving of textiles by artisans who live and work in houses scattered along the dirt road running parallel to the river. Today, however, local artisans have also taken to producing attractive *sa* paper, which is made from the bark of the mulberry, or sa, tree. Here, visitors can watch local craftsmen and women at work, and purchase products directly from the makers.

> **The milky waters rush over natural limestone formations, falling into clear turquoise-colored pools that are ideal for swimming and bathing.**

24

Tat Sae Waterfalls

🅰B2 ⏰11 miles (18 km) SE of Luang Prabang 🚌From Ban En 🕒8am–5:30pm daily

Located on a tributary of the Nam Khan, a tuk-tuk ride from Luang Prabang, are the beautiful Tat Sae Waterfalls. The milky waters rush over natural limestone formations, falling into clear turquoise-colored pools that are ideal for swimming and bathing. In the dry season, though, they are reduced to a mere trickle. Nevertheless, it continues to be a popular spot.

The area around the falls is usually quite busy on the weekend; for a more peaceful experience, visit mid-week. Other attractions in the area include a zipline tour that takes adventure-seekers high above the forest canopy.

25

Tat Kuang Si Waterfalls

🅰B2 ⏰20 miles (32 km) SW of Luang Prabang 🚌From Luang Prabang, then tuk-tuk 🕒8am–5:30pm daily

The spectacular, multitiered Tat Kuang Si Waterfalls make an ideal day trip from Luang Prabang, either by road or by boat along the Mekong. Water gushes over the 197-ft- (60-m-) high limestone form-ations, and collects in azure pools at the base of the falls.

The lower levels are great for a picnic, with food vendors offering the usual grilled fish or chicken. A trail ascending to the left of the falls leads to a much quieter set of pools above the main falls, and a second trail leads to more pools and a cave. Take care while climbing as the area around the falls is slippery.

Tat Kuang Si Waterfalls, near Luang Prabang

A SHORT WALK
OLD TOWN

Distance 1.4 miles (2.2 km) **Nearest Ferry Pier** Off Suvanbanlang **Time** 30 minutes

The southern end of the Luang Prabang peninsula has several attractions: the Mekong and Nam Khan rivers, a vibrant morning market, and religious and secular architecture. The National Museum Complex, which lies between the Mekong and Mount Phou Si, was constructed by the French between 1904 and 1909 as a residence for King Sisavang Vong. It can be reached by a staircase lined with frangipani trees. The wats here range from the rustic Wat Siphoutabath to the splendid Wat Mai Suwannaphumaham. This area also has an assortment of shops, boutique hotels, art galleries, cafés, and restaurants.

MEKONG RIVER

SUVANBANLANG

SOTIKA KOMAN RD

SISAVANG VONG ROAD

Two Chinese gods guard the entrance to **Wat Choum Khong** *(p178), which was completed in 1856. The temple is surrounded by a verdant garden, ideal for relaxing. The sim is encircled by sculptures of the Buddha in various poses.*

A unique blend of French and Lao architectural styles, the **National Museum** *building (p174) houses the sacred Phabang statue. Of equal interest is the throne room with its glass mosaics, as well as the royal artifacts on display.*

Elaborate gilded bas-reliefs, which depict scenes from the Phra Lak Phra Lam, the Lao version of the Ramayana, *adorn the front veranda of* **Wat Mai Suwanna-phumaham** *(p177).*

START

Did You Know?

Luang Prabang's signature dish is a soup known as *lam*. Try it in a restaurant like Tamarind *(p181)*.

0 meters 100
0 yards 100

N ↑

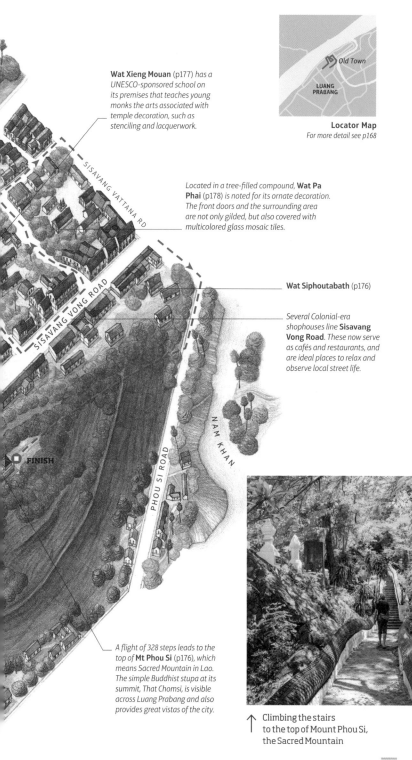

Wat Xieng Mouan (p177) *has a UNESCO-sponsored school on its premises that teaches young monks the arts associated with temple decoration, such as stenciling and lacquerwork.*

SISAVANG VATTANA RD

SISAVANG VONG ROAD

Locator Map
For more detail see p168

Old Town

LUANG PRABANG

Located in a tree-filled compound, **Wat Pa Phai** (p178) *is noted for its ornate decoration. The front doors and the surrounding area are not only gilded, but also covered with multicolored glass mosaic tiles.*

Wat Siphoutabath (p176)

Several Colonial-era shophouses line **Sisavang Vong Road***. These now serve as cafés and restaurants, and are ideal places to relax and observe local street life.*

PHOU SI ROAD

NAM KHAN

FINISH

A flight of 328 steps leads to the top of **Mt Phou Si** (p176), *which means Sacred Mountain in Lao. The simple Buddhist stupa at its summit, That Chomsi, is visible across Luang Prabang and also provides great vistas of the city.*

↑ Climbing the stairs to the top of Mount Phou Si, the Sacred Mountain

NORTHERN LAOS

Northern Laos may seem isolated, but it lies at a political and geographical crossroad, sharing borders with Thailand, Myanmar, Vietnam, and China. This strategic geographic location has resulted in great periods of turbulence in its history. While the region benefited from regular cross-border trade with the Thais and the Vietnamese, it also had to endure hostility, not only from its trading partners, but also from the Burmese, who periodically invaded Laos during the 16th century. Westerners, such as the French and the Dutch, have coveted the resources and river routes of Northern Laos, and its location as a strategic buffer zone cost it dearly during the 19th century. Today, the region's many wonders, from its charming towns to thickly forested hills and mountains, are slowly opening up to tourism, and visitors will find an enchanting array of places and activities to choose from.

NORTHERN LAOS

Must Sees
1. Vang Vieng
2. Muang Sing
3. Plain of Jars

Experience More
4. Phonsavan
5. Sam Neua
6. Vieng Xai
7. Nong Khiaw
8. Muang Ngoi
9. Muang Khua
10. Phongsali
11. Luang Nam Tha
12. Ban Nam Di
13. Nam Ha National Protected Area
14. Bokeo Nature Reserve

Ban Nakhua

Phou Sam Sao

Son La

Tran Phu

Vinh Yen

Ma

Hat Lot

Ban Thai

Moc Chau

Hoa Binh

MUANG NGOI

Nam Mai

Ban Nahoy

Ban Sop Long

Muong Khen

Ban Kenpha

Ban Sop Hao

Vieng Kham

SAM NEUA 5   6 VIENG XAI

VIETNAM

Pak Xeng

Ban Sakok

Phu Leuy 6,765 ft (2,062 m)

Nam Sam

Nam Xoi

Phou Luang

Taat Saloei

Phu Nampa 5,997 ft (1,828 m)

Phu Bo 5,712 ft (1,741 m)

Ngoc Lac

Vieng Thong

Ban Khong

Sam Tai

Tho Xuan

Phu Phasiphu 003 ft (1,525 m)

HUA PHAN

XIENG KHUANG

Nam Neun

Muang Kham

Ban Soplan

Ban Tao

Phu Huatt 2,452m

Nhu Xuan

ang Sui

Ban Pakho

Hieu

Quy Chau

Xieng Khouang Airport

PHONSAVAN

Nong Haet

Tuong Duong

Ca

Thai Hoa

PLAIN OF JARS 3   4

Ban Xieng Di

Muang Khoun

Ban Xiang Khong

Phu Muang Nga 7,894 ft (2,406 m)

Tan Ky

Dien Chau

Phu Samsum 8,599 ft (2,621 m)

Do Luong

Ban Hatdiat

Annam Highlands

Muang Huong

CENTRAL AND SOUTHERN LAOS p204

Vinh

Bolikham

BOLIKHAMSAI

Phu Luang 4,816 ft (1,468 m)

Lak Sao

ong River

Ban Namsang

Ban Boneng

Nong Waeng

THAILAND

Songkhram

Mekong River

Phen

Sawan Daen Din

Akat Amuai

0 kilometers   50

0 miles   50

N

don Thani

Udon Thani International Airport

Limestone karsts surrounding the Nam Song river at dusk in Vang Vieng ↑

❶ VANG VIENG

Ⓐ C2 Ⓐ 90 miles (150 km) N of Vientiane 🚌 Bus Route 13
ℹ️ Luang Prabang Street; (023)-511-707

Surrounded by majestic limestone karst peaks, Vang Vieng has long been a magnet for visitors to Laos. The place is no longer the quiet riverside village that first caught travelers' attention, but in the past decade or so the emphasis has shifted from no-holds-barred budget partying to classy mid-range accommodations and well-organized outdoor adventures. The main attractions are beyond Vang Vieng itself – with hiking, rock climbing, and a range of river activities available.

①
Tham Jang

Ⓐ 1 mile (1.5 km) SW of Vang Vieng Ⓒ 8–11:30am & 1–4:30pm daily

The surrounding limestone peaks are riddled with caves, and Tham Jang is one of the most easily accessible, located a short distance across the Nam Song. The cave was used as a bunker during the invasion of Chinese marauders in the late 19th century. Today it is approached by a flight of stairs leading to its mouth. Visitors can follow the well-marked path within, and emerge at a second, higher entrance, which offers a fantastic view over the valley.

It is also possible to swim in the spring at the mouth of the cave and follow it for about 160 ft (50 m) inside.

②
Tham Phu Kham

Ⓐ 5 miles (8 km) W of Vang Vieng Ⓒ 8am–4:30pm daily

This atmospheric cave makes a fascinating destination for a half-day trip from Vang Vieng. The cave is considered sacred

↑ Buddhist shrine in the main cavern of Tham Phu Kham

BLUE LAGOONS

Although much of the action in Vang Vieng takes place along the main Nam Song river, there are other relaxing places to go for a dip here. So-called Blue Lagoon 1 lies to the west of town near the Nam Xay viewpoint, and is often busy with tourists swimming and tubing. Blue Lagoon 2 lies further south and is much quieter, while Blue Lagoon 3, around 11 miles (17 km) from town, is even lesser known, and often empty. The names are misleading, though; these are not lagoons but streams. They are, however, very blue.

Did You Know?

During the Vietnam War, the US built an air force base in Vang Vieng, known to pilots as Lima Site 6.

by locals, and it houses a large bronze reclining Buddha, as well as several other smaller Buddha images. Tunnels branch off the main cavern and shrine, which visitors can explore if they bring a flashlight or if they are on an organized tour.

Tham Phu Kham is also known as the Blue Lagoon because of an azure stream running in front of the cave. It's a great spot for a refreshing dip among the fishes after you've explored the cave. There are also various stalls nearby selling drinks and snacks.

The journey from Vang Vieng to the cave passes through majestic karst landscapes, and can be made on foot, by bicycle, or in a hired tuk-tuk.

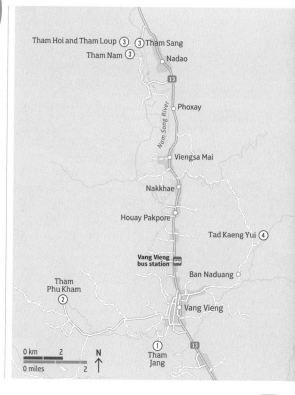

Tham Hoi and Tham Loup ③ ③ Tham Sang
Tham Nam ③
Nadao

Nam Song River

Phoxay

Viengsa Mai

Nakkhae

Houay Pakpore

Tad Kaeng Yui ④

Vang Vieng bus station

Ban Naduang

Tham Phu Kham ②

Vang Vieng

0 km   2
0 miles   2

N

① Tham Jang

EAT

A.M.D. Restaurant

Although it lies away from the center of town, the hearty food at this family-run place always draws the crowds.

📍 Viengkeo Rd, Vang Vieng 📞 (020)-553-012-38

Crabe d'Or

Overlooking the Mekong in the Riverside Boutique Resort, this place serves superb Lao classics like *kaeng juud look sin kai* (ginger and chicken soup). There's also a Western menu.

📍 Ban Viengkeo 🌐 riversidevang vieng.com

Tham Sang Triangle

📍 8 miles (13 km) N of Vang Vieng ⏰ 8am–4:30pm daily

A group of four caves, the Tham Sang Triangle is a popular spot for day-trippers. The first of these caves is called Tham Sang, Elephant Cave, due to the pachyderm-shaped stalagmites within. A clearly marked path from here leads to the entrances of Tham Hoi and Tham Loup. Tham Hoi is a sacred cave with a large Buddha image at the entrance, while Tham Loup, the more attractive of the two, has a series of impressive stalactite formations. The final stop is Tham Nam, meaning water cave, a quarter of a mile (400 m) south of Tham Hoi. Depending on the season, it is possible to wade into the cave or to rent a tube to go in.

Tad Kaeng Yui

📍 4 miles (6 km) N of Vang Vieng

These two 100-ft- (30-m-) high waterfalls make for a peaceful and picturesque half-day trip from Vang Vieng. Set deep in the forest, Tad Kaeng Yui remains relatively off the beaten track, and is accessed by a small dirt track from Vang Vieng. The terrain is rough and steep to climb, so unless you are an experienced hiker it is best to take a tuk-tuk, or hire a motorbike for the journey. There's a car park next to the waterfalls, with a handful of stalls selling barbecued food and drinks. The bamboo shelters around the cascades are perfect for a cool, refreshing picnic. Farther down from the waterfalls there is a deep pool that is great for swimming in.

↑ Sunset over the magnificent karst landscape surrounding Vang Vieng

ACTIVITIES IN VANG VIENG

Vang Vieng is the adventure sports capital of Laos. The most straightforward activities involve exploring the network of trails through the countryside on foot or on a rented motorbike, but there are plenty of more adventurous options.

Tubing
Tubing along the Nam Song is Vang Vieng's signature activity, and these days it comes without the dangerous addition of alcohol. Inflated tractor inner tubes are available for rent in town, with a drop-off 3 miles (5 km) north of town included in the fee.

Mountain Biking
Cycling is a great way to explore the region. The trails on the west side of the Nam Song are idyllic, although tough in places. Bikes are available to rent in town, and most places provide a basic map of the area showing the main trails.

Rock Climbing
Vang Vieng has emerged as one of the top climbing destinations in the region. The most developed spots are near Tham Non, north of town. Sports climbing dominates here, and most established routes are bolted. Beginners can learn the ropes with several climbing schools based in town.

Kayaking
Kayaking has now surpassed tubing as the must-do Vang Vieng river activity. For beginners, gentle guided trips on the Nam Song include stops to explore caves and villages. More serious paddlers can tackle the rapids on the nearby Nam Ngum. Green Discovery (www.greendiscoverylaos.com) is one of the most reputable kayaking operators.

Ziplining
Ziplines around Vang Vieng are no longer lax affairs rigged up by riverside party bars. Instead, serious tour operators have installed proper harnessed cables that allow for thrilling rides over forest or water.

1. Tubing down the Nam Song.

2. Mountain bikers on the rural trails around Vang Vieng.

3. Rock climber in Tham Non.

4. Kayakers on the Nam Song.

5. Ziplining over the Nam Song near Vang Vieng.

↑ Vendors selling fresh produce from baskets at the Morning Market

2

MUANG SING

🅰 B1 🅒 42 miles (68 km) NW of Luang Nam Tha
🚌 Near Morning Market 🛈 Route 17b; (086)-213-021

Tranquil Muang Sing is the archetypal provincial Lao town, set on a broad plain and ringed by green hills. It remains off the tourist radar, which is something of a mystery, given its beautiful setting, ample hiking opportunities, and lively Morning Market. The Chinese border is just 5 miles (8 km) to the north, and the influence of the gargantuan northern neighbor is increasingly obvious on the streets here.

①

Muang Sing Exhibition Museum

🅰 Northern left corner of Route 17b 🕘 9am–4pm Mon–Fri

Housed in the former home of a local prince, the well-proportioned wooden structure of Muang Sing Exhibition Museum is as impressive as the exhibits within. The museum focuses on the area's many different communities, with displays of clothing, musical instruments, religious artifacts, and tools. Upstairs, there are panels explaining the history of Muang Sing and its important

role on the ancient trade route to China and Myanmar. There's an extra fee to watch an interesting 40-minute video on Akha culture.

↑ Buddha image and altar in Wat Luang Ban Xieng Jai

②

Morning Market

🅰 Northwest of town, near to bus terminal 🕘 7am–7pm daily

In the north of town, close to the bus station, this is a bustling hub for the people of the surrounding countryside, with no concessions made to tourists. The market operates all day, but is at its busiest between 7am and 10am, when women from outlying villages sell fresh greens from baskets. The permanent sections of the market, featuring mostly dry goods, are housed under tin roofs. There's plenty of street food available here for the adventurous, especially in the morning.

---

③

Wat Luang Ban Xieng Jai

🅰 Off Route 17b, behind the Muang Sing Exhibition Museum 🕘 8am–5pm daily

Located just behind the museum, this wat is among the most popular religious sights in town. It attracts hordes of worshipers, especially early in the morning, when it is

OPIUM: THE GOLDEN TRIANGLE

Muang Sing was once at the center of the Golden Triangle, the infamous region straddling the borders of Laos, Myanmar, and Thailand that was the main source of the world's opium. During the colonial era the drug became a major cash export, and in the 20th century heroin production stepped up a gear. Production has been greatly reduced since the early 21st century, though pockets of poppy-growing remain in remote areas.

particularly busy with locals from the outlying villages coming to worship and pay their respects. The wat's architectural style is typically Thai Lue, with silver-painted filigree fretwork on the exterior, and dramatic triple-headed *nagas* (serpents) on the balustrades. The interior is even more flamboyantly decorated, with colorful thongs (long prayer flags) hanging from the roof around the central Buddha image, which sits on a multicolored mosaic altar.

---

 ④

Former French Garrison

🏛 Off Route 17b, W of Kaysone Memorial
🚫 To the public

Once an important base for Moroccan and Senegalese troops posted here as part of the French army, this garrison is the most obvious Colonial-era relic in Muang Sing. Now belonging to the Lao Army, its crumbling brick ramparts and gateways are all that remain of what was once a strategic point where the spheres of French, British, and Chinese influence met. As an active army base, the garrison itself is off-limits, and photography is not permitted. But visitors can catch a glimpse of the atmospheric ruins from the street. A former French hospital also stands nearby.

⑤

Wat Nam Kaew Luang

🏛 Off Route 17b, near the beginning of the road to Xieng Kok ⏰ 8am–5pm daily

On the southern edge of town, this Buddhist temple sits in a compound shaded by palms and banyans. There are two beautifully decorated sims (prayer halls),

the smaller of which features a towering golden roof spire, and the larger of which has a lavish entrance porch decorated with carvings of *nagas*. The compound also includes a golden stupa. The monks' quarters were formerly a *wihan* (assembly hall). The complex is typical of the architectural style of the Thai Lue, who once dominated this area.

Ancient sandstone funerary jars scattered across the Plain of Jars ↑

3

PLAIN OF JARS

🗺 C2 ⏱ 6 miles (10 km) SW of Phonsavan ℹ Anfa Rd, Phonsavan; (061)-312-217; 8am–4pm daily

A region of gently rolling hills, the area southwest of Phonsavan is home to one of the great archaeological enigmas of Southeast Asia. Scattered across the countryside here are the mysterious stone jars that give the area its name. The largest are around 9 ft (3 m) tall, and it is thought that they were used as tombs, from around 2,500 years ago. The area was heavily bombed during the Vietnam War, but several thousand jars survived the onslaught. Unexploded landmines are still dotted around the countryside, so visitors must stick to the three official sites and not stray from marked paths.

①
Site 1: Thong Hai Hin

A total of 331 jars are scattered across a hillside at this, the most accessible site in the area, looking out over Phonsavan's airport. Among them is the single largest discovered jar, Hai Jeuam, weighing around 6 tons (5,445 kg). Local

legend has it that this vast receptacle was the wine cup of the mythical King Khun Cheum. The traces of more recent history are also plain to see here, with multiple bomb craters pocking the ground between the jars. As warning signs attest, unexploded ordinance also remains a problem so make sure you stick to the marked paths.

②
Site 2: Hai Hin Phu Salato

More than 90 jars sit across the slopes of two low, wooded hills here. The largest concentration lie on the eastern hillock, accessed by pathways branching off from a central

LOCAL LEGENDS

Various legends have sought to explain the existence of the huge urns that dot the Plain of Jars. The commonest tale has it that the area was once ruled by a benign giant, Khun Cheum, who created the jars to hold his vast supply of rice wine. Another legend, once taken seriously by archaeologists, has it that the jars were made to store rainwater to supply to passing travelers. A more likely explanation is that the jars were used in prehistoric burial rituals.

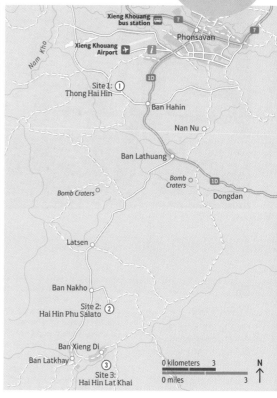

lane. Look out for a much-photographed jar through which a tree has grown, splitting the carved stone into several pieces. Another jar here has a curious marking resembling a frog. From the western hillock there are fine views across the surrounding meadows and rice fields, and the start of a

path that leads through beautifully bucolic countryside to Hai Hin Lat Khai. On the way, there are a number of pretty Hmong villages to explore. Near the entrance to Site 3, there is also a simple wooden monastery, Wat Xieng Di, with a large bomb-damaged Buddha.

Did You Know?

The Plain of Jars is peppered with bomb craters and unexploded landmines from the Vietnam War.

③

Site 3: Hai Hin Lat Khai

With an attractive location at the top of a hill offering fabulous views of the surrounding countryside, Site 3 lies on the outskirts of Ban Xieng Di, a village inhabited by the Phuan. From the ticket booth, a path crosses a small stream to the hilltop where the main cluster of jars is to be found. From here, other paths lead south and east to further clusters of jars. Be sure to stick to the paths here, as there may still be unexploded ordinance in this area – as suggested by several large bomb craters.

←
Bomb crater, created during the Vietnam War, in the Plain of Jars

←

Exploring the extraordinary caves at Vieng Xai

EXPERIENCE MORE

④ Phonsavan

🗺️ C2 🚗 132 miles (220 km) SE of Luang Prabang ✈️ 🚌 From Vientiane or Luang Prabang ℹ️ (061)-312-217

Capital of Xieng Khuang province, Phonsavan was built after the Vietnam War ended in 1975. With an airport offering transport links, it's a good jumping-off point for the Plain of Jars (p198) – though there is much more to see besides. The Mines Advisory Group's (MAG) Visitor Information Center, on Main Street, is an enlightening place. Although the war memorabilia on display can be disturbing, there is a wealth of absorbing information here. The surrounding hilltops, two of which are crowned by memorials to the Lao and Vietnamese wars, provide magnificent views of the town, hills, and plains.

Visitors will find **Mulberries Silk Farm** an inspiring stop. A fair-trade company dedicated to recreating a sustainable local economy, the organic farm grows mulberry bushes and spins its own silk, which is then hand-dyed and woven into garments and scarves. A number of classes and workshops are available.

Mulberries Silk Farm

🏠 No. 7 Rd, Ban Li, Meuang Pek District ⏰ 8am-4pm Mon-Sat 🌐 mulberries.org

⑤ Sam Neua

🗺️ C2 🚗 132 miles (220 km) NE of Phonsavan 🚌 From Phonsavan ℹ️ (064)-312-567

The capital of the northeast province of Hua Phan, Sam Neua lies nestled in a small valley that is often shrouded in fog. On clear days, however, the sparkling Nam Sam, which flows through this quiet town, is a pleasure to behold. This makes a pleasant stop on the way to the nearby Vieng Xai caves. Sam Neua is famous for the intricacy of its hand-woven textiles, which can be bought in the market close to the river, or at the homes of the weavers themselves. Directions to the weavers' homes are provided by the town's excellent local tourist office on the main street.

⑥   Vieng Xai

🗺️ D2 🚗 20 miles (32 km) E of Sam Neua 🚌 From Sam Neua ℹ️ Kaysone Phomvihane Memorial Cave Tour Office; (064)-314-321; open for guided tours only: 9am-1pm

Tucked away among the karst mountains of the Annamite Mountain Range near the Vietnamese border, this spectacular valley initially served as the shelter and hiding place for Pathet Lao leaders, including Kaysone Phomvihane (p154) and Prince Souphanouvong, during the Vietnam War (1954–75). The caves in the valley were used not just as their homes, but as communication centers, hospitals, and small factories. Also used as a secret military area, they were the location of prison camps where key members of the former regime, notably the royal family, were incarcerated.

It is also possible to visit another huge cave nearby where mass political rallies, and Socialist musical and theatrical performances were held.

> ### KARST LIMESTONE
>
> Northern Laos is home to ranks of impressive toothy peaks rearing over forests and rice fields. These karst outcrops are the result of water erosion over several million years. Mildly acidic rain forges tiny channels in the soluble limestone, which in time develop to become a fantastical network of caves and overhangs.

7

Nong Khiaw

C1 78 miles (126 km) NE of Luang Prabang From Luang Prabang From Luang Prabang or Muang Ngoi

The town of Nong Khiaw straddles the Nam Ou, split by an impressively tall bridge built by Chinese engineers in 1976. Most travelers arrive here from Luang Prabang by boat or road – the well-surfaced Route 13 runs along the river most of the way and offers pictur-esque views.

The Tham Pha Tok caves, located 2 miles (3 km) east of the town, where villagers hid from B-52 bombers during the Vietnam War, attract many visitors. The village of the Indigenous Khamu group, a short distance east along the same route, is also a popular spot. On longer stays, adventure-seekers can opt for trekking and mountain-bike excursions.

8

Muang Ngoi

C1 20 miles (32 km) NE of Nong Khiaw From Nong Khiaw or Muang Khua

A serene village, Muang Ngoi nestles on the east bank of the Nam Ou. Owing to its location on a small plain, it is ideally placed for growing rice in an otherwise moun-tainous area. Inaccessible by road, Muang Ngoi has no electricity, and no cars – factors that contribute to its appeal. Local attractions, apart from its charm and impressive scenery, include a few caves in a forested area, reached by fording a mountain stream about 3 miles (5 km) east of the village. The caves are best explored with a local guide.

9

Muang Khua

C1 67 miles (107 km) N of Muang Ngoi From Luang Prabang From Nong Khiaw or Hat Sa

Farther upstream on the Nam Ou lies the bustling riverside town of Muang Khua. With precipitous mountains on either side of the river, Muang Khua resembles Nong Khiaw, but the atmosphere is much less placid – a steady stream of goods-laden trucks from Vietnam pour into the town's busy commercial center. To escape the hustle and bustle, cross the wooden suspension bridge spanning the Nam Phak (a tributary of the Nam Ou) to visit the local temple, Wat Srikkhounmoung, known for its *Ramayana*-based bas-reliefs and statues reflecting the syncretic nature of Lao Buddhism. It also has a temple bell fashioned from an American cluster bomb.

Sunset over Nong Khiaw, as seen from a hilltop viewpoint ↓

STAY

Pou Villa

Half-timbered villas on a forested hillside, with lovely views overlooking the valley.

 B1 Luang Nam Tha
(020)-292-926-26

$ $ $

Zuela Guesthouse

Lovely guesthouse where motorbike rentals and tours are also available.

 B1 Luang Nam Tha
(020)-220-638-88

$ $ $

 10

Phongsali

B1 240 miles (386 km) N of Luang Prabang From Udomxai From Nong Khiaw

At 4,290 ft (1,430 m), the town of Phongsali is the highest provincial capital in Laos, giving it an agreeable climate in summer, but making it less than comfortable during the misty winter. Reached only via a rough ten-hour drive from Udomxai, or a two-day boat trip from Nong Khiaw, the town is off the tourist track.

The province is home to 22 different communities, the largest being a Sino-Tibetan group called the Phunoy. Many of these communities are famed for their skilled crafters. The Phongsali Provincial Museum of Ethnic Minority Cultures in the heart of the town recounts the history of these groups; note that it's open weekdays only.

Visitors can also stroll through the cobblestone roads crisscrossing the Phunoy village to the nearby morning market. On the northeast edge of the town, Phou Fa, or Sky Mountain, has a stupa at the top, reached by climbing a flight of 400 steps.

Located 9 miles (4 km) southeast of town toward Udomxai is Ban Komaen, where a 400-year-old tea tree stands in the midst of a modern tea plantation. Local teas are available for tasting.

Farther afield, to the northeast of the province, the 506-sq-mile (1,310-sq-km) Phu Den Din National Protected Area (NPA) offers spectacular trekking terrain.

 11

Luang Nam Tha

B1 124 miles (200 km) NW of Luang Prabang From Vientiane From Huay Xai, Muang Sing, or Luang Prabang luang namtha-tourism.org

This provincial capital was the scene of fierce fighting during the Civil War, and the current town is actually the result of construction that began in 1976. Happier times reign today, and Luang Nam Tha has emerged as an important center of ecotourism. The town is located within the boundaries of the Nam Ha National Protected Area and attracts adventure seekers for activities such as trekking, boating, and cycling. The town itself, often shrouded in mist until afternoon, is pleasant, with good restaurants, a small night market, as well as the **Wat Vieng Neua**, a small but beautifully gilded temple adorned with colorful statues.

For a taste of semi-rural village life, visitors can head to the prosperous villages on the opposite bank of the Nam Tha, reached by crossing a bamboo footbridge over the river.

Four miles (6 km) southeast of Luang Nam Tha is That Phum Phuk, a gilded stupa that sits atop a hill overlooking the valley. The original stupa was destroyed by aerial bombing.

Wat Vieng Neua

Center of town, two blocks west of the river
8am–5pm

 12

Ban Nam Di

B1 4 miles (6 km) E of Luang Nam Tha

Located just off Route 1 on the road to Luang Prabang, the village of Ban Nam Di is known for the unique paper made by the Lanten people. This paper is not only used to hold their Taoist religious

↑ Hikers in the Bokeo Nature Reserve, and (inset) gibbon resident

Nam Ha National Protected Area

🅰B1 🏔10 miles (16 km) W of Luang Nam Tha
🌐ecotourismlaos.com

One of the 20 National Protected Areas (NPAs) established by the Lao National Tourism Authority with assistance from UNESCO, this protected area covers 859 sq miles (2,224 sq km) and extends all the way to the Chinese border. The project aims to protect the environment by using sustainable ecotourism as

texts, but has also become a source of income as a handicraft item. An attractive waterfall lies a short distance from the village.

a means to supplement villagers' incomes, and to deter them from taking part in activities that can harm the environment.

The area is a watershed for four rivers, notably the Nam Ha, which gives the NPA its name. The Nam Ha NPA is rich in both flora and fauna. A large variety of animals, such as clouded leopard, tiger, gaur, a muntjac species, and the Asian elephant, as well as 228 bird species, can be found here. Tour agencies in Luang Nam Tha are active partici-pants in the project and a couple of them offer a variety of tours in the NPA, ranging from one-day trips to several-day excursions, which can be undertaken on foot, by kayak, or bicycle.

14 🛶 Ⓜ

Bokeo Nature Reserve

🅰B1 🏔68 miles (110 km) SW of Muang Sing 🌐gibbon experience.org

Covering a stretch of 475 sq miles (1,230 sq km) of mixed deciduous forests, the Bokeo reserve is home to endangered animals such as the black-crested gibbon, migrating wild buffalo, elephants, and several species of birds.

The only way to visit the reserve is through the Gibbon Experience. As part of two- or three-day tours, visitors can trek deep within the forest and stay in the multistory tree houses that serve as the base camp. These are reached by an exhilarating zipline. The elusive black gibbon, and a wide variety of flora and fauna, can be observed on day treks before returning to the base camp in the evening.

A CULTURAL PATCHWORK

Home to a number of communities with varied languages, northern Laos is one of the most culturally diverse regions in Southeast Asia. The mountainous geography and tangle of nearby borders explain this complexity, and there has been much movement into the area from China and Myanmar within the last few hundred years. Known collectively as Lao Sung or "Highland Lao" within Laos, these distinct communities include the Hmong, Mien, and Akha. Many are known for their sophisticated handicrafts, such as Hmong textiles.

← Simple rural dwellings in the hills surrounding Phongsali town

CENTRAL AND SOUTHERN LAOS

Central and Southern Laos has not only been molded by a number of communities and cultures that have settled here from time to time, but also by its geography. The transport and food sources afforded by the mighty Mekong encouraged many civilizations, notably the Champa, Chenla, and Khmer empires, to flourish along its banks from the 5th century CE onward. The French settled the three major towns of Thakhek, Pakse, and Savannakhet during the early 20th century, leaving behind a distinct cultural imprint. At the same time, the Vietnamese entered the country from the east across the narrow band of land between the South China Sea and the Mekong. The Vietnamese put down roots here, intermingling with the local population and contributing to the cultural melting pot that is Southern Laos.

The Mekong River has provided an efficient means of transport and trade with neighboring countries such as Thailand and Vietnam. Despite this, much of the region, except for the three main towns along its banks, was off most tourist itineraries due to poor infrastructure. With the construction of the Friendship Bridge in 1994, however, there has been an increase in visitors, and today the region is slowly opening its treasures to the world.

NORTHERN
LAOS
p188

VIENTIANE

VIENTIANE
p156

CENTRAL AND
SOUTHERN LAOS

Must Sees

❶ Si Phan Don
❷ Wat Phu Champasak
❸ Savannakhet

Experience More

❹ Thakhek
❺ That Sikhot
❻ Mahaxai Caves
❼ Kong Leng Lake
❽ Tham Kong Lo
❾ Pakse
❿ Champasak
⓫ Ho Nang Sida and Hong Tha Tao
⓬ Don Daeng
⓭ Wat Tomo
⓮ Bolaven Plateau
⓯ Dong Phu Vieng National
　Protected Area
⓰ Xe Pian National Protected Area

0 kilometers 50

0 miles 50

N

CENTRAL AND
SOUTHERN LAOS

Dien Chaau

Vinh
International Airport

Vinh

Ha Tinh

Phu Laoko
7,506 ft (2,288 m)

Ky Anh

Thanh Hoa

Hoa Binh

Phu Viatyo
6,056 ft (1,846 m)

Pheo

Bo Trach

Ban
angdao

Ban Heu

Ban Ban

Ban Naden

Xuan Duc

Gulf
of Tonkin

KHAMMUAN

Xai Bua Thong

Phu Laak
3,058 ft (932 m)

Vinh Linh

phangthong

Ban Lampoy

Sepon

Ban Dong

Quang Tri

SAVANNAKHET

Muang Phin

Lao Biao

VIETNAM

Hue

Vinh Thanh

Xonbuli

DONG PHU
VIENG NPA

Phu Bai
International Airport

Xebanghiang

Phu Mali
2,572 ft (784 m)

Phu Lek
4,035 ft (1,230 m)

Atguat
Plateau

Prag

Danang

Da Nang
International Airport

Tahoy

Hoi An

Tumlan

SALAVAN

Ban Nongkung

Vapi

Salavan

Ban Hung

Phu Katoe
5,210 ft (1,588 m)

Ban Dak Euy

Thanh My

Tien Ky

Khong Sedon

SEKONG

Kham Duc

Sanasombun

Phu Phiamay
5,584 ft (1,702 m)

Sekong

Ban Daktiam

se International
Airport

Tat Fane

Tat Yuang

BOLAVEN PLATEAU

Ban Thakanat

Dak Chum

PAKSE

CHAMPASAK

Ban Sok

ATTAPEU

WAT PHU
AMPASAK

CHAMPASAK

Ban
Taew

Attapeu

DON DAENG

WAT TOMO

O NANG SIDA
AND HONG
THA TAO

Sanamxai

Huay Lamphu

Se Xv

Ban Antum

Ban Xayden

Plei Kan

XE PIAN
NPA

Phu Kokdon
3,159 ft (963 m)

Ban Kham
Dorang

Kontum

Ban Paksong

SI PHAN DON

Muang Khong

Phu Mailai
912 ft (278 m)

NORTHERN
CAMBODIA
p110

RATANAKIRI

Phleu Leu

Phu Hoa

Pleiku

lu Prey

STUNG TRENG

Voen Sai

Tang Se

Chu Ty

Did You Know?

The borassus palms on the islands are tapped for sugar, the main agricultural export of Si Phan Don.

1

SI PHAN DON

E5 81 miles (135 km) S of Pakse From Pakse to Don Khong and Ban Nakasang Between Don Khong & Don Det and Don Det & Don Khon; not available during the dry season

As it approaches the Cambodian border, the Mekong splits into a maze of islands – a region known as Si Phan Don, or Four Thousand Islands. Most accommodation is on three islands – Don Khong, Don Det and Don Khon – though explorations to other parts of the archipelago are possible by boat or kayak.

①

Don Khong

Tha Hae Rd

Don Khong, the largest island in the archipelago, is a place of lush green fields, low hills, and sugar palms. The main settlement is Muang Khong, a quiet little town that serves as a ferry port for boats arriving from the mainland. There are a few Colonial-era mansions here, including one that doubles as the tiny Don Khong History Museum. The best way to explore the beautiful island is on a bicycle or motorbike.

Don Khong History Museum

Muang Kong 8:30-11:30am & 1-4pm Mon-Fri

②

Don Det

Don Det can be reached either by a scenic two-hour boat ride from Don Khong or a quick trip from the mainland village of Ban Nakasong. This pretty little island has the highest concentration of accommodation in Si Phan Don, with a cluster of backpacker guesthouses and a mellow party scene (note that bars tend to shut by 11:30pm) at the northern-most tip in the village of Ban Hua Det. The rest of the island is thoroughly tranquil, crisscrossed by a network of quiet lanes.

LOCAL LEGENDS

The waters of Si Phan Don are central to life, with fishing the livelihood for over 95 per cent of the families here. But the river is also said to harbor deathly dangers. Lao legend has it that they are infested with *ngeuak*, a type of fearsome water serpent that is said to gorge on drowning victims, and is an object of dread for local fishers.

Sunset over stilt houses lining the Mekong on Don Khong

STAY

Golden Hotel Don Det

Don Det's finest hotel has rooms with teak floors and furniture in villa-style buildings set around a pleasant pool.

 West side of Don Det
(020)-557-592-52

$$$$$$

Sala Done Khone

This place offers the best accommodation on the islands. Choose from rooms in a French-era bungalow, or opt for a pretty floating studio, set just inches above the water.

 Northern end of Don Khon W sala laoboutique.com

$$$$$$

③
Don Khon

Linked to Don Det by a bridge, Don Khon is home to an unlikely relic of the colonial era in the form of a defunct railway. Built by the French in the early 20th century, there are 7 miles (12 km) of tracks which originally allowed river cargo ships to circumvent the waterfalls blocking passage for loaded boats. The island also features a string of pretty beaches, including those at Li Phi and Xai Kong Nyai, and the Khon Pa Soi and Tat Sophamit rapids.

with vast quantities of water roaring over a series of rocky ledges and outcrops. It's a top tourist attraction and a popular picnic spot for locals, best accessed from Ban Nakasong.

④
Khon Phapeng Waterfalls

🕐 8am–5pm daily

Approached from the mainland on the eastern bank of the Mekong, these thunderous waterfalls are among the biggest in Southeast Asia. What they lack in height, they make up for in volume, especially in the rainy season,

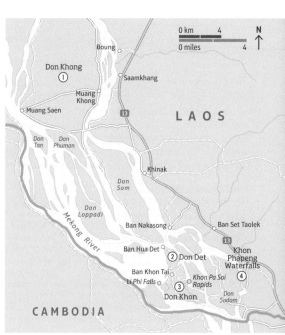

Aerial view of Wat Phu Champasak's two pavilions and *barays* ↑

2 ⊛ ⊛

WAT PHU CHAMPASAK

🗺 D5 🚗 5 miles (8 km) S of Champasak 🕐 8am–5pm daily; open late for sound and light shows during full moon 🌐 vatphou-champassak.com

Named a World Heritage Site by UNESCO in 2001, Wat Phu, meaning Mountain Temple, is located in the foothills of the Lingaparvata Mountain, now known as Phu Phasak. Sacred to at least three different cultures, the temple is believed to have been revered by the Champa Empire during the 5th–8th centuries. Most of the present edifices, however, are pre-Angkorian, built around the beginning of the 9th century.

The Lower Levels

The first level of the complex begins beyond a large *baray* (ceremonial pond), with a causeway passing between two smaller *barays*. These are now normally dry pits, except during monsoon months. The second level is marked by a trio of beautiful pavilions, with the approach route first passing between the Worship Pavilions, notable for their detailed bas-reliefs. Archaeologists believe that these served as separate worship facilities for men and women. Beyond these lie the smaller Nandi Pavilion, dedicated to the sacred bull Nandi, the mount of Shiva

(the statue of Nandi itself is in the small site museum near the main entrance).

The Main Temple

The main temple stands at the uppermost part of the complex. Intricately carved lintels above the 12 entrances depict Hindu and Buddhist deities. The innermost part of the main temple, meanwhile, is the Shiva lingam sanctuary. A stone statue, clad in Buddhist robes, stands guard over the inner sanctum. According to local lore it portrays the legendary founder of Wat Phu. Wat Phu

EXPERIENCE Central and Southern Laos

THE CROCODILE STONE

On the hillside behind the main sanctuary stands the enigmatic Crocodile Stone, a life-sized outline of a crocodile, deeply indented in a large boulder. No similar carving has been recorded in other Khmer temples, and while crocodiles were semi-divine creatures in Khmer culture, its existence is something of a mystery. One popular, though entirely unproven, theory (suggested through interpretation of a 6th-century Chinese text) has it that this was a place of human sacrifice.

was originally a Hindu temple, dedicated to Shiva, but it was later converted to Buddhism, and the sanctuary now houses a large Buddha statue. It is regularly visited by devotees with offerings.

← Buddha statue in the Shiva lingam sanctuary

Crumbling exterior of the Main Temple at ↓ Wat Phu Champasak

Behind the Main Temple

Behind the main temple sanctuary is a bas-relief, carved into a large boulder, depicting the Hindu trinity of Brahma, Vishnu, and Shiva. Nearby is a holy spring which once fed a channel that delivered holy water to the Shiva lingam via a stone spout.

↑ Cycling past a crumbling Colonial-era building in Savannakhet

 3

SAVANNAKHET

🏛D4 🚌80 miles (130 km) S of Thakhek 🚏Makhasan Rd, 1 mile (2km) N of town ✈Connections to Vientiane and Bangkok ℹChaleun Muang Rd; (041)-212-755

Set on the banks of the Mekong and connected to Thailand by a bridge, Savannakhet's tranquil atmosphere belies its importance as a border town. The downtown area is still home to countless Colonial-era buildings, many of them falling apart, but others restored. There's also a Taoist temple and a Catholic church, St. Theresa's. Savannakhet was the birthplace of Laos's Communist patriarch, Kaysone Phomvihane, whose childhood home is located in the town center.

 ①

Chao Mahesak Shrine

🏛Tha Hae Rd 🕐8am–5pm daily

Built under the shade of a huge banyan tree and perpetually wreathed in incense smoke, the Chao Mahesak Shrine is a revered religious landmark. Locals come here to pay respects to a diverse pantheon of deities and spirits, including Chao Mahesak, who is mythically linked to the town's founding, and the Chinese Goddess of Mercy.

 ②

Wat Sainyaphum

🏛Tha Hae Rd 🕐8am–5pm daily

Lying across the street from the Chao Mahesak Shrine, Wat Sainyaphum is the largest Buddhist temple in town. The architecture displays European and Chinese influences, and the building is adorned with striking bas-reliefs of mythical animals. A small factory toward the riverside entrance of the temple turns out gold-painted statues.

  3

Savannakhet Dinosaur Museum

🏛Khanthabuli Rd 🕐8–11:30am & 1:30–4pm daily

The area around Savannakhet has proved fertile territory for dinosaur hunters since the 1930s, when the first major French-run excavations began turning up significant fossil remains. The Savannakhet Dinosaur Museum displays parts of a large brontosaurus and other specimens found in the province. The signage is all in Lao and French, but

↑ Stupa at That Ing Hang, a structure of great religious importance

the curators are happy to explain the background and show visitors around.

④

Wat Rattanalangsi

🏠 Chao Kim Rd 🕐 8am-5pm daily

Situated in a pretty tree-filled complex, Wat Rattanalangsi was built in 1951. The temple includes a statue of Brahma, the Hindu God of Creation – a good example of Hindu-Buddhist syncretism. Look for the three-level gilded drum-and-gong-tower at the back of the compound and the large Reclining Buddha.

⑤

That Ing Hang

🏠 10 miles (16 km) NE of Savannakhet 🚌 From town 🕐 7am-6pm daily

Lying north of town, this towering temple is of great religious significance. The origins of the site may go back to the 10th-century Khmer empire of Sri Khotabura, with further connections to King Chao Fa Ngum's return from Cambodia in the 14th century, though the current structure, with its attractive four-tiered edifice with a lotus bud-shaped pinnacle, largely dates from the 16th century. The complex is surrounded by a covered gallery containing 329 identical images of the Buddha. Women are not permitted into the inner sanctum surrounding the stupa.

⑥

Dong Natad Protected Area

🏠 10 miles (16 km) NE of Savannakhet

Easily accessed from Savannakhet, Dong Natad is one of the smallest National Protected Areas in Laos. It has verdant forests and several pristine lakes, as well as two friendly villages where homestays are available.

Must See

EAT

Pilgrim's Kitchen

This popular, convivial guesthouse and restaurant serves hearty plates of nachos, wraps and quesadillas, and cold beer. An excellent place to meet fellow travelers.

🏠 Khantabuli Rd
📞 (020)-221-337-33

$$$

Lin's Café

A smart café that's been welcoming travelers for years. Lin's serves crispy spring rolls, moreish cakes, and really top-notch coffee.

🏠 Latsaphanit Rd
📞 (020)-998-816-30

$$$

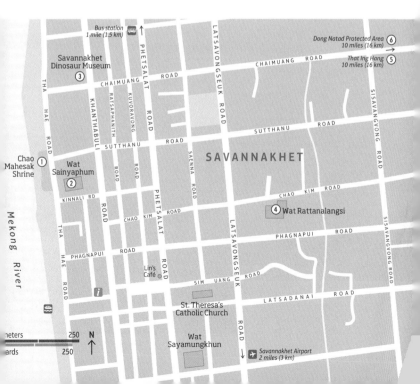

EXPERIENCE MORE

Thakhek

 D3 220 miles (350 km) S of Vientiane Vientiane Rd

Capital of Khammuan province, Thakhek was settled by the French in the 1920s. Although there are no major tourist attractions here, it remains a pretty settlement surrounded by majestic karst mountains and the meandering Mekong River. Thakhek is an excellent resting point for visitors traveling around Southern Laos, and a crossover point for travelers to and from neighboring Thailand and Vietnam. The third of four Friendship Bridges across the Mekong provides a highway link from Thakhek to Nakhon Phanom province in Thailand.

Thakhek is a convenient base from which to organize trips to the caves, waterfalls, and soaring limestone mountains of the **Phu Hin Pun**

National Protected Area. This huge, spectacularly beautiful preserve is home to a number of endangered species, such as the douc langur, François langur, Assamese macaque, 43 species of bat, sooty babbler, and limestone leaf warbler. There are exciting adventure and ecotourism facilities here too, including trekking and kayaking. Trips can be organized by visitors on their own or through tour operators such as Green Discovery, whose office is located in the Inthira Hotel Sikotabong on Chao Anou Road. The local tourism office is also helpful.

Phu Hin Pun National Protected Area

3 miles (5 km) N of Thakhek ecotourismlaos.com

That Sikhot

D3 4 miles (6 km) S of Thakhek 8am–6pm daily

This stupa and the adjacent wat occupy a site that dates from the Khmer principality of Sri Khotabura. The iconic lotus bud-shaped stupa is

> HIDDEN GEM
> ### The Thakhek Loop
>
> One of the best ways to explore the area around Thakhek is by following part or all of the Thakhek Loop, a self-drive motorbike route that stops off at atmospheric caves, lagoons, and spectacular karst landscapes.

→ Thai Lao Friendship Bridge across the Mekong at Thakhek

of considerable religious significance to the Lao people, and pilgrims come from across the country to the annual fair, Boun That Sikhot, held in February.

Mahaxai Caves

△D3 **⬚Off Route 12, 5 miles (8 km) E of Thakhek** **◷8:30am–4:30pm daily**

A few miles east of Thakhek, the landscape along Route 12 begins to change, with sheer karst formations looming on both sides of the road. These cliffs are riddled with caves, several of which are quite impressive, and all a cool respite from the heat of the day. The first, 5 miles (8 km) east of Thakhek, is Buddha Cave, Tham Pa Fa; locals come to venerate the 229 Buddha statues here, some of which are 500 years old. Another

4 miles (6 km) along Route 12 lies Tham Xiang Liab. This cave is about 656 ft (200 m) long and emerges in an isolated valley with pools ideal for swimming. Further on this route is Tham Nong Aen, famous for the constant flow of cool air from its depths.

Kong Leng Lake

△D3 **⬚30 miles (48 km) N of Thakhek** **◷8:30am–4:30pm daily**

This isolated lake, over 21 ft (70 m) deep in the center, lies in the foothills of the Phu Hin Pun NPA. Depending on the weather, the lake is either an emerald green or deep blue in color. Sacred to locals, it is believed to be inhabited by spirits capable of ringing a gong on full moon nights; Kong Leng means "evening gong." Fishing is not allowed, and swimming is restricted to certain areas. The best way to visit the lake is as part of an organized trip from Thakhek.

Tham Kong Lo

△D3 **⬚Off Route 8, 50 miles (80 km) N of Thakhek** **⬚◷8:30am–4:30pm daily**

A visit to this dramatic cave, a magnificent creation of nature, is the highlight of any

↑ Flat-bottomed boats at the entrance to the Tham Kong Lo cave

trip into the karst highlands of Central Laos. It is entered on a motorboat, from the downstream end of the Nam Hin Boun river, which flows through the cave for 4 miles (6 km). The short boat ride includes a stop at a hidden valley on the upstream end, and the entire trip takes about two hours. Once back, visitors can enjoy a swim at any one of the large pools located close to the entrance, or buy great picnic food from vendors stationed here. Decent guesthouses in the area make this an excellent overnight trip from nearby Thakhek.

HO CHI MINH TRAIL

The so-called Ho Chi Minh Trail was a vast system of tracks, paths, and bridges running parallel to the Vietnam border from Kammuan province through to the Cambodian frontier. During the Vietnam War, it served as a vital supply route for the North Vietnamese Army, despite enduring a daily barrage of US bombs. Several tours take in sections of the trail, still studded with war debris.

Carved lintel depicting Vishvakarma, Champasak Provincial Museum, Pakse

Pakse

🅰E5 📍140 miles (230 km) S of Savannakhet 🚐🚌
ℹ Thanon 11 Rd; (031)-312-120-21

Located at the confluence of the Don and Mekong rivers, Pakse, capital of Champasak province, was founded by the French in 1905. The Colonial-era Art Deco-style architecture of Pakse's downtown area, with several high-rise buildings, makes it more urban than the other towns along the Mekong. The completion of a bridge across the Mekong, just south of town, has enabled brisker trade with Thailand.

Although Pakse serves as a jumping-off point for sights such as Wat Phu Champasak (p210) and Si Phan Don (p208), the town has attractions of its own. The Dao Heuang Market, close to the bridge, is a huge complex rivaling Vientiane's Talat Sao (p164), where local textiles and produce, such as coffee from the Bolaven Plateau (p219), are on offer. Another interesting sight is the Champasak Palace Hotel on the corner of Route 13 and Road 1. It was built as a palace for Chao Boun Oum Na Champasak, a prince who held ceremonial sway in the area until the Communists seized power in 1975. The most interesting stop, however, is the **Champasak Provincial Museum**, which has some excellent Khmer lintels taken from sites throughout the province. A walk along the riverfront esplanade is also always a pleasure.

Champasak Provincial Museum
🔖 📍Route 13 🕗8–11:30am & 2–4pm Mon–Fri

Champasak

🅰E5 📍21 miles (34 km) SW of Pakse 🚌From Pakse 🚤From Ban Muang ℹPakse

A small town on the west bank of the Mekong, Champasak was the royal capital of the Na Champasak principality, which ruled much of Southern Laos. Popular due to its proximity to the majestic Wat Phu Champasak ruins (p210), and as a jumping-off point for Don Daeng, Champasak today is a quiet town with the only remnants of royalty being two Colonial-style royal residences that can be found just south of the fountain in the center of town. Due west of these buildings lies Wat Thong, the temple where the town's sovereigns performed religious rites, and where their cremated ashes now lie. The town is a pleasant place in which to relax after a tiring day exploring the magnificent sights of Wat Phu.

Ho Nang Sida and Hong Tha Tao

🅰E5 📍1 mile (2 km) S of Wat Phu Champasak

Although not as magnificent or significant as the Wat Phu complex (p210), the two Khmer sites of Ho Nang Sida and Hong Tha Tao are an interesting side trip to any visit to Wat Phu. Located south of Wat Phu, they are accessed by turning left just before the two main galleries on the first level of the complex. The first, Ho Nang Sida, dates to the 10th century and is venerated by locals. A tree growing through the center of this crumbling shrine is festooned with Buddhist prayer flags put up by devotees who come here to pray. A mile farther south lies the site of Hong Tha Tao, that once used to be a rest house for travelers venturing to and from the ancient capital of Angkor. Although neither of these sites are of much architectural interest, they are quite atmospheric and certainly worth a visit.

> **SPIRIT HOUSES**
>
> Outside many Lao homes you'll spot a miniature wooden building, set on a platform fixed to a wall or tree, or supported on a wooden pillar. These are "spirit houses," shrines for the worship of *phi*, local spirits of place. Putting offerings in the spirit house is an ancient folk tradition, today interwoven with Buddhist practice.

EAT

Daolin

A bustling restaurant at a busy junction, Daolin has great coffee, ice creams, baguettes, pasta and some tasty Thai dishes at very attractive prices.

E5 Route 13, Pakse (020)-557-331-99

$$\textcircled{\$}\textcircled{\$}$$

Le Panorama

With sweeping views in all directions, this rooftop hotel restaurant is the most atmospheric dining option in town, serving up excellent Asian and European cuisine.

E5 Pakse Hotel, St 5, Pakse hotel pakse.com

$$\textcircled{\$}\textcircled{\$}$$

⓬ Don Daeng

E5 Half a mile (1 km) E of Champasak From Pakse From Ban Muang

Located in the middle of the Mekong River, across from Champasak, Don Daeng is an appealing option for those wanting to stay on a river island.

The island is ringed by eight separate villages, which are all connected by an unpaved track. Sights around the island include the beautiful Wat Ban Boung Kham, situated on the southwest coast. The wat was built over a former Khmer shrine, which is thought to date back to the time of Wat Phu Champasak.

Visitors will find adequate accommodation facilities at the community guesthouse in the village of Ban Hua Daeng, which is located on the northern edge of Don Daeng. There is also a top luxury hotel, La Folie Lodge, a mile south, on the west coast. Don Daeng provides easy access to the forested precincts of Wat Tomo nearby.

⓭ Wat Tomo

E5 30 miles (48 km) S of Pakse From Champasak or Don Daeng 8am–5pm daily

Lying on the east bank of the Mekong River, a short distance south of Wat Phu Champasak *(p210)*, the Khmer ruins of Wat Tomo, also known as Ou Muang, date from the 9th century. This wat was built in honor of Rudrani, the wife of Shiva, God of Destruction. It is constructed of laterite, and while the best lintels are now in the Champasak Provincial Museum in Pakse, some artifacts remain, including a unique *mukha-linga*, which is an ornately carved *lingam* (phallic statue). Situated in a shady forest, the wat makes an excellent day trip by boat from Champasak or Don Daeng. In the dry season, it's a 15-minute walk from the river bank, but after the rains, boats can land within 100 ft (30 m) of the temple. It is also accessible by land from the east side of the Mekong River.

↓ A traditional matted trackway leading to fishing boats on Don Daeng island

←
Climbing up to the
Bolaven Plateau
from Tat Yuang falls

Bolaven Plateau

🅰 E5 🅰 47 miles (78 km)
E of Pakse

The Bolaven Plateau is an elevated region in Champasak province crossed by several rivers and renowned for its numerous waterfalls. The French colonialists found the temperate climate and rich soil here particularly suitable for habitation and cultivation. They planted the area with coffee, cardamom, and vegetables. This region can be explored from the town of Paksong, which lies 14 miles (23 km) south of the plateau. Although small, Paksong styles itself, with pride, as the "coffee capital" of Laos and there are roasting workshops and coffee farm tours on offer.

Bolaven literally means Home of the Laven, which is the largest community that lives here. Other Indigenous minorities here include the Alak and the Katu.

The plateau was the site of intense battles during the Vietnam War and some areas, especially the Attapeu province, remain uncleared of UXO (Unexploded Ordnance). Today, the area's waterfalls are a draw for visitors. Among the more popular are Tat Fane, a 360-ft- (120-m-) high cascade, and the 120-ft- (40-m-) high Tat Yuang, which is great for swimming. Travelers who wish to explore the area further can stay at the Tadlo Lodge, which is close to a few of the waterfalls. Treks to nearby villages and markets can be arranged from here as well.

↑ Floating across the lush Kiet Ngong wetland in the Xe Pian National Protected Area

Dong Phu Vieng National Protected Area

🅰 E4 🅰 110 miles (180 km)
E of Savannakhet
ℹ Savannakhet Eco-Guide Unit, Ratsaphanith Rd, Savannakhet; www.weare lao.com/trekking-savannakhet

This remote NPA is home to a small Mon-Khmer minority called the Katang, who even today remain unaffected by modernization, steeped as they are in their own distinct culture and belief systems. It is possible to visit this area as part of a tour organized by the Savannakhet Eco-Guide Unit, which works with the local people. The demanding trek begins at Muang Phin on Route 9 heading toward Vietnam. Visitors spend a couple of nights in the Katang villages, and the journey culminates with a boat trip on the Se Bang Hieng River.

Xe Pian National Protected Area

🅰 E5 🅰 30 miles (48 km) S of Pakse 🚌 from Pakse ℹ Kingfisher Ecolodge; www. kingfisherecolodge.com

Beginning roughly at Wat Tomo and continuing south to the Cambodian border, Xe Pian National Protected Area covers some 1,000 sq miles (2,600 sq km). It sustains a variety of wildlife, including tigers, Asiatic black bears, banteng, wild oxen, gibbons, hornbills, and cranes. The area is best explored by arranging a trek from the Kingfisher Ecolodge, near the village of Kiet Ngong at the north-eastern corner of the NPA.

A SANCTUARY FOR WILDLIFE

Southern Laos is the country's wildlife stronghold. The sparsely populated Bolaven Plateau, the inaccessible mountains, and the dense forests of the border regions all provide refuge for wild animals. Several new mammal species have been discovered in the area within the last few decades, including the Laotian rock rat and the saola. Asiatic black bears, yellow-cheeked crested gibbons, and a small number of Indochinese tigers also survive here.

NEED TO KNOW

Motorcyclists crossing the Old Bridge in Luang Prabang, Laos

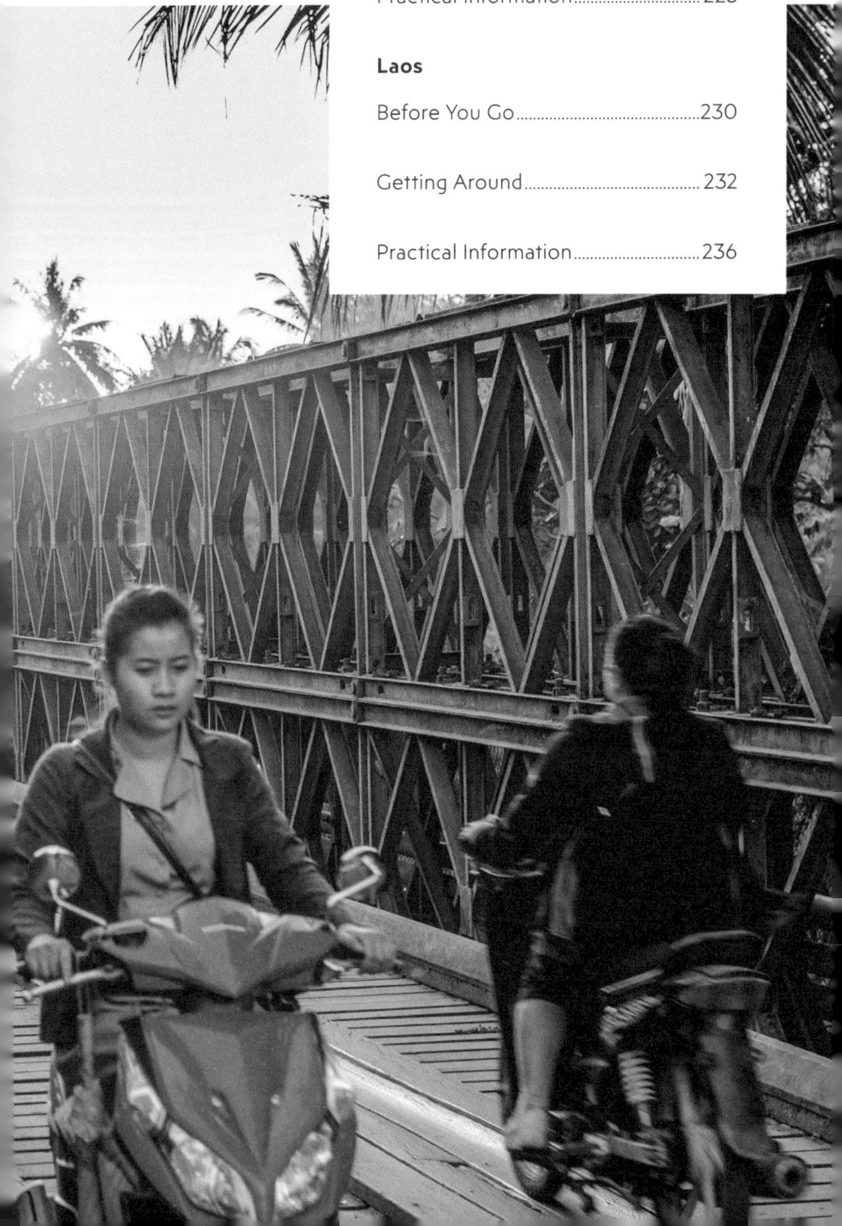

BEFORE YOU GO
CAMBODIA

Things change, so plan ahead to make the most of your trip to Cambodia. Be prepared by considering the following points before you travel.

AT A GLANCE

CURRENCY
Riel (KHR)   US Dollar ($)

AVERAGE DAILY SPEND

SAVE $30   SPEND $60   SPLURGE $ 100+

BOTTLED WATER $0.50   COFFEE $1   BEER $1.50   DINNER FOR TWO $15

ESSENTIAL PHRASES

Hello	Joom reapsooa
Please	Soom
Thank you	Awkoon
Excuse me	Suom dtoh
I don't understand	Khnyom min yul tee

ELECTRICITY SUPPLY

Power sockets are mainly type C, fitting two-pin, round-pronged plugs. Flat-pronged type A plugs are also used. Standard voltage is 220v.

Passports and Visas

For entry requirements, including visas, consult your nearest Cambodian embassy or check the Cambodian **e-visa** website. Most travelers, including citizens of the UK, US, Canada, Australia, New Zealand, and the EU, can usually obtain a 30-day tourist visa on arrival at Cambodian airports and land borders for a fee of $30. A passport photo is required. Citizens from other ASEAN countries don't need a visa to visit as a tourist.
E-visa
W evisa.gov.kh

Government Advice

Now more than ever, it is important to consult both your and the Cambodian government's advice before travelling. The **UK Foreign, Commonwealth & Development Office**, **US State Department**, **Australian Department of Foreign Affairs and Trade**, and **Tourism of Cambodia** websites offer the latest information on security, health, and local regulations.
Australian Department of Foreign Affairs and Trade
W smartraveller.gov.au
Tourism of Cambodia
W tourismcambodia.com
UK Foreign, Commonwealth & Development Office
W gov.uk/foreign-travel-advice
US State Department
W travel.state.gov

Customs Information

You can find information on the laws relating to goods and currency taken in or out of Cambodia on the Tourism of Cambodia website.

Insurance

We recommend taking out a comprehensive insurance policy covering theft, loss of belongings, medical care, cancellations and delays, and read the small print carefully. Check coverage includes medical evacuation as well.

Vaccinations

Discuss vaccinations with your doctor at least eight weeks before traveling. Vaccinations against hepatitis, tetanus, and typhoid are recommended. Proof of yellow fever vaccination is required when arriving in Cambodia directly from an infected area. Mosquito-borne malaria and dengue are present in the country, although the former is largely found in remote areas. Seek current advice from a doctor about suitable prophylaxis for both.

Money

Two currencies are in everyday use in Cambodia – the Cambodian riel and the US dollar (the latter are used for prices in this guide). Generally, dollars are used to pay for accommodations and high-end purchases, while riel are more useful for minor purchases. Note that change is usually given in riel, and US dollar notes need to be in pristine condition, otherwise they may not be accepted. However, the currencies are often used interchangeably. Credit cards are broadly accepted, and ATMs are widely available. QR code payments are common among local banks.

Tipping is not expected, but it is common to tip wait staff 5–10 per cent and tour guides 10 per cent.

Booking Accommodation

For most accommodations in Phnom Penh, Siem Reap, and other large towns, online booking is available. For more remote destinations (such as the offshore islands) online booking is not always reliable, so call ahead.

The cooler months from November to March are peak season in Cambodia. During the rainy season, from April to October, online deals are available, especially in Siem Reap and Sihanoukville.

Travelers with Specific Requirements

Cambodia has limited facilities for travelers with specific requirements. The pedestrian crossings in Sihanoukville and Siem Reap have been made far more wheelchair-friendly in recent years, but it's still difficult to get around the capital Phnom Penh as most venues outside of five-star hotels don't provide ramp access.

The following tour operators can make specialist arrangements:

About Asia
W aboutasiatravel.com
Accessible Holidays
W disabledholidays.com

Language

Khmer is the official language in Cambodia. English is widely spoken in places such as Siem Reap and Sihanoukville; Chinese has also become more prevalent. Learning a few words of Khmer will always be appreciated.

Opening Times

> Situations can change quickly and unexpectedly. Always check before visiting attractions and hospitality venues for up-to-date opening hours and booking requirements.

Saturday Banks usually close at lunchtime.
Sunday Banks and some museums close.
Public holidays Banks and government offices close, but most private businesses are open.

PUBLIC HOLIDAYS

1 Jan	New Year's Day
7 Jan	Victory Day
19 Feb	Meak Bochea
8 March	Women's Day
13-15 Apr	Cambodian New Year
19 Apr	Visak Bochea
1 May	International Labor Day
23 May	Royal Ploughing Ceremony (May)
13-15 May	King Sihamoni's Birthday
18 June	Queen Mother's Birthday
24 Sept	Constitution Day
27-30 Sept	Bon Pchum Ben
15 Oct	Commemoration Day of King's Father
29 Oct	Coronation Day
11 Nov	Independence Day
12-13 Nov	Bon Om Tuk
10 Dec	Human Rights Day

GETTING AROUND
CAMBODIA

Whether you are making a flying visit, or heading off on a lengthy adventure, discover how best to travel like a pro in Cambodia.

AT A GLANCE

PUBLIC TRANSPORT COSTS

PHNOM PENH

$2

100 mins
Tuk-tuk fare

SIEM REAP

$15

100 mins
1-day *moto* charter

SIHANOUKVILLE

$10

100 mins
Bus from Phnom Penh

TOP TIP
Make sure you agree tuk-tuk, *moto*, and cyclo fares before you begin your journey.

SPEED LIMITS

MOTORWAY	DUAL CARRIAGEWAYS
100 km/h (60 mph)	**60** km/h (35 mph)

SECONDARY ROAD	URBAN AREAS
90 km/h (55 mph)	**40** km/h (25 mph)

Arriving by Air

The two main international gateways for Cambodia are Phnom Penh International Airport and Siem Reap-Angkor International Airport, with regular flights to regional hubs such as Bangkok, Kuala Lumpur, and Singapore, and onward connections worldwide. Both Phnom Penh and Siem Reap are well served by regional budget airlines such as AirAsia, making a visit as part of a wider exploration of Southeast Asia straightforward.

A third airport at Sihanoukville mainly receives international flights from Kuala Lumpur and various cities in China.

The table opposite lists popular transport options to and from Cambodia's main airports. Note that tuk-tuks are fixed at the same price as taxis within the airport grounds at Phnom Penh and Siem Reap-Angkor; if you walk just outside the airport gates in Phnomh Penh, you should find tuk-tuk drivers prepared to offer a reduced fare, but in Siem Reap, your best bet is the airport bus ($8 into town, or $15 return trip). In Sihanoukville, all tuk-tuk journey prices are fixed and prices are high – a taxi, bus, or shared taxi are probably your best options.

Arriving by Land

Many visitors arrive in Cambodia overland from neighboring countries. Visas on arrival are usually available at all official entry points, though e-visas are only valid for entry at the most important crossings.

There are several border crossings with Thailand, of which by far the most important is that at Poipet, west of Siem Reap on the main highway. There are train connections from Bangkok on the Thai side of the border, and onward buses to Phnom Penh, Siem Reap, and Battambang on the Cambodian side. While there is a train line that runs from Poipet to Phnom Penh, it may not operate at short notice, so check in advance. Hundreds of travelers typically cross this frontier each day, and the crossing has a reputation for hassle – particularly inflated visa fees charged by bogus

GETTING TO AND FROM THE AIRPORT

Airport	Distance to City	Taxi Fare	Public Transport	Journey Time
Phnom Penh	6 miles (9 km)	$20	bus	30 mins
Siem Reap	28 miles (45 km)	$35	bus	1 hr
Sihanoukville	9 miles (15 km)	$25	bus	40 mins

officials, and money-changing scams. To minimize problems, make sure you apply in advance for an e-visa. Other less busy crossings with Thailand include Koh Kong, Pailin, and Anlong Veng.

There are seven official crossings on the Cambodia–Vietnam border, of which the crossing at Bavet is the most popular. This is usually plied by modern, air-conditioned coaches connecting Phnom Penh directly with Ho Chi Minh City – a journey of around six hours along a modern highway. An appealing alternative route is the boat journey between Phnom Penh and Chau Doc in Vietnam's Mekong Delta via K'am Samnar. Note that Cambodian e-visas are only accepted for entry from Vietnam at Bavet.

There is only one border crossing between Cambodia and Laos, at Trapeang Kriel, north of Stung Treng. Although cross-border buses sometimes run between Stung Treng and Si Phan Don in Laos, crossing this frontier typically involves using a combination of local transport on either side of the frontier.

Domestic Air Travel

Scheduled domestic air travel in Cambodia is limited to three routes, connecting Phnom Penh, Sihanoukville, and Siem Reap. The Phnom Penh–Siem Reap route is well served, with up to ten flights a day, though taking into account check-in time and journeys to and from the airports, it is often almost as quick to travel by bus. The Siem Reap–Sihanoukville route is more useful as a way of avoiding a long and roundabout overland journey.

One-way fares on internal routes typically start at around $200 on the Phnom Penh–Siem Reap route, though it is possible to book at short notice. Advance booking, particularly at busy times or during the peak holiday season, is advisable on the other routes. **Cambodia**

Angkor Air is the most reliable operator, with online booking available.
Cambodia Angkor Air
w cambodiaangkorair.com

Train Travel

Cambodia's battered Colonial-era rail network has had an injection of investment in recent years, with services now running between Phnom Penh and Sihanoukville, and a second line from Phnom Penh to the Thai border at Poipet with on and off operations. Travel by train is slow compared to flying or taking direct long-distance buses, but it does make a relaxing alternative to the hectic highways.

Train tickets can only be booked at the stations in Phnom Penh, Sihanoukville, or at the intervening stops.

Boats and Ferries

Ferries were once a major form of public transport in Cambodia, but with greatly improved intercity highways, their importance has declined. Boat services maintained for tourists still operate between Siem Reap and Battambang, and Siem Reap and Phnom Penh, and scheduled speedboats connect Sihanoukville with the offshore islands.

By Road

Although traveling by road in Cambodia can still be a chaotic affair, these days highways and a planned network of express-ways – like the one between Phnom Penh and Sihanoukville – between major cities have improved hugely, cutting journey times and making for much smoother rides. In more remote areas, however, expect slow trips and plenty of bumps in the road.

Long-Distance Buses

Bus transport in Cambodia is privately run, with multiple companies serving the major routes. Between main hubs, modern air-conditioned buses, run by companies such as **Mekong Express** and **Giant Ibis**, are available, as well as cheaper and less comfortable options. In rural areas, buses tend to be cramped and badly maintained.

Online booking is available for a few of the deluxe bus services via an online booking agent like **12Go**, but generally booking in person is the most straightforward option. Bus company offices tend to be widely scattered, so the easiest option is often to book through a travel agent, or via a hotel or guesthouse. Such bookings often include a transfer by *moto* or tuk-tuk to the point of departure.

Mekong Express
w catmekongexpress.com
Giant Ibis
w giantibis.com
12Go
w 12go.asia

Minibuses and Shared Taxis

Minibuses and shared taxis serve most of the major routes also covered by buses, as well as a far wider array of minor destinations. They are sometimes slightly more expensive than buses, and though faster, they are not necessarily more comfortable. They tend to leave when full from specific stops within towns, so they are a good option if you're moving on at short notice. Deluxe minibuses will often pick up directly from hotels and drop off at a specific destination within a city.

Driving

It is very difficult for non-resident foreigners to rent a car for self-drive. A Cambodian license is required, which is only available for residents, and there are very few formal rental agencies. Cars with drivers, however, are widely available, and are best arranged through hotels or travel agents. They can be very good value, though if you wish to charter a car for multiple days, you will need to cover the cost of the driver's food and accommodation.

Motorbikes

Motorbikes are widely available for rent, with many guesthouses and general travel agencies in places such as Siem Reap renting out 125cc automatic or semiautomatic scooters for a few dollars a day. These bikes are easy to ride, and a great way to explore. Bikes can be particularly good for getting around in more isolated areas, such as the northeast, where public transport

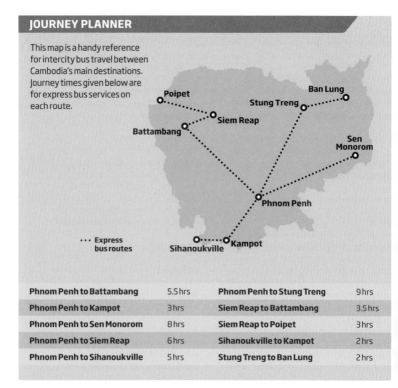

JOURNEY PLANNER

This map is a handy reference for intercity bus travel between Cambodia's main destinations. Journey times given below are for express bus services on each route.

··· Express bus routes

Phnom Penh to Battambang	5.5 hrs	**Phnom Penh to Stung Treng**	9 hrs
Phnom Penh to Kampot	3 hrs	**Siem Reap to Battambang**	3.5 hrs
Phnom Penh to Sen Monorom	8 hrs	**Siem Reap to Poipet**	3 hrs
Phnom Penh to Siem Reap	6 hrs	**Sihanoukville to Kampot**	2 hrs
Phnom Penh to Sihanoukville	5 hrs	**Stung Treng to Ban Lung**	2 hrs

is limited. Road and traffic conditions can be hazardous, however, so inexperienced riders should think twice before renting a bike.

It is illegal to ride without a helmet, and Cambodian police are zealous about enforcing this law. In theory, an international driving permit valid for motorbikes is required. In practice, renters and police rarely check. However, be aware that travel insurance policies will not cover any unlicensed motorbike riding.

Public Transport

Apart from a basic bus service in Phnom Penh, there is no organized public transport within cities and towns, so getting around relies on things like taxis, tuk-tuks, and *motos*.

Tuk-tuks

There are two types of tuk-tuk available in Cambodia. The standard Cambodian tuk-tuk, known locally as *remork-moto*, is a trailer with seats that are hitched to the back of a motorbike. They comfortably seat four, though you'll often see them crammed with six people or more. They're most commonly found outside of the big cities, or outside of hotels.

More recently, Indian-style three-wheel auto-rickshaws have arrived in Cambodia's big cities, especially in Phnom Penh. They are faster but smaller than the *remork-motos*.

Both types of tuk-tuk can be booked via mobile hailing apps such as Grab, PassApp, and Tada, all of which offer fixed fares. Travelers spending a good deal of time in Phnom Penh should consider buying a SIM card and down-loading one of these apps. Tuk-tuks can also can be hailed anywhere on the street. However, unlike when using the above apps, fixed fares do not exist, so it's always essential to agree a price before boarding – a short trip within a town should cost no more than a couple of dollars.

Custom-made three-wheeler tuk-tuks, designed to take a larger number of passengers, sometimes run between towns and outlying bus or ferry terminals.

Motos

Motos are simply motorbikes with a driver, serving as one-passenger taxis. They congregate at street corners in most towns, and can also be flagged down in passing. They can also be chartered, say for a day's exploration of the Angkor temples. Helmets are legally required for pillion passengers, so insist that your driver provides one.

Drivers are adept at handling large loads, and can usually cram a suitcase or backpack up front. However, rides through busy traffic can be alarming. Fares need to be agreed in advance to avoid overcharging.

Although mainly used for travel within cities, motos are often the only option for getting to infrequently visited outlying attractions.

Cyclos

Traditional, green-painted cycle-rickshaws, known as cyclos in Cambodia, are still a feature of Phnom Penh. Only really useful for short journeys, passengers sit up front in a bucket seat with an unobstructed view of the street.

Taxis

Metered taxis are not generally available in Phnom Penh, but cars can be ordered via the mobile hailing app Grab.

Addresses

Navigating Cambodian towns is relatively easy by the standards of the region, as most places are laid out on a grid, with numbered streets. Local drivers may not always know the numbers of individual streets, however, so it's worth identifying a nearby landmark when giving your destination, rather than simply stating an address, or consider buying a SIM card so you can use Google Maps.

Cycling

A bicycle is a great way to explore quieter areas – though extreme caution must be exercised on busy roads, where bikes are at the very bottom of the traffic hierarchy, and on quieter routes where potholes and other obstacles abound.

Bicycles are readily available for rent in Siem Reap and Battambang, where the surrounding countryside is helpfully flat. Mountain bikes are available in Kratie and Stung Treng for explor-ations along the Mekong. Guided bicycling tours are also available in several locations.

Rules of the Road

Although the condition of the roads in most major towns and on main intercity routes is decent, the traffic itself can be hectic. Cambodia drives on the right, in theory, but smaller vehicles over-taking and anarchic intersections are the norm.

Police checkpoints are frequent, with fines – official or unofficial – levied for violations, such as riding a motorbike without a helmet.

Walking

Despite some improvements, Phnom Penh is not a very walkable city, though the riverside offers a scenic place for an evening stroll. Following sub-stantial infrastructure investment, both Siem Reap and Sihanoukville are more pedestrian-friendly, while the historic heart of Battambang is a delight to walk around. For a hike, Kep National Park provides the best trails and vistas.

PRACTICAL INFORMATION
CAMBODIA

A little local know-how goes a long way in Cambodia. Here you will find all the essential advice and information you will need during your stay.

AT A GLANCE

EMERGENCY NUMBERS

AMBULANCE	POLICE
119	**117**

FIRE SERVICE

118

TIME ZONE
GMT +7, as in Thailand and Vietnam; no daylight saving.

TAP WATER
Tap water is not safe to drink in Cambodia; use bottled water or refill from hotel and restaurant dispensers.

WEBSITES AND APPS

Tourism of Cambodia
The official government tourism website has information on destinations and events (*tourismcambodia.org*).

Khmer Times
The website of Cambodia's main English-language newspaper has all the latest news (*khmertimeskh.com*).

Audio Khmer
Translate basic communications between English and Khmer with this free app.

Personal Security

Although violent crime is rare, bag-snatchings occur, especially in Phnom Penh. Be very careful with your belongings, especially when riding a tuk-tuk or *moto*. Pickpocketing is also an issue in busy markets.

If you have anything stolen, report the crime as soon as possible at the nearest police station and take ID with you. Get a copy of the crime report to claim on your insurance. Contact your embassy or consulate if your passport is lost or stolen, or in the event of a serious crime or accident.

Be very careful about straying from marked trails when exploring the countryside – unexploded ordinance is still a significant problem in Cambodia.

As a rule, Cambodians are accepting of all people, regardless of their race, gender or sexuality. Compared to some other countries in the region, Cambodia is a relatively LGBTQ+-friendly place, with no legal restrictions on same-sex relationships, and a reasonable degree of social acceptance in urban areas. There are lively gay scenes in Phnom Penh and Sihanoukville, and a number of gay-friendly hotels and bars around the country. Public displays of affection are not appropriate for couples of any orientation, however, and attitudes in rural areas are much more conservative – though more likely to result in bemusement than overt hostility. If you do feel unsafe, the **Safe Space Alliance** pinpoints your nearest place of refuge.
Safe Space Alliance
W safespacealliance.com

Health

Healthcare provision is generally poor in Cambodia, though there are good – if expensive – private clinics in Phnom Penh, including the **Royal Phnom Penh Hospital.** There's also the Sunrise Hospital, Raffles Medical and Intercare Medical Center. Pharmacies can often provide advice for minor ailments.

It is important to organize comprehensive insurance prior to traveling that includes

medical care. Check that medical evacuation is part of the policy, as the treatment of serious conditions may necessitate an emergency transfer to Bangkok in Thailand.

Minor stomach upsets, caused by unfamiliar food and climate, and poor hygiene, are the commonest issue. Rest and rehydration are the main treatments; seek advice from a pharmacy or clinic if there is no improvement after a couple of days.

Mosquitoes are a nuisance in Cambodia, particularly toward the end of the monsoon. Cover up in the evenings and use repellent. If travelling outside of the cities it is also wise to seek current advice from a doctor about suitable prophylaxis for the mosquito-borne diseases of malaria and dengue.

Royal Phnom Penh Hospital
Ⓦ royalphnompenhhospital.com

Smoking, Alcohol, and Drugs

Smoking is banned in public places such as bars and restaurants, though this rule is often ignored. Alcohol is socially acceptable – though homebrew liquor is sometimes dangerously tainted and so best avoided. The legal limit for drivers is 0.05 per cent BAC (blood alcohol content). Breaking this law can result in fines or imprisonment.

It's not unusual for tourists to receive unsolicited offers of illegal drugs on the streets, especially in Phnom Penh and Sihanoukville, but possession can result in lengthy prison sentences – or extortion by corrupt officials.

ID

Tourists are not legally required to carry ID, though it is advisable to carry at least a photocopy of some form of official identification, particularly when traveling outside of towns.

Local Customs

The *sompeyar* (a slight bow with palms pressed together) is a traditional greeting, and will be appreciated by locals, although handshakes are becoming more common.

Despite the apparent relaxed atmosphere around some tourist areas, especially those on the coast, Cambodia is a conservative society. Public displays of affection are inappropriate.

Neat, relatively modest dress (covered shoulders and below-the-knee shorts for both men and women) will make a good impression. Noisy or aggressive behavior is considered improper.

Visiting Temples

Cambodian temples are open to non-Buddhists, but respectful behavior is essential. Shoulders and legs should be covered for both men and women, and shoes should be removed before entering any buildings within a temple complex. Be aware that monks are forbidden to touch women – a rule that includes handshakes or contact while posing for photos.

Cell Phones and Wi-Fi

Wi-Fi is now ubiquitous in bigger towns, with virtually every hotel, restaurant, and café providing a free connection. Some intercity buses now also have on-board Wi-Fi. Connection speeds are not particularly fast, but usually adequate for browsing or using social media.

International GSM mobile phones usually have coverage in Cambodia – though check with your provider before travelling. Pre-paid local SIM cards are also readily available from phone shops. It is necessary to show proof of ID to buy a card, and vendors will generally set it up for you if you have an unlocked phone.

Post

Post offices are available in all but the smallest towns. Letters and postcards can take anywhere from two weeks to two months to reach destinations outside of Asia, but postage is very cheap. It is possible to send parcels through post offices, but couriers such as DHL and UPS, which have agents in Siem Reap and Phnom Penh, are faster and more reliable.

Taxes and Refunds

A 10 per cent sales tax is usually included in the marked price of retail goods, though some hotels and high-end restaurants do not include it in posted prices and add it to the bill at the end. No tax refunds are available for departing visitors, and duty-free items on sale at airports are sold at dramatically marked-up prices.

BEFORE YOU GO
LAOS

Plan ahead to make the most of your trip to Laos. Consider the following points before you travel so you're prepared for all eventualities.

AT A GLANCE

CURRENCY

Kip

US Dollar

AVERAGE DAILY SPEND

SAVE	SPEND	SPLURGE
$30	$60	$120+

BOTTLED WATER	COFFEE	BEER	DINNER FOR TWO
$0.50	$1	$1.50	$20

ESSENTIAL PHRASES

Hello	Sabaidee
Please	Kaluna
Thank you	Khobjai
Do you speak English?	Jaw vaw pasa anggit bor?
I don't understand	Khoy bauw khaojai

ELECTRICITY SUPPLY

Power sockets are mainly type C, fitting two-pin, round-pronged plugs. Flat-pronged type A plugs are also used. Standard voltage is 220v.

Passports and Visas

For entry requirements, including visas, consult your nearest Laos embassy or check the Laos **eVisa** website. Most travelers, including citizens of the UK, US, Canada, Australia, New Zealand, and the EU, can obtain a 30-day tourist visa on arrival (fee varies by nationality, from $30 to $42). A passport photo and address of your first accommodation in Laos are required. Citizens from other ASEAN countries don't need a tourist visa.
eVisa
🌐 laoevisa.gov.la

Government Advice

Now more than ever, it's important to consult both your and the Laos government's advice before traveling. The **UK Foreign and Commonwealth Office**, the **US State Department**, the **Australian Department of Foreign Affairs and Trade**, and the **Laos Ministry of Foreign Affairs** offer the latest information on security, health and local regulations.
Australia
🌐 smartraveller.gov.au
Laos Ministry of Foreign Affairs
🌐 mofa.gov.la
UK
🌐 gov.uk/foreign-travel-advice
US
🌐 travel.state.gov

Customs Information

You can find information on the laws relating to goods and currency taken in or out of Laos on the **IATA** website.
IATA
🌐 iata.org

Insurance

We recommend taking out a comprehensive insurance policy covering theft, loss of belongings, medical care (including medical evacuation), cancellations and delays, and read the small print carefully.

Vaccinations

Discuss vaccinations with your doctor at least eight weeks before traveling. Vaccinations against hepatitis, tetanus, and typhoid are recommended. Proof of yellow fever vaccination is required when arriving directly from an infected area. The risk of malaria is relatively low, particularly in Vientiane and Luang Prabang, but prophylaxis may be recommended if you plan to visit more remote areas. For information regarding COVID-19 vaccination requirements, consult government advice.

Money

Three currencies are in use in Laos. The official currency is the Lao kip, which is used for minor transactions. The Thai baht is regarded as an acceptable form of alternative payment, especially in border towns. The US dollar (used for prices in this guide) is also accepted, and is preferred when paying for hotels and high-end purchases.

Credit cards can be used in higher-end hotels, restaurants, and shops, and ATMs are available in larger towns. Contactless payments are being introduced in Laos, but are not yet common.

It is usual to tip wait staff 5–10 per cent, hotel porters $1 per bag, and tour guides 10 per cent.

Booking Accommodation

Online booking is now available for most accommodations in Vientiane and Luang Prabang. Accommodations in remote areas may not appear on online, however; even if they do, the systems are not always reliable, so confirm by phone.

During the drier, cooler months (November to March), prices tend to increase and advance booking is advisable. The best deals are available during the monsoon, from May to September.

Travelers with Specific Requirements

Laos does not cater well for travelers with specific requirements. Even in pedestrian-friendly cities like Luang Prabang, uneven pavements can present difficulties to visitors with limited mobility; there is also a lack of accommodations and restaurants with ramp access. Traveling to Laos requires careful planning, and will be smoothed by using guides and private transport. **Mobility**

International USA and **Wheelchairtraveling.com** have useful information. In addition, **Traveleyes**, a travel company that pairs blind and sighted travelers together, periodically runs trips to Laos.

Mobility International USA
w miusa.org
Traveleyes
w traveleyes-international.com
Wheelchairtraveling.com
w wheelchairtraveling.com

Language

Laos has great linguistic diversity. The official language is based on the dialect spoken around Vientiane, and is widely understood throughout the country. Locals appreciate visitors' efforts to speak Lao, if only a few words. Basic English is widely spoken around major tourist destinations.

Opening Hours

Situations can change quickly and unexpectedly. Always check before visiting attractions and hospitality venues for up-to-date opening hours and booking requirements.

Weekends Banks and post offices close.
Public holidays All banks close.

PUBLIC HOLIDAYS	
1 Jan	New Year's Day
6 Jan	Pathet Lao Day
20 Jan	Army Day
8 Mar	Women's Day
22 Mar	Lao People's Party Day
14–16 Apr	Lao New Year
1 May	International Labor Day
1 Jun	Children's Day
16 Jul	Boun Khao Pansa
20 Jul	Lao Women's Union Day
13–14 Oct	Boun Ok Pansa
11 Nov	Boun That Luang
2 Dec	National Day

GETTING AROUND
LAOS

Whether you are visiting Laos for just a few days or plan on touring the country, discover the best way to reach your destination.

AT A GLANCE

PUBLIC TRANSPORT COSTS

VIENTIANE

$2.50

100 mins
Public *jumbo* fare

LUANG PRABANG

$5

100 mins
Tuk-tuk fare

SAVANNAKHET

$10

8-10 hours
Bus from Vientiane

TOP TIP
The Laos section of the Laos–China railway is a great way to cross the country.

SPEED LIMITS

MOTORWAY

130 km/h
(80mph)

RURAL ROADS

90 km/h
(55mph)

SECONDARY ROAD

90 km/h
(50mph)

URBAN AREAS

40 km/h
(25mph)

Arriving by Air

The main airports in Laos are Vientiane's Wattay International Airport and Luang Prabang International Airport. Both are well served by regional budget airlines such as AirAsia. Vientiane has better long-haul connections, though it may be cheaper to make Bangkok the initial destination, then book an onward flight from there.

The smaller airports at Savannakhet and Pakse have limited regional connections, which can be useful for travelers heading directly to southern Laos, particularly from Bangkok.

In Vientiane, Luang Prabang, and Pakse, fixed-price taxis and minibuses should be booked at the taxi counter by the exit to the arrivals hall. The shuttle bus runs every 40 minutes from outside the airport at Vientiane. At Pakse, tuk-tuks can be hailed outside the airport and prices are negotiable. In Savannakhet, it is best to ask your accommodation to arrange a private transfer.

Arriving by Land

Laos has many border crossings with Thailand. The most heavily used is that between Vientiane and Nong Khai, which is served by trains from Bangkok. It is also possible to cross into northern Laos at several points, including Huay Xai en route to or from Chiang Rai in Thailand, and into southern Laos at Savannakhet or Pakse, with connections to and from Bangkok.

There are various border crossings with Vietnam. The most popular is at Dansavanh, which has direct bus services for the long journey between Vientiane and Hanoi or Ho Chi Minh City.

A single border with Cambodia is served by buses, running from Pakse to Stung Treng.

Visas are available on arrival at all official entry points, but e-visas may not be valid at the more minor crossings.

Domestic Air Travel

Laos's domestic flight network is a good way to avoid long-haul road journeys, although it is, of course, less environmentally friendly.

GETTING TO AND FROM THE AIRPORT

Airport	Distance to City	Taxi Fare	Public Transport	Journey Time
Vientiane	2 miles (4 km)	$8	bus	30 mins
Luang Prabang	2 miles (4 km)	$10	-	20 mins
Pakse	2 miles (3 km)	$5	-	15 mins

The northern part of Laos has a good number of domestic airports, including Huay Xai, Luang Nam Tha, Luang Prabang International, Phongsali, Xiengkhouang (in Phonsavan), Nathong (in Sam Neua), and Udomxai (in Muang Xi). Almost all flights, however, originate in Vientiane, so travelling between places within Laos by air generally involves transiting through the capital. The one exception is the direct route between Luang Prabang in the north and Pakse in the south.

Two airlines operate within Laos – **Lao Airlines**, the main domestic and regional operator, and **Lao Skyway**, which competes on the main domestic routes and also serves minor destinations not covered by Lao Airlines. Domestic flights are generally not as cheap as the regional routes covered by budget carriers. Fares between Vientiane and Luang Prabang typically start at around $70. Both airlines have online booking, but it is always a good idea to confirm bookings in person, particularly those to or from more remote destinations. If booking in person at an airline office, payment in US dollars is required.

Most domestic routes are served by twin-propeller planes, and cancellations are not unusual, particularly during the rainy season, so it is essential to allow plenty of time for alternative arrangements.

Lao Airlines
W laos-airlines.com
Lao Skyway
W laoskyway.com

Boats and Ferries

Regular passenger boats once plied the Mekong in Laos, but these have been superseded by buses in the last decade as road conditions improved. The last main ferry service links Luang Prabang with Pak Beng and Huay Xai. There are also many imprecisely scheduled services, usually provided by small open boats, on shorter stretches of the Mekong and Nam Ou, and around Si Phan Don.

Public Transport

Journey times in Laos are slow, especially during the monsoon, but a new high-speed rail network is revolutionizing transport. Within urban areas, public transportation is limited to a few minibuses and large shared tuk-tuks and jumbos running on fixed routes.

Trains

For a long time, Laos's rail network was limited to the short stretch of track across the Friendship Bridge from Nong Khai in Thailand. The opening of the Laos–China high-speed railway network in 2021 has changed everything. Running from Boten on Laos's northern border with China to Vientiane, the new high-speed rail makes it possible to cross the northern half of the country in around 5.5 hours, cutting journey times between Vientiane, Vang Vieng, and Luang Prabang to around a fifth of what they were before. Tickets can be bought up to three days in advance, either in person or via the LCR Ticket app, although this requires a local phone number.

Long-Distance Buses

Government buses serve all the major routes. They are usually basic affairs with hard seats and no air-con. For tickets, it is often possible simply to turn up at the bus station on the day.

Along the country's main transport spine, Route 13, which runs from Luang Prabang south to the Cambodian border, there are also many private operators while the website of **12Go** is another useful resource for booking journeys. Tickets are best booked through hotels or travel agents. Always be clear about the type of bus you'll be traveling on. VIP buses serving destinations off Route 13 may not meet any serious expectations of luxury.

12Go
W 12go.asia

Minivans

Air-conditioned minivans also serve major routes, typically departing when full and accommodating around ten passengers. Fares are usually slightly higher than on the buses, but journey times are often shorter on the same routes. They can also be chartered for a negotiable fee, which can be an excellent option for those traveling in a small group.

As with VIP buses, it is usually best to book through a hotel or travel agent, as private operators often use their own depots away from the main bus stations. Some travel agents include a transfer to the point of departure in the price.

City Buses

Vientiane has a city bus network, known as Vientiane City 2 Bus, which runs on fixed routes from the Talat Sao terminal. Single fares on Vientiane city routes are 15,000 kip (around $1.30), and route information can be found via the bus network's social media.

Tuk-tuks

Most travelers end up using tuk-tuks to get around cities. Tuk-tuks are ubiquitous in Laos, but they are markedly more expensive than in most neighboring countries, with drivers often demanding inflated fares from foreigners.

The typical Lao tuk-tuk is sometimes known locally as a *samlaw* ("three wheels"), and is similar to those found in Thailand. They comfortably seat two passengers. A few have a sidecar-style passenger seat.

Since tuk-tuk drivers mainly serve foreign travelers, many have evolved into self-appointed guides offering tours of local sights, particularly those out of town, such as waterfalls. If you find a good tuk-tuk driver, it is worth taking their cell phone number so you can call them to arrange this sort of excursion.

Jumbos

Jumbos look little different from tuk-tuks, though they are larger. Passengers usually board from the back, rather than the side, and they normally have two narrow benches where passengers sit facing one another, between stacks of tightly packed baggage. They run on roughly fixed routes and essentially serve as miniature city buses. Fares are low, but routes are aimed at local commuters rather than tourists and are not particularly useful for sightseeing.

Songthaews

Songthaews are like a scaled up version of a jumbo – a flatbed pickup truck with open sides, a roof canopy for shade, and a double

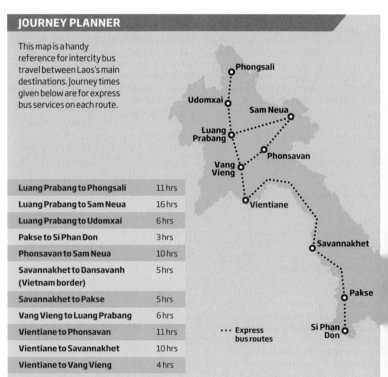

JOURNEY PLANNER

This map is a handy reference for intercity bus travel between Laos's main destinations. Journey times given below are for express bus services on each route.

Luang Prabang to Phongsali	11 hrs
Luang Prabang to Sam Neua	16 hrs
Luang Prabang to Udomxai	6 hrs
Pakse to Si Phan Don	3 hrs
Phonsavan to Sam Neua	10 hrs
Savannakhet to Dansavanh (Vietnam border)	5 hrs
Savannakhet to Pakse	5 hrs
Vang Vieng to Luang Prabang	6 hrs
Vientiane to Phonsavan	11 hrs
Vientiane to Savannakhet	10 hrs
Vientiane to Vang Vieng	4 hrs

Phongsali

Udomxai

Sam Neua

Luang Prabang

Phonsavan

Vang Vieng

Vientiane

Savannakhet

Pakse

Si Phan Don

••• Express bus routes

row of benches for passengers. They mainly run between villages in rural areas, and to the outlying suburbs of towns, with passengers flagging them down and hopping on and off along a loosely fixed route.

Taxis

Taxi services are generally provided by unmetered private vehicles, so it's always necessary to negotiate and fix a fare before you travel. Vientiane is the only place where taxis are readily available on the streets, with drivers often hanging around outside major hotels or tourist attractions. Vientiane also has a fleet of modern, metered yellow taxis, which can be called in advance for pickups.

In other places it is possible to find a car with a driver, but this usually needs to be arranged in advance of your visit, or via a travel agent or your hotel. Mobile transport hailing apps have yet to arrive in Laos.

Private Transport

Having your own transport allows for great deal of freedom when it comes to traveling in Laos. Unscheduled stops, detours, and getting off the beaten track become easy.

Driving in Laos

Although few foreign travelers rent cars during their visit to Laos, it is possible to do so. Vientiane has several local agencies, and **Avis** has branches in Luang Prabang, Pakse, and Savannakhet, as well as in Vientiane. Prices are not particularly cheap by international standards, and for short excursions it's often cheaper to charter a car with a driver via any hotel or travel agency. But for longer explorations, having your own vehicle can be a great option. A valid international driving permit is required to rent a car.

Avis

W avis.la

Motorbikes

Rented motorbikes are a far more common means of transport for tourists in Laos, with easy-to-ride 125cc scooters available in all major tourist destinations. In smaller towns it is usually also possible to arrange an informal rental – ask at hotel or guesthouse receptions. Bikes typically cost between $5 and $10 a day, with significant discounts available for longer rental periods.

Helmets are essential and, though traffic conditions are relatively calm by Southeast Asian standards, it is vital to take great care at all times. Although neither renters nor police commonly ask to see driving licenses, an international driving permit valid for motorbikes is required. It is also essential to have a valid license to be covered by travel insurance for motorbiking.

Cycling

The relatively light traffic in Laos makes it a great place for getting around by bicycle, and a bike can be a particularly good option to avoid the high tuk-tuk fares if you are spending several days exploring Luang Prabang.

Basic bikes suitable for exploring towns and the nearby countryside are available for a few dollars a day from numerous travel agencies and guesthouses in Luang Prabang and Vang Vieng, and in Si Phan Don. It is also possible to rent mountain bikes for more serious off-road explorations from operators in Luang Prabang.

Rules of the Road

Although the once quiet streets of Vientiane have become considerably more chaotic in recent years as private vehicle ownership booms, road conditions in Laos are generally far less daunting than in Thailand, Cambodia, or Vietnam. Even in regional centers such as Savannakhet and Luang Prabang, traffic is relatively light, and rural roads are very quiet.

Lao traffic travels on the right, though don't expect tuk-tuk and motorbike drivers to respect rules about overtaking, indicating, or giving way. It is important to be very cautious at intersections, and to remember the unspoken rule that "might is right," and that buses and trucks are unlikely ever to give way to smaller vehicles.

Road conditions in major towns, and along Route 13, are generally good, but in rural areas stretches of road may be unsurfaced, and potholes are a common hazard.

Walking

In keeping with Laos's comparatively quiet roads, the country's main urban centers are surprisingly walkable compared to some cities in Southeast Asia. Large vehicles like coaches are banned from Luang Prabang's historic core (and for the most part wouldn't fit through the narrow streets anyway), while Vientiane's riverside streets have been pedestrianized, allowing for markets, parks and play areas as well as easy walking; on Saturdays, the additional closure of the adjacent three-lane highway makes this area even more pedestrian-friendly.

Hiking in the Lao countryside, particularly the national parks, is a delight, but it is essential you stick to marked trails. The amount of unexploded ordnance in Laos means that you risk coming across it whenever you stray from waymarked paths.

PRACTICAL INFORMATION
LAOS

A little local know-how goes a long way in Laos. Below you'll find all the essential advice and information you will need during your stay.

AT A GLANCE

EMERGENCY NUMBERS

AMBULANCE	POLICE
1195	**1191**

FIRE SERVICE

1190

TIME ZONE
GMT +7, as in Thailand and Cambodia; no daylight saving.

TAP WATER
Tap water is not safe to drink in Laos; use bottled water.

WEBSITES

Laos Simply Beautiful
Laos's informative official tourism website *(tourismlaos.org)*

Vientiane Times
The main English-language news site for Laos *(vientianetimes.org.la)*.

HoboMaps
Detailed maps covering destinations throughout northern and central Laos *(hobomaps.com)*.

Personal Security

Laos is one of the safest countries for foreigners in Southeast Asia. Violent crime targeting tourists is virtually unknown, and overall crime rates are relatively low. Bag-snatching and pickpocketing do occur, however, especially in Vientiane. Be very careful with your belongings, particularly when riding in a tuk-tuk or visiting a crowded area. Thefts from hotel rooms are sometimes reported in Vang Vieng, so avoid leaving valuables unattended.

If you have anything stolen, report the crime as soon as possible at the nearest police station and take ID with you. Get a copy of the crime report to claim on your insurance. Contact your embassy or consulate if your passport is lost or stolen, or in the event of a serious crime or accident.

Tourist scams are far less common in Laos than in neighboring countries, and generally go no further than overcharging by tuk-tuk drivers. Do, however, be wary of any pleas for help with school fees or medical bills from strangers.

Unexploded ordinance is still a serious issue throughout the eastern border regions of Laos. It is very important to not stray from clearly defined trails when walking or cycling in these areas.

As a rule, Laotians are accepting of all people, regardless of their race, gender or sexuality. Although same-sex relations are not illegal in Laos, and there is little obvious public hostility, the vibrant gay scene of Thailand and Cambodia is not replicated here. A few low-key gay-friendly bars and restaurants exist in Vientiane and Luang Prabang. Public displays of affection are not appropriate for couples of any orientation, as Laos is a traditional society. Men and women should dress conservatively.

Health

Healthcare facilities in Laos are poor. There are some reputable private clinics in Vientiane, but any serious injuries or illnesses

are better treated across the border in Bangkok, Thailand. Therefore it is important to ensure you have comprehensive insurance that covers medical evacuation.

Minor stomach upsets, caused by unfamiliar food and climate, and poor hygiene, are the commonest health issue for travelers. Rest and rehydration are the main treatments; seek advice from a pharmacy or clinic if there is no improvement after a couple of days.

The risk of malaria is low in urban areas, but it is present in the countryside. Cover up in the evenings, use repellent, and consider taking anti-malaria medication for lengthy stays in remote regions.

Smoking, Alcohol, and Drugs

Smoking is officially banned in indoor public places, including restaurants, and on public transport. In practice, these rules are frequently violated – though they are generally observed in indoor tourist restaurants and VIP buses.

As well as the ubiquitous Beerlao, local moonshines are widely available in Laos. These are best avoided, as they are sometimes dangerously tainted with ethanol and other chemicals that can cause serious illness or even death. Although Laos has drink-driving laws (with a blood-alcohol-content limit of 0.08 per cent, as in the UK), drunk drivers are still a major cause of accidents.

As part of the Golden Triangle, it's not surprising that illegal drugs are widely available in Laos, and tourists may be offered cannabis and even opium by street hustlers in Vientiane. The country has strong anti-drug laws and these are strictly enforced. A former universal tolerance of drug use in Vang Vieng is now very much a thing of the past, and arrests of foreigners for possession are not unusual.

ID

Police and other officials sometimes request to see ID. A photocopy is acceptable if you don't wish to carry your passport with you.

Local Customs

The traditional Lao greeting is the *nop* (a slight bow with palms pressed together).

Despite the relaxed atmosphere, Laos is a traditional society, and religious values are important. Public displays of affection are unacceptable, and prestige and the concept of "saving face" is taken seriously. Direct confrontation, even in the case of serious dispute, will seldom lead to a satisfactory outcome, and aggressive behavior is considered particularly inappropriate.

Visiting Temples

Lao temples are open to non-Buddhists, but in this deeply religious country, respectful behavior is essential. Shoulders and legs should be covered for both men and women, and shoes should be removed before entering an inner building. Monks are respected figures, and should be treated as such.

Cell Phones and Wi-Fi

Wi-Fi is widely available in the main towns, with virtually every café and bar in Vientiane, Vang Vieng, and Luang Prabang offering free connections to visitors. In smaller towns and more remote areas, however, it is harder to get online and connection speeds are likely to be much slower.

International GSM mobile phones usually have coverage in Laos, and pre-paid local SIM cards are very cheap; it is often worth buying one for the duration of your stay.

Post

The postal service in Laos is slow, but fairly reliable. Valuable items and large packages are best sent via DHL or FedEx, which have agents in Vientiane. Postal and courier services are generally cheaper and more reliable in neighboring Thailand.

Taxes and Refunds

A 10 per cent sales tax is usually included in the marked price of retail goods, though some hotels and high-end restaurants do not include it in posted prices and add it to the bill at the end – check in advance if you are in any doubt. No tax refunds are available for departing visitors from Laos.

INDEX

PHRASE BOOK
CAMBODIA

Khmer or Cambodian is the language of the Khmer people and the official language of Cambodia. It is a widely spoken Austroasiatic language. Khmer has been considerably influenced by Sanskrit and Pali, especially in the royal and religious registers, through the vehicles of Hinduism and Buddhism. It is also the earliest recorded and written language of the Mon-Khmer family, predating Mon and, by a significant margin, Vietnamese. Khmer has influenced and also been influenced by Thai, Lao, Vietnamese, and Cham - many of which form a pseudo-sprachbund in peninsular Southeast Asia, since most contain high levels of Sanskrit and Pali influences. Additionally, during and after the French occupation, Khmer was strongly influenced by French. Hence, some of the medical, legal, and technical terminology is borrowed from it. The Khmer alphabet consists of 28 consonants and about 38 vowels. Unlike English, Khmer has a vowel for almost every sound, and is a phonetic language in both oral and written forms. It consists of long and short vowels with distinctive pronunciation. Unlike its Southeast Asian counterparts, Khmer does not have intonation.

GUIDELINES FOR PRONUNCIATION

The consonants are pronounced as follows:

k	is equivalent to the French pronunciation of k
kh	is equivalent to the English pronunciation of k
c	is a sound that is between c and j in English
ch	is equivalent to the English pronunciation of ch
ng	is equivalent to the English ending sound of ng
ny	is equivalent to the Spanish pronunciation of ñ
t	is equivalent to the French or Spanish pronunciation of t
th	is equivalent to the English pronunciation of t
p	is equivalent to the French or Spanish pronunciation of p (bi-labial, nonfricative)
ph	is equivalent to the English pronunciation of p
អ	is a representation of a consonant that has a vowel-like sound. Unlike English, Khmer cannot begin any word with a vowel. Hence this consonant "អ" is used

Vowels are pronounced as follows:

/a/ or /aa/	is equivalent to the French or Spanish pronunciation of /a/. The single /a/ is short while the double /aa/ is long.
/i/ or /ii/	is equivalent to the French or Spanish pronunciation of /i/. The single /i/ is short while the double /ii/ is long.
/o/ or /oo/	as in "zone," "cone," or "bone." The single /o/ is short while the double /oo/ is long.
/u/ or /uu/	as in "tune," "soon," or "cube." The single /u/ is short while the double /uu/ is long.
/aw/	as in "saw" or "thaw"
/y/ or /yy/	is a sound that does not exist in the English language. It is made in the epiglottis; a high sound made in the back of the oral cavity.
/ɛ/ or /ɛɛ/	is equivalent to the short /a/ or /ă/ of the English language. The single /ɛ/ is short while the double /ɛɛ/ is long.
/uh/	as in "doctor," "master," or "pasture"
/u/	as in the English sound "schwa"

A single vowel is a short vowel using the glottal stop to distinguish it from the long vowel.

A double or two vowels make a long vowel.

Akhosa is any consonant that ends with (aw) while choosa is any consonant that ends with (oo).

The former has a low sound while the latter is high. Hence, the tones change depending upon which of the two consonants is used.

IN AN EMERGENCY

Help!	ជួយផង!	Cuay phawng!
Fire!	ភ្លើងឆេះហើយ!	Phluhng cheh!
Where is the... nearest hospital?	តើ... មន្ទីរពេទ្យ បន្ទាប់នៅទីណា?	Tau montii peet kbae nih nuv tii naa?
Call an ambulance!	សុំហៅ ឡានពេទ្យ!	Som hau laan peet!
Call the police!	សុំហៅ ប៉ូលីស!	Som hau poolis!

COMMUNICATION ESSENTIALS

Hello!	សួស្ដី	Joom reapsooa!
Goodbye!	លាសិនហើយ	Joom reapleah!
Yes	បាទ / ចាស	Baat / caas
No	ទេ	Tee
Please	សូម	Soom
Thank you	សូមអរគុណ	awkoon
I don't understand	ខ្ញុំមិនយល់ទេ	Khnyom min yul tee
Sorry/excuse me	សូមអភ័យទោស !	Soom aphpheytoos
What?	អ្វី?	Aawey aawey?
Why?	ហេតុអ្វី?	Haet aawey?
Where?	នៅទីណា?	Nuv tii naa?
How?	ដោយរបៀប ៉ ្រ៉បណា?	Doay roobiab naa?

USEFUL PHRASES

How are you?	តើ អ្នកសុខសប្បាយ ទេ?	Tau neak sok sabaay cia tee?
How do I get to...?	តើ ខ្ញុំអាចទៅ ៉ ទៅ...?	Tau khnyom aac tuv ae...?
Where is the restroom/toilet?	តើ...នៅកន្លែងណា? បន្ទប់ទឹក?	Tau...nuv tii kawnlaeng naa? bawntub tyk?
Do you speak English?	តើ អ្នកចេះនិយាយភាសា អង់គ្លេសទេ?	Tau neak niyiay phiasaa awngkles ryy tee?
I can't speak Khmer/Lao	ខ្ញុំមិននិយាយភាសា ខ្មែរ / លាវទេ	Khnyom min niyiay phiasaakhmae/ liaw tee

USEFUL WORDS

open	បើក	bauk
closed	បទ	bet
left	ខាងឆ្វេង	khaang chweeng
right	ខាងស្ដាំ	khaang sdam
straight ahead	ខាងមុខ	khaang muk
near	ក្បែរនេះ	kbae nih
far	ឆ្ងាយ	chngaay
entrance	ផ្លូវចូល	phlow cool
exit	ផ្លូវចេញ	phlow cenya

MONEY

I want to change US$100 into 100 Cambodian/Lao currency.	ខ្ញុំចង់ប្ដូរលុយ ១០០ដុល្លា រ ទ ៉ក្នុង ១០០ លុយខ្មែរ/លាវ	Khnyom cawng bdoo luy muayrooy dollaa tuv knong luy khmae/ liaw.
exchange rate	ទំរង់នៃការប្ដូរ	dawmlay ney kaabdoo
bank	ធនាគារ	thooniakia
money/cash	លុយ / លុយសុទ្ធ	luy/ lut sot
credit card	កាតក្រេឌីត	kaatkreedit

KEEPING IN TOUCH

I'd like to make a telephone call.	ខ្ញុំចង់ ្រ៉ ទូរស័ព្ទ	Khnyom cawng prau tuurosap.
I'd like to make an international phone call.	ខ្ញុំចង់ស្រុកទៅ្រក្រ ្រ ៉ ១បរទេសោ	Khnyom cawng tuurosap cenya tuv prawteh.
cell phone	ទូរស័ព្ទដៃ	tuurosap day

SHOPPING

How much does this cost?	តើ នេះមានតម្លៃ ៉ ៉ ?	Tau nih mian daw- mlay ponmaan?

I would like...	១.ញ្ញាច្ន់..់	*Khnyom cawng...*
Do you take credit cards?	តើ.អ្នកយកគ្.រ.ចេឌិតកាតទេ?	*Tau neak yook kreedit kaat ryy tee?*
What time do you open/close?	តើ.ពេលណាអ្នកបេ.ក៣.ក រឺទិ.ព.ក?	*Tau peel naa neak bauk twia ryy but twia?*
market	ផ្.សា	*phsaa*
pharmacy	ឱសៃស្.ហាន	*oasawtthaan*
souvenir store	ហាងលក់អនុស្.សាវរីយ៍	*haang luk ahnuhsaawoorii*
souvenirs	អនុស្.សាវរីយ៍	*ahnuhsaawoorii*

SIGHTSEEING

beach	ឆាងស់មទ្.រ	*moat sawmut*
island	កោ.ះ	*koh*
lake	បជឹ	*bung*
mountain	ភ្.នំ	*phnom*
museum	សារមន្.ទី	*saamontii*
tourist office	ការិយាល័យទេសចរណ៍	*kaariyaalay tehsacaw*
travel agent	ភ្.នាក់ងារទេសចរណ៍	*phneak ngia tehsacaw*

TRANSPORTATION

A ticket to...please.	សម្.ចូបត្.រ.ទៅ ១...	*Soom tinya... sawbot tuv.*
Where is the bus stop?	តើ.ចុទ្ធីសរាប់ប៍ស៍ នៅ ១ឯណ៍ា?	*Tau weetikaa sawmrab bus nuv tii naa?*
train station	ស្.ថានីយ៍រទេះភ្.លេ.ឹង	*sthaanii rootehphluhng*
airport	៣លយន្.ដហោ.ះ	*wial yunhawh*
bus station	ស្.ថានីយ៍ប៍ស	*sthaanii bus*
ticket	សប៍ត្.រ	*sawmbot*
one-way ticket	សប៍ត្.រសៃកទសិ	*sawmbot aektys*
round-trip ticket	សប៍ត្.រ.ទ្រ្របម៍ករ៍ញ	*sawmbot trawlawb niik winya*
taxi	តាក់ស្ឺ	*taksii*
car rental	ការជ្ឈូ ល្ញ្ហាន	*kaacual laan*
plane ticket	លិខិត្.យេរ៖ ហោ.ះ	*likhet yunhawh*
motorcycle	ម៩ូ	*mootoo*
bicycle	កជ៍	*kawng*

ACCOMMODATIONS

Do you have a vacant room?	តើ.មានបន្.ទប់ទំនេរទេ?	*tau mian bawntub tumnee ryytee?*
I have a reservation	១.ញ្ញាច្ន់ធ្.វ្ក៍ា រ៉ាវុ៣ទុកជាមុ	*Khnyom cawng thwuhkaa bawm-rong tuk cia mun*
double/twin room	បន្.ទ្របំរាប់បុស្. សណីនក្	*bawntub sawrab moonuh pii neak*
single room	បន្.ទ្របំរាប់បុស្. សម.ន្ត្ាក់	*bawntub sawrab moonuh mneak*
hotel	សណ្.ឋាការ	*sawnthaakia*
guesthouse	បន្.ទប់ទទួលភ្ញ្រ.ឱ្	*bawntub tootual phnyiaw*
air conditioning	ម៉ាស្ឺនត្.រជាក់	*maasin trawceak*
bathroom	បន្.ទប់ទ៍ក	*bawntub tyk*

EATING OUT

May I see the menu?	១.ញ្ញាស៍ម្ឹ.លមញ្ញ ជី៣ហារបានទេ?	*Khnyom som muhl aahaa baan tee?*
Can I have the check, please?	តើ.ខ្.ញ្ញាអ៍កបានលុយវិត្. លុយៃ៍?	*Tau khnyom bann likhut luy ryy tee?*
baguette	ន៍ប៍ង	*num pang*
beef	សាចៃ.ក.រ	*sac koo*
beer	បៃ.រ	*bia*
chicken	សាច្ម៍ាន់	*sac moan*
chopsticks	ឆ្ន.ក៍ស៍	*cawngkus*
coffee	ការ៉េ.ស្	*kaafee*
egg	ពងមាន់	*poongmoan*
fish	សាចៃ.ត្.រ	*sactrey*
fork	សៃម	*sawm*
meat	សាច់	*sac*

mineral water	ទ៍កសាប	*tyk saab*
noodles	គុយទា៉	*kuytiaw*
pork	សាចជ៍. រ្ក	*sac crook*
prawn	បង្.គា	*bawngkia*
restaurant	ភ្.ៃ៣ជនីយដ្.ឋាន	*phoocooniithaan*
rice	អង្.ករ រ៍ ៃ៣យ	*awngkaw/ baay*
spicy (hot)	ហឹរ៉ុណ.ស់	*hel nas*
vegetables	បន្.ល្ក៍	*bawnlae*
water	ទ៍កសាប	*tyk saab*
Western food	៣ហាររម៍រិកិ៌ង	*aahaa aameerikang*

HEALTH

I do not feel well	១.ញ្ញាមិន.ស្រូ៉ល.ខ្លុន	*khnyom min srual khluan*
I have a fever	១.ញ្ញាក៍.រ្ន	*khnyom krun*
I'm allergic to antibiotics	១.ញ្ញាក្ន្ទោស់ ៦.ន្ម៍ាំង៍ប់ផៃ.រក	*khnyom min toas thnam rumngoab meerook*
blood pressure (high/low)	ឈាម (ឡ្ឺ.ង រ៍ ៃ៉ះ)	*chiam (laum/cos)*
diabetes	ជំង៍ទ៍ីករា៉យភ្.អៃម	*cumngyy tyknoomph-aem*
diarrhea	រា៉ត	*riak*
food poisoning	ការឈ្ម៉ឹ៣ហារ	*kaapul aahaa*
headache	ការឈ្ម៍.ក្បាល	*kaachyy kbaal*
malaria	ជំង៍ី.រ្គុតចាញ៉	*cumngyy krun canya*
prescription	សប៍ត្.រ៦.ន្មពៃ.ទ្.យ	*sawmbot thnam peet*
temperature	៣៣តអុកាស	*thiat aakas*

TIME AND DAY

minute	៣៣ទ្ឺ	*niatii*
hour	ម៍ៃ៉ង	*moang*
day	៦.ង្ៃ៉	*thngay*
week	៣អាទិ.ត្.យ	*aatit*
month	៩រ	*khae*
year	ឆ្.ន៉ា	*chnam*
Monday	៦.ង្ៃចៃន.ទ្	*Thngay can*
Tuesday	៦.ង្ៃអ៉ង្.ការ	*Thngay awngkia*
Wednesday	៦.ង្ៃពុធ	*Thngay put*
Thursday	៦.ង្ៃព្.រ៉ហស្.បត៍	*Thngay proohoas*
Friday	៦.ង្ៃសៃក្.រ	*Thngay sok*
Saturday	៦.ង្ៃស៉ៃ.រ៍	*Thngay sau*
Sunday	៦.ង្ៃអាទិ.ត្.យ	*Thngay aatit*
What time is it?	តើ.ម៍ៃ៉ងប៉ុន្ម៉ាំ៣ហើ.យ?	*Tau moong ponmaan hauy?*
morning	ព្.រ៍ក	*pryk*
afternoon	៦.ង្ៃរៃ៉.ស៉ៃ.ល	*thngay roosial*
evening	ល្.ង៉ាច	*lngiac*
night	យប់'	*yub*

NUMBERS

1	ម៍ូយ	*muay*
2	៣ឺ	*pii*
3	ប៍ី	*bey*
4	៣ន	*buan*
5	៣.រា៉	*pram*
6	៣.រ៉ម៍ូយ	*prammuay*
7	៣.រ៉ពី.រ៍	*prampii*
8	៣.រ៉ប៍ី	*prambey*
9	៣.រ៉ប៍ូន	*prambuan*
10	ដប់	*dawb*
20	ម្.ៃ៉	*muayphey*
30	សាមស៍ប់	*saamseb*
40	ស៍ៃ.ស៍ប់	*saeseb*
50	ហាស៍ប់	*haaseb*
60	ហុ៣ស៍ប់	*hokseb*
70	៣ឹ៣ស៍ប់	*cetseb*
80	៣ៃ៉ស៍ប់	*paetseb*
90	កៃ ៉ស៍ប់	*kawseb*
100	ម៍ូយរយ	*muayrooy*
1,000	ម៍ូយ៣.ន់	*muaypoan*
10,000	ម៍ូយម៍ឺ	*muaymuhn*
1,000,000	ម៍ូយល៉ាន	*muaylian*

PHRASE BOOK LAOS

Lao or Pasa Lao, the official language of Laos, is a tonal, generally monosyllabic language. Thus having good pronunciations and tonal sounds is essential for communication. It is a part of the Tai sub-group of the Sino-Tibetan group of languages, and its written form evolved from an ancient Indian script called Pali. Just like English, Lao is read from left to right and follows the subject-verb-object word order. In addition, most Lao letters are pronounced just like the sounds that exist in English. However, Lao differs from English in that it has little grammar, no plurals, few articles, and regularly omits the subject pronouns (I, he, she) when the context is understood.

GUIDELINES FOR PRONUNCIATION

Lao consonants below have been divided into three groups according to the tone in which they are spoken. The consonants are pronounced as follows:

Aksone sung (high sounding consonant)

ຂ	**kh**	like 'c' in "cat" (aspirated)
ສ	**s**	like 'ss' in "hiss"
ຖ	**th/t**	like 't' in "top"
ຜ	**ph**	like 'p' in "pig" (aspirated)
ໝ	**m**	similar to 'm' in "mother"
ຫຼ	**l**	similar to 'l' in "long"
ຫວ	**w**	like 'w' in "weight"

Aksone kang (middle sounding consonant)

ກ	**k/g**	like 'k' in "skate" (unaspirated)
ຈ	**ch/j**	like 'ch' in "chop"
ດ	**d/t**	like 'd' in "dog"
ຕ	**t**	like 't' in "stab"
ບ	**b**	like 'b' in "bed"
ປ	**p**	like 'p' in "spit" (unaspirated)
ຢ	**y**	like 'y' in "yes"
ອ	**o**	like 'o' in "top"

Aksone tum (low sounding consonant)

ງ	**ng**	like 'ng' in "sing"
ຊ	**s/x**	like 'z' in "zoo"
ຍ	**nh/y**	like 'y' in "yes"
ຟ	**f**	like 'f' in "fan"
ມ	**m**	like 'm' in "mother"
ຣ	**r**	like 'r' in "room"
ລ	**l**	like 'l' in "love"
ວ	**v**	like 'v' in "vacant"
ຫ	**h**	like 'h' in "help"
ນ	**n**	like 'n' in "nice"

Lao vowels are pronounced as follows:

ິ	**i**	like 'i' in "nit"
ີ	**ii**	like 'ee' in "feet"
ະ	**a**	like 'u' in "gum"
າ	**aa**	like 'a' in "father"
ແະ	**ae**	like 'a' in "fat"
ແ	**e**	like 'e' in "fence"
ເ	**eh**	like in 'ai' in "bait"
ຸ	**u**	like 'u' in "fruit"
ູ	**ou**	like 'oo' in "mood"
າວ	**aw**	like 'aw' in "saw"
ຳ	**am**	like 'um' in "drum"
ເິ	**oe**	similar to the 'uh' in "huh"
ເ	**eu**	like 'eu' in the French "deux"

IN AN EMERGENCY

Help!	ຊ່ວຍແດ່!	Suoy dae!
Fire!	ໄຟໃໝ້!	Fai mai!
Where is the nearest hospital?	ໂຮງໝໍໃກ້ສຸດຢູ່ໃສ?	Hong Mor Kai Sud Yu sai?
Call an ambulance!	ໂທຫາລົດຂົນສົ່ງຄົນເຈັບແດ່!	Towha lod khonsong khonchep dae!
Call the police!	ໂທຫາຕຳຫຼວດແດ່!	Towha tum luot dae!
Call a doctor!	ໂທຫາທ່ານໝໍແດ່!	Towha thanmor dae!

COMMUNICATION ESSENTIALS

Hello!	ສະບາຍດີ!	Sabaidee!
Goodbye!	ລາກ່ອນ!	Lakhon!
Yes	ແມ່ນ	Maen
No	ບໍ່	Bauw
Please	ກະລຸນາ	Kaluna
Thank you	ຂອບໃຈ	Khobjai
No, thank you	ບໍ່, ຂອບໃຈ	Bauw, Khobjai
I don't understand	ຂ້ອຍບໍ່ເຂົ້າໃຈ	Khoy Bauw Khaojai
Sorry/excuse me	ຂໍໂທດ!	Khauwthod
What?	ແມ່ນຫຍັງ?	Maen yang?
Why?	ຍ້ອນຫຍັງ?	Yonyang?
Where?	ຢູ່ໃສ?	U sai?

USEFUL PHRASES

How are you?	ເຈົ້າສະບາຍດີບໍ?	Jaw Sabaidee Bor?
Very well, thank you – and you?	ຂ້ອຍສະບາຍດີ, ຂອບໃຈ – ເຈົ້າເດ?	Khoy sabaidee, Khobjai – Jawdee?
How do I get to...?	ຂ້ອຍຈະໄປ... ໄດ້ແນວໃດ?	Khoychapai ....ai neo day?
Where is the restroom/toilet?	ຫ້ອງນ້ຳຢູ່ໃສ?	Hongnam u sai?
Do you speak English?	ເຈົ້າເວົ້າພາສາອັງກິດບໍ?	Jaw Vaw Pasa Anggit Bor?
I can't speak Khmer/Lao	ຂ້ອຍບໍ່ສາມາດເວົ້າພາສາກຳປູເຈຍ/ພາສາລາວໄດ້	Khoy bor sa mart vaw pasa gampuchia/ pasa Lao dai.

USEFUL WORDS

woman/women	ແມ່ຍິງ	mae ying
man/men	ຜູ້ຊາຍ	phu xai
child/children	ເດັກນ້ອຍ	dek noy
open	ເປີດ	peurt
closed	ປິດ	pit
left	ຊ້າຍ	sai
right	ຂວາ	khoua
near	ໃກ້	kai (high falling short)
far	ໄກ	kai (mid to long)
entrance	ເຂົ້າ	khao
exit	ອອກ	ork

MONEY

I want to change US$100 into 100 Cambodian/Lao currency.	ຂ້ອຍຕ້ອງການປ່ຽນ 100 ໂດລາເປັນເງິນ ກຳປູເຈຍ/ເງິນກີບລາວ	Khoy tong kan pien neung hoy do la pen ngeun kampuchia/ngeun kip lao.
exchange rate	ອັດຕາແລກປ່ຽນ	aat ta laek pien
I'd like to cash these traveler's checks.	ຂ້ອຍຕ້ອງການແລກ ໃບເຊັກທ່ອງທ່ຽວ ເຫຼົ່ານີ້ເປັນເງິນສົດ	Khoy tong kan laek bai sek thong thieu nee pen ngeun sot.
bank	ທະນາຄານ	thanakhan
money/cash	ເງິນ/ເງິນສົດ	ngeun/ngeun sot
credit card	ບັດເຄດິດ	bat khe dit

KEEPING IN TOUCH

I'd like to make a telephone call.	ຂ້ອຍຢາກໂທລະສັບ	Khoy yark tow la sap.
cell phone	ໂທລະສັບມືຖື	tow la sap meu theu
public phone booth	ຕູ້ໂທລະສັບສາທາລະນະ	tu tow la sap sa tha la na

SHOPPING

English	Lao	Transliteration
How much does this cost?	ອັນນີ້ລາຄາເທົ່າໃດ?	An nee la kha thao dai?
What time do you open/close?	ເຈົ້າເປີດ/ປິດເວລາ ກໍ່ໂມງ?	Jaw peurt/pit vei la chak moung?
size	ຂະໜາດ	kha nat
market	ຕະຫຼາດ	ta lat
pharmacy	ຮ້ານຂາຍຢາ	han khai ya
souvenir store	ຮ້ານຂາຍຂອງທີ່ ເບິກ	han khai khong tee la neuk

SIGHTSEEING

English	Lao	Transliteration
cave, grotto	ຖ້ຳ	tham
lake	ໜອງ	nong
mountain	ພູເຂົາ	phu khao
river	ແມ່ນ້ຳ	nam
tourist office	ຫ້ອງການທ່ອງທ່ຽວ	hong kan thong thieu
travel agent	ຄົວແທນທ່ອງທ່ຽວ	tou thaen thong thieu

TRANSPORTATION

English	Lao	Transliteration
A ticket to...please.	ເອົາປີໄປ.... ໃຫ້ແດ່.	Aw pii pai ... hai dae.
Where is the bus stop?	ບ່ອນຈອດວົດເມຍຢູ ໃສ?	Bon chot lot mei u sai?
arrivals	ຂາເຂົ້າ	kha khao
airport	ສະໜາມບິນ	sa nam bin
one-way ticket	ປີ້ຂາໄປ	pii kha pai
round-trip ticket	ປີ້ໄປກັບ	pii pai kub
taxi	ວົດແທກຊີ	lot taek xee
car rental	ການເຊົ່າວົດ	kan sao lot
plane ticket	ປີ້ຍົນ	pii nhon
motorbike	ວົດຈັກ	lot chak
bicycle	ວົດຖີບ	lot theep

ACCOMMODATIONS

English	Lao	Transliteration
Do you have a vacant room?	ເຈົ້າມີຫ້ອງຫວ່າງບໍ່?	Jaw mee hong vang bor?
I have a reservation	ຂ້ອຍໄດ້ຈອງໄວ້ແລ້ວ	Khoy dai chong vai laeo
double/twin room	ຫ້ອງຕຽງຄູ່/ສອງຕຽງ	hong tieng khou/ song tieng
single room	ຫ້ອງຕຽງດ່ຽວ	hong tieng dieu
hotel	ໂຮງແຮມ	hoong haem
guesthouse	ເຮືອນພັກ	heuan pak
air conditioning	ເຄື່ອງປັບອາກາດ	kheuang pap aakard
bathroom	ຫ້ອງອາບນ້ຳ	hong arb nam
passport number	ວາງຫົວໜັງສືຜ່ານ ແດນ	Leik tee nang su phan daen

EATING OUT

English	Lao	Transliteration
May I see the menu?	ຂ້ອຍຂໍເບິ່ງເມນູໄດ້ບໍ່?	khoy khor beung mei nu dai bor?
Can I have the check, please?	ກະລຸນາ ເອົາບິນໃຫ້ ແດ່?	Ka lu na ao bin hai dae?
baguette	ເຂົ້າຈີ່ກ້ອນຍາວ	khao chii kon yao
beef	ຊີ້ນງົວ	xeen ngua
chopsticks	ໄມ້ຖູ່	mai thu
chicken	ໄກ່	gai
coffee	ກາເຟ	ka fei
crab	ປູ	pu
egg	ໄຂ່	khai
fish	ປາ	pa
fork	ສ້ອມ	som
fruit	ໝາກໄມ້	mark mai
meat	ຊີ້ນ	xeen
mineral water	ນ້ຳແຮ່	nam hae
milk	ນົມ	noom
noodles	ເສັ້ນ	mee
pepper	ໝີກໄທ	pik thai
pork	ຊີ້ນໝູ	xeen mou
prawn	ກຸ້ງ	kung
restaurant	ຮ້ານອາຫານ	han aa han
rice	ເຂົ້າ	khao
salt	ເກືອ	keua
spicy (hot)	ເຜັດ	fet

HEALTH

English	Lao	Transliteration
spoon	ບ່ວງ	boang
sugar	ນ້ຳຕານ	nam tan
tea	ຊາ	xaa
vegetables	ຜັກ	fak
water	ນ້ຳ	nam
Western food	ອາຫານຕາເວັນຕົກ	aa han ta ven tok

HEALTH

English	Lao	Transliteration
I do not feel well	ຂ້ອຍຮູ້ສຶກບໍ່ສະບາຍ	Khoy hu seuk bor sa bai
It hurts here	ມັນເຈັບຢູ່ບ່ອນນີ້	Man cheb bon nee
I have a fever	ຂ້ອຍເປັນໄຂ້	Khoy pen khai
I'm allergic to antibiotics	ຂ້ອຍແພ້ ຢາຕ້ານເຊື້ອ	Khoy pae ya tan xeua
blood pressure (high/low)	ຄວາມດັນເລືອດ (ສູງ/ຕ່ຳ)	khoam dun luot (sung/tum)
cough	ໄອ	i
diabetes	ເບົາຫວານ	bao wan
diarrhea	ຖອກທ້ອງ	thok thong
food poisoning	ອາຫານເປັນພິດ	aa han pen pit
headache	ເຈັບຫົວ	cheb hua
illness	ການເຈັບປ່ວຍ	kan cheb puoy
malaria	ໄຂ້ມາເລເຣຍ	khai ma la ria
prescription	ໃບສັ່ງຢາ	bai sang ya
toothache	ເຈັບແຂ້ວ	cheb khaeo

TIME AND DAY

English	Lao	Transliteration
minute	ນາທີ	na tii
hour	ຊົ່ວໂມງ	xou mohng
day	ມື້	meuh
week	ອາທິດ	aa thit
month	ເດືອນ	deuan
Monday	ວັນຈັນ	Van chan
Tuesday	ວັນອັງຄານ	Van ang khan
Wednesday	ວັນພຸດ	Van phut
Thursday	ວັນພະຫັດ	Van pa hat
Friday	ວັນສຸກ	Van suk
Saturday	ວັນເສົາ	Van sao
Sunday	ວັນອາທິດ	Van aa thit
What time is it?	ເວລາຈັກໂມງແລ້ວ?	Vei la chak mohng laeo?
morning	ຕອນເຊົ້າ	ton xao
afternoon	ຕອນບ່າຍ	ton baii
evening	ຕອນແລງ	ton laeng
night	ກາງຄືນ	kang keun

NUMBERS

1	ໜຶ່ງ	neung
2	ສອງ	song
3	ສາມ	saam
4	ສີ່	sii
5	ຫ້າ	ha
6	ຫົກ	hok
7	ເຈັດ	jet
8	ແປດ	paet
9	ເກົ້າ	kao
10	ສິບ	sip
20	ຊາວ	xao
30	ສາມສິບ	saam sip
40	ສີ່ສິບ	sii sip
50	ຫ້າສິບ	ha sip
60	ຫົກສິບ	hok sip
70	ເຈັດສິບ	jet sip
80	ແປດສິບ	paet sip
90	ເກົ້າສິບ	kao sip
100	ໜຶ່ງຮ້ອຍ	neung hoy
1,000	ໜຶ່ງພັນ	neung pan
10,000	ສິບພັນ	sip pan
1,000,000	ໜຶ່ງລ້ານ	neung laan

ACKNOWLEDGMENTS

DK would like to thank Tim Hannigan, David Chandler, Peter Holmshaw, Iain Stewart, Richard Waters and Hilary Bird for their contribution to the previous edition.

The publisher would like to thank the following for their kind permission to reproduce their photographs:

Key: a-above; b-below/bottom; c-center; f-far; l-left; r-right; t-top

123RF.com: Nuwat Chanthachanthuek 198-9t; Niti Kantarote 14t; Kwanchai Khammuean 30t; Somchai Rakin 41cla.

4Corners: Stefano Coltelli 94-5t; Daniele Coppa 201b; Kristel Richard 27cl; Luigi Vaccarella 106-7b.

Alamy Stock Photo: Arcaid Images 153bl; Brian Atkinson 31clb; BE&W agencja fotograficzna Sp. z o.o. 171tr; Pawel Bienkowski 35cla, 56cl; Tibor Bognar 59bl; Guy Brown 37tr; Paul Brown 178bl; Michele Burgess 196bc; Chronicle 86fbr; Classic Image 60bl; David Coleman 155tr, 200tl; Max Dominik Daiber 215tr; David Noton Photography 2-3; dbimages 171clb; Danita Delimont 160cr; Everett Collection Historical 61bl, 154-5t; Stephen Ford 85br; Philip Game 150bl; David Gee 203t, 203cla; Alexey Gnilenkov 160cb, 161; Mike Goldwater 199bl; Paul Hayman 59tl; Hemis 33b, 142-3b; hemis.fr / Guiziou Franck 44-45t; imageBROKER 25tr, 29cl, 182bl, 211c, 212br; Image Source Limited / Rosanna U 39cl; Jack Malipan Travel Photography 116br, 130t; Jon Arnold Images Ltd 90cl; Keystone Pictures USA 60tl, 60br; Lena Kuhnt 187br; Mat Ladley 8-9; Jason Langley 177br; Lazyllama 91cr; Leslie Garland Pictures 86fclb; Yadid Levy 70bl; LOOK Die Bildagentur der Fotografen GmbH 33cl; M@rcel 175cr; M.Sobreira 97fclb; mauritius images GmbH 79tl; Neil McAllister 163br; John Michaels 18-9ca; Michiel Bosch (BKK Photography) 151cr; Raquel Mogado 109bc; NiceProspects-Prime 46-7b; Stuart Pearce 25cla; Peter Ptschelinzew 162bc; Paul Quayle 63br; Radius Images 59ca; Sergi Reboredo 35crb; Lionela Rob 37crb; robertharding 162-3t; robertharding / Yadid Levy 39br; Norbert Scanella 6-7, 24-5t, 192br, 218; Andy Selinger 32bl; Valerii Shanin 182-3t; Kumar Sriskandan 24tl; Steve Davey Photography 151tr; Komal Thadani 88bl; Aroon Thaewchatturat 61br; Ariadne Van Zandbergen 98tr; Mireille Vautier 151tl; Vedrana2701 39t; Steve Vidler 171br; Germán Vogel 76tr; Matthew Wakem 49br; wanderworldimages 152bc; Terry Whittaker 36br; Steve Whyte 90c; Darren Wilch 122bl; Jan Wlodarczyk 50–51; Xinhua 57cr, 150cla, 151bl; Joanna Yee 47tl; Ron Yue 91c; ZUMA Press Inc. 28cra; ZUMA Press Wire / SOPA Images / Peerapon Boonyakiat 61cra

Angkor Photo Festival: Irène Yap 57br.

AWL Images: Aurora Photos 176cra; Matteo Colombo 12ca, 57cl; Bertrand Gardel 54cl, 54-5, 69; Katie Garrod 216tl; Franck Guiziou 104t; Jason Langley 4, 16cl, 96, 172-3b, 179t; Tim Mannakee 210-1t; Michele Falzone 195crb; Alex Robinson 45tr; Travel Pix Collection 98bl; Ian Trower 71tr.

Bridgeman Images: History 58br; Musee National de Phnom Pen, Cambodia 97fclb; Pictures from History 153tr, 154bl, 154fbr; Veneranda Biblioteca Ambrosiana, Milan, Italy / De Agostini Picture Library 152t.

Depositphotos Inc: actionbleem 44bl.

Dorling Kindersley: Green Discovery Laos / Linda Whitwam 195cr, 195br.

Dreamstime.com: Addimaging 153cla; Rui Baião 174br; Beibaoke1 106tc; Blagodeyatel 22-3t; Blanscape 29cr; Jaromír Chalabala 16clb; Bundit Chotsuwan 30-1b; Chrishowey 55clb, 124-5; Karin De Mamiel 115cra; Luke Derriman 86clb; Digitalpress 202br; Dinozzaver 38cra, 136-137t 118-9t; Donyanedomam 13t; Stefano Ember 38tl; F11photo 14-5b; Filmlandscape 20tl; Gkasabova 36tl; Tatsiana Hendzel 62-63t; Oliver Hitchen 37cl; Soon Img 115t; Jackmalipan 8cla, 8cl, 32-3t, 77b, 132-3t; John6863373 26-7b; Prasert Krainukul 140tl; Krajinar 120crb; Alain Lauga 15br; Nhut Le Quang 21tl; Fabio Lamanna 38b; Madrugadaverde 174-5t; Aliaksandr Mazurkevich 195tr; Luciano Mortula 59tr; Phuongphoto 141b; Pradit Pinyopasakul 86cra; Pixattitude 98-9t; Platongkoh 173crb; Pnichaya 58bc; Tawatchai Prakobkit 101cr; Presse750 43br, 73tr, 121tl, 165tc, 212t; Psstockfoto 27br; Matyas Rehak 63crb; Buntoon Rodseng 43cl; Dmitry Rukhlenko 18tl; Sergeychernov 26t; Alexander Shalamov 47br; Skolton 23tr, 40b; Sutiponmm 144-5; Theerapong28 184-85; Aleksandar Todorovic 19tr; Tortoon 20-1ca, 194b; Tith Vannarith 56bl; James Wagstaff 31bc; Teerachakorn Watthakawimol 118bl.

Getty Images: AFP 57tl / Tang Chhin Sothy 57tr; 61tr; Glen Allison 173tr; Anadolu Agency 56cla; Andy Teo aka Photocillin 74-5; Elizabeth Beard 43tr, 108t; Anders Blomqvist 219tr; Bloomberg 155cra; Tessa Bunney 45crb; John Seaton Callahan 137br; Sayan Chuenudomsavad 105b; Cultura Exclusive / Matt Dutile 120b; DAE / Biblioteca Ambrosiana 97crb; Luis Dafos 148cl, 156-7; Dave Stamboulis Travel Photography 217b; Pascal Deloche 59bc; Grant Dixon 18tr; Thierry Falise 57bl; Godong 97clb, / Catherine Leblanc 29tl; Manfred Gottschalk 29cla; David Greedy 151cl; Historical Picture Archive 58t; Keystone-France 154tl; Philippe Le Tellier 154br; LightRocket / Ben Davies 197tr; Lonely Planet Images / Grant Dixon 123tr; Michael Melford 48-9t; Roland Neveu 60–61t; Kyodo News 155crb; Athit Perawongmetha 150cra; Sino images 91tl; Satoshi Takahashi 56cra; Stone / Andrea Pistolesi 34br; Andrew JK Tan 54bl, 80-1; Carlina Teteris 24cla, 48bl; The Image Bank / Matthew Micah Wright 149t, 188-89; ullstein bild 155bc; Sebastian Voigt 208-9t; Matthew Wakem 15cr; Matthew Micah Wright 49cl.

Getty Images / iStock: 13672071 214-5b; 1905HKN 31tr, 86crb; aluxum 150cl; boule13 40–41t; carstenbrandt 20tr; davidionut 181b; Matthew Digati 92-3t; egadolfo 78bl; elmvilla 173cra; fbxx 149bl, 204–05; fototrav 13cr; guenterguni 24cra; Gwengoat 88-9; holgs 22-3ca, 84t; JEN_n82 114bl; joakimbkk 86cr; Kewadee 94br; Kintarapong 27tr; KulikovaN 16t; LordRunar 100bl; manx_in_the_world 173cr; Jacqueline Michelle 12–13bc; nickfree 28-9b; Noppasin 16crb; Oleh_Slobodeniuk 89tr; OSTILL 90-1c; PhotoTalk 14clb; piccaya 92br; rchphoto 34-5t; RibeirodosSantos 150br; rmnunes 195cra; Rufous52 160bl; rweisswald 171bc; SanerG 97cra; saylakham 211b; sihasakprachum 42–3b; Supamon R 8clb; swissmediavision 21tr; tegmen 164-5b; tortoon 170bl; traveler1116 42tl; urf 150cr; yenwen 88tr.

Kampot Traditional Music School: Steve Porte 132bc.

Luang Prabang Film Festival: 151crb.

Malis Restaurant: 47tr.

Picfair.com: Dmitry Rukhlenko 87; Ferry R Tan 100-1t.

Robert Harding Picture Library: Nathalie Cuvelier 15t, 116t; Jason Langley 72b; Kay Maeritz 148bl, 166-7; Alex Robinson 135b; Eric Rorer 153tl; Frank Waldecker 19tl.

Shutterstock.com: Em7 12bl; EPA / Heng Sinith 56br / Mak Remissa 56cr; PICH Makthora 134tr; Gianni Dagli Orti 172cr; Peter Stuckings 196t; Tonkinphotography 128t; Kong Veasna 138-39; venusvi 22tl; VladislavPichugin 45cl.
SuperStock: age fotostock / Clickalps SRLs 102-3, / Norbert Scanella 192-3t, 220-1; Glasshouse Images 41crb; Hemis / Bertrand Gardel 128br; robertharding / Alex Robinson 55t, 110-1.

Teuk Skor: 47clb.

Front flap:
123RF: Nuwat Chanthachanthuek br; **Alamy:** imageBROKER cla; Jack Malipan Travel Photography cb; Leisa Tyler cra; Mat Ladley tc; **Robert Harding Picture Library:** Kay Maeritz bl.

Cover images:
Front and Spine: **Alamy Stock Photo:** Jon Arnold Images Ltd / Michele Falzone.
Back: **Alamy Stock Photo:** Jon Arnold Images Ltd / Michele Falzone b; **123RF.com:** Sangkhom Hungkhunthod tr; **4Corners:** Stefano Coltelli cla; **Getty Images:** Andy Teo aka Photocillin c.

All other images © Dorling Kindersley Limited

Mapping:
Base mapping supplied by Kartographie Huber, www.kartographie.de and Lovell Johns Ltd, www.lovelljohns.com

Maps to Phnom Penh, Vientiane and Luang Prabang are derived from © www.openstreetmap. org contributors, licensed under CC-BY-SA.

For further information see: www.dkimages.com

Illustrators: Chingtham Chinglemba, Sanjeev Kumar, Surat Kumar Mantoo, Arun Pottirayil, Guatum Trivedi.

This edition updated by

Contributors Simon Ostheimer, Daniel Stables
Senior Editors Dipika Dasgupta, Alison McGill
Senior Art Editor Stuti Tiwari
Project Editor Anuroop Sanwalia
Assistant Editors Ilina Choudhary, Abhidha Lakhera
Assistant Art Editor Bineet Kaur
Proofreader Stephanie Smith
Indexer Helen Peters
Assistant Picture Research Administrator Manpreet Kaur
Senior Picture Researcher Nishwan Rasool
Publishing Assistant Simona Velikova
Jacket Designer Laura O'Brien
Project Cartographer Ashif
Cartography Manager Suresh Kumar
Senior DTP Designer Tanveer Zaidi
Senior Production Controller Samantha Cross
Managing Editors Shikha Kulkarni, Beverly Smart, Hollie Teague
Managing Art Editor Gemma Doyle
Senior Managing Art Editor Priyanka Thakur
Publishing Director Georgina Dee

MIX
Paper | Supporting responsible forestry
FSC
www.fsc.org   FSC™ C018179

This book was made with Forest Stewardship Council™ certified paper – one small step in DK's commitment to a sustainable future.
Learn more at **www.dk.com/uk/ information/sustainability**

First edition 2011

Published in Great Britain by Dorling Kindersley Limited,
DK, One Embassy Gardens, 8 Viaduct Gardens,
London SW11 7BW, UK

The authorised representative in the EEA is
Dorling Kindersley Verlag GmbH. Arnulfstr.
124, 80636 Munich, Germany

Published in the United States by DK Publishing,
1745 Broadway, 20th Floor, New York, NY 10019, USA

Copyright © 2011, 2024 Dorling Kindersley Limited
A Penguin Random House Company

24 25 26 27 10 9 8 7 6 5 4 3 2 1

The publishers cannot accept responsibility for any consequence arising from the use of this book, nor for any material on third party websites, and cannot guarantee that any website address in this book will be a suitable source of travel information.

A CIP catalog record for this book
is available from the British Library.

A catalog record for this book is available
from the Library of Congress.

ISSN: 1542 1554
ISBN: 978 0 2416 7721 6

Printed and bound in Malaysia.

www.dk.com

A NOTE FROM DK
The rate at which the world is changing is constantly keeping the DK travel team on our toes. While we've worked hard to ensure that this edition of Cambodia and Laos is accurate and up-to-date, we know that opening hours alter, standards shift, prices fluctuate, places close and new ones pop up in their stead. So, if you notice we've got something wrong or left something out, we want to hear about it. Please get in touch at travelguides@dk.com